Mindful Wandering

Mindful Wandering

Nature and Global Travel through the Eyes of a Farmgirl Scientist

Rebecca J. Romsdahl

The Digital Press at the University of North Dakota
Grand Forks, ND

2021 The Digital Press @ The University of North Dakota

Library of Congress Control Number: 2021951148
The Digital Press at the University of North Dakota, Grand Forks, North Dakota

ISBN-13: 978-1-7364986-4-4 (paperback)
ISBN-13: 978-1-7364986-5-1 (Ebook/PDF)

For my parents
Thank you for all your love, for supporting my curiosity,
and for giving me a love of books.

Table of Contents

Preface

How does life on a farm shape the essence of a girl? Farm life teaches a girl to be mindful, to pay attention to the world around her, to be considerate of other people and creatures. A farm embodies contours of change with a veneer of stability, like a prairie river meandering through its watershed, subtly shifting its boundaries within the landscape, simultaneously ever constant.

Farm life is saturated by changing seasons. Seasons of life, family, and nature. Summer brings apples to harvest and freeze, and tomatoes for canning; these family activities bring the taste of summer into long, cold winters. The rhythms of farm life harmonize with the seasons and become imbued in a girl's understanding of how to live in the world.

Life on a farm teaches her to observe and record the activities of the seasons. Barn swallows build nests in the barns in spring, fly aerobatics across the yard catching insects and feeding chicks in summer, gather their flocks in fall, and disappear for the winter. She also observes overlaps between natural and social systems. Farm families keep records of details, like bills and payments, harvested crops, and bags of seeds. They also record relationships with the land, weather, and their animals, as well as social ties with family, friends, and neighbors.

My grandmother and my father would write notes on a weekly calendar about weather, family events, and any remarkable activity they wanted to remember. The calendars were kept from year to year. Following this example, as a young teenager I began keeping journal records of my life and relationships with the world. As a professor, I teach my students through journaling. Putting thoughts into words on a page helps us not only archive the details of our life story, but also to better understand ourselves and our relationships.

My process of writing has been daily at some points in my life, and at other times months will pass between entries. The writing itself is more than just an account of activities. It is often a practice in mindful wandering, calming anxieties, soothing grief, memorializing milestones, and recording the story of an adventure. As the words fill pages, my mind lets go of emotional weight. The pages carry old memories so that my mind can make space for new ones.

As a farmgirl and university professor, I write as a scientist, nature interpreter, and advocate. I am trained as a translational ecologist, and my education includes a Bachelor of Arts degree in Environmental Studies, a Master of Science degree in Resource Development, and a doctorate in Environmental Science and Public Policy. My teaching and research examine different ways that environmental science is translated in the policymaking process and how our human values for the natural environment are included or left out. I try to raise awareness and self-reflection about the complexities and challenges we face in managing the environment and society, so that we humans can hopefully make decisions that are informed by science and our myriad values. And I admit to promoting strong support for protecting the natural environment.

The desire to write this book has been skulking around the back of my brain since 1995. But the actual idea of it only began to take shape and form after I returned from living half a year in the United Kingdom. I wanted to pull on some of the threads of my life and weave them together. Reflecting on thousands of journal pages written so far, I have gone back through time and across the world to extract musings, observations, and stories to share. This resulting collection of essays is an exercise in mindful wandering. How has my understanding of the world changed over the past 25 years, living in different watersheds, visiting different countries, growing from a farmgirl to a scientist? But mindful wandering is not just a personal activity. While wandering the globe, I contemplate ideas of sustainability and resilience and advocate that we (especially those of us privileged enough to travel) must expand our mindful considerations to include all the other inhabitants of this beautiful Earth. Several of these essays first appeared on my blog, BlueMarble notes (https://bluemarblenotes.wordpress.com/), and have been revised and updated for this book.

This book is organized into seasonal chapters to reflect the seasonality of life and nature. The chapters include essays from trips or events that occurred in each season, roughly in chronological order. I think seasonally, travel seasonally, and I am trying to eat more seasonally. I feel we have lost many connections with the natural world because we do not really live seasonally in our modern lives. Many of us can control our indoor temperatures to a constant 72 degrees Fahrenheit, we expect fresh fruits and vegetables to be available year-round, and we now believe Amazon.com can deliver anything to our doorstep within a day or two. But many of us also fail to understand how these conveniences may have far-reaching consequences that are detrimental to the ecological health of our planet and our own human health. I practice mindful wandering to try to be a better global citizen and reduce my impacts on the world around me.

There is also a local-to-global narrative in my writing as I experience new places through the lens of my farmgirl background. How do we reconnect with the local, seasonal rhythms of life, while caring about the whole Earth as our home? One approach I have applied here is to establish location in each essay by watershed, instead of or in addition to city and nation. Environmental problems do not recognize lines on any map. Global problems like the climate crisis have severe consequences across national boundaries and into our local neighborhoods and watersheds.

My travel companion is my life partner, Mick Beltz. He is my navigator, good weather charm, and best friend since we began discussing big philosophical questions under a big starry sky during college.

I hope you enjoy the insights of this farmgirl scientist as she reflects on seasonality, sustainability, and resilience from local to global scales. I also hope to inspire reflection. How mindful are you about your values, decisions, and the actions that you can take within your own watershed? If we all got in the habit of considering how we affect the natural environment and people inside and outside our communities, we could make changes toward a more sustainable and resilient future, both in our daily lives and in our travels across this amazing planet.

Author's family farm in the 1980s.
Photo credit 2021 Rebecca J Romsdahl.

Through the Eyes of a Farmgirl

Watonwan River watershed, United States, July 2016

Farm life gave me an early relationship with the ideas of sustainability and resilience. In my childhood, recycling and reusing items was nothing trendy, it was a normal part of daily life. Small glass jars of screws, washers, and nails of multiple sizes lined the weathered, old countertop of my grandfather's workshop. In my parents' house, you could always find collections of rubber bands, buttons, twist ties, scratch paper, boxes and paper bags for storage, and wrapping paper for gifts. Practically nothing was discarded, and even food scraps were fed to the pigs or the garden. Clothes and shoes were handed down from older to younger children, across siblings and cousins. Everything, from kitchen appliances and winter coats to toys and tractors, was repaired when possible and used until they were worn out. But sustainability is about more than just frugality and respecting your resources.

Sustainability refers to systems and processes that are able to function over long time frames, like the legacy of handing a family farm down from father to son to granddaughter. Sustainability is also about recognizing that all things are connected. As scientist, author, and advocate Rachel Carson wrote: "In nature, nothing exists alone." For example, a thriving farm requires balanced inputs from healthy soils, plants, and animals; a well-managed budget; and happy, vigorous people working the land with equal opportunities for success and equal share in the resources and rewards.

When I teach about sustainability, I talk about three systems in particular: environment, economy, and society. Think of each system as representing a leg on a step stool. If one leg/system is not equal to the others, then the stool is unstable and we risk falling off. So how do we cope with the challenge of standing on that wobbly step stool until we fix it? As humans, we have some natural abilities to adapt to change, but we must also learn new ways to be resilient.

Growing up on a farm taught me that change is a constant force in life. Managing a farm is all about adapting to change, and that is where resilience comes into play. Resilience is often described as the capacity for a system (like an ecosystem, a business, or a community) to absorb some amount of change or disturbance and then bounce back into good condition after a shock. Think of it like a rubber band. You stretch it, release it, and then it snaps back to its original shape. But resilience is more than just a simple return to normal. The rubber band is a helpful tool, but we also need to be mindful that every system has its limits. Like a rubber band stretched too far or damaged by age and use, it can lose its resilience and break.

In farming, I see resilience as the creative ability of farmers to be flexible and adjust to the constant changes thrown at them. Farming requires adaptive thinkers who can tackle such challenges as fixing their own machinery, replanting sections of fields destroyed by fickle or severe weather, building a makeshift stretcher to transport an injured animal back to the barn, or learning to decode the financial tea leaves of the global market to decide when to sell or store crops. Lessons can be passed from one generation to the next of strategies that work well for common problems, but each generation will also need to adapt to new challenges, such as the current climate crisis.

Resilience is composed of awareness that change is normal in systems; planning to manage changes; and innovation and experimentation that are needed to test new ideas for adapting to changes. All of these components need to be managed together, holistically, in order to chart a path to the kind of sustainable and resilient future we might want. In mapping our route, we can draw lessons from our past and present.

On a gravel road in southern Minnesota, surrounded by fields of corn and soybeans, there is a small cluster of farmhouses, a few red barns, and other outbuildings. One house is ranch-style, light gray with white trim. This is the house in which I grew up. It sits neatly on a clipped summer lawn with a grove of trees behind it, a mix of elms, cotton-woods, and walnuts.

Walnut trees create distinct childhood observations. First, you learn to not be afraid of things that go bump in the night. In late summer, when walnuts are ripe, they fall from their branches, hitting the roof of the house with a loud *thunk* and rolling down the shingles with a *clickity-clack* that echoes softly through the wooden attic beams. Then with a quick *pip*, they hit the edge of the roof, jump off, and land with a soft *thump* on the ground outside your bedroom window. Second, in spring the walnut trees are the last to fill out their leaves and in autumn they are the first to drop their gold colors at the slightest breeze. For much of the year, the house is framed by their naked, black branches. Some days in winter, the little house seems to fold itself into the matching landscape of gray sky and white snow, inviting you to stay inside where there is warmth and color.

My worldview was originally formed in this small farming community. This is my touchstone in life. In all my world travels, I see and hear and understand new cultures and experiences through the frame of my own background. I often find myself wondering, "How would my family relate to this scenario?" My sense of place has grown from the rolling hills of farm fields under big open sky to a global view of the entire Earth as my home.

The journey began when I jumped at the first chance to travel to a new country. As a 19-year-old college student, I flew over the rainbow and landed in Japan for a four-month study-abroad adventure. Being immersed in a foreign culture and language was fascinating, exciting, and intoxicating. I was hooked. Since then, I have visited many more countries, and lived seven months in the United Kingdom as an exchange scholar. But, like Dorothy in the *Wizard of Oz*, my heart is always home on the farm. This is where I first learned how to think about sustainability and resilience, and how to observe life through the lens of seasons.

Spring on the farm is snowmelt, rain showers, the smell and sight of soft new green growth, and everywhere is a feeling of exuberance, from migrating birds to farmers' eagerness in planting seeds.

> *March 1988. The snow is all melting away! We only have about four or five inches left on the ground—but there is enough mud, mud, mud everywhere to replace the snow! The geese are coming back and the dogs and horses are shedding like crazy, so spring is on the way!*

> *May 1985. My two favorite cats, Snow and Dottie, have kittens again! Snow has three soft gray kittens with stripes, just like mama. Dottie is black and white. She has four kittens and they are all different colors- so pretty! One is calico with bright orange and brown spots on white. Another is mostly white with a few black spots. Another is foggy gray with white feet. The last one is tiger orange with white stripes and a white bib under his neck. They are all just a few days old I think, because their eyes are still shut. I'm very good at finding where the mamas hide their nests. I follow Snow or Dottie up into the hayloft. I can mew just like the tiny kittens. Then I watch where mama goes to see if the kittens are safe and why they might be crying (but it's just me mewing). I wonder how long it takes Snow and Dottie to find a good hiding space in the haybales. Sometimes I have to move several haybales to find a nest. It's fun to check on the kittens when I get home from school each day. They are so tiny and their fur is so soft! In a few weeks they will be big enough to play with me, I can't wait! They are so cute when they scamper and chase and pounce on each other!*

Summer is filled with life: kittens and baby birds, playing in tallgrass, swatting mosquitos, weeding bean fields, the smell of hay in the big red barn, long sunlight hours, and refusing to go to bed because of a desire to enjoy every minute of daylight.

June 1988. Yesterday, mom called us to the back porch as Dusty was barking like crazy. There my sister and I found a curious baby red squirrel. The squirrel wanted to play in Dusty's doghouse even though we tried several times to place him safely up on a tree branch and encourage him to scamper away. Eventually, he got tired of teasing us and raced out into the grove of trees behind our house.

Today, I rescued a sparrow from drowning in the horses' water tank. When I pulled her out, she could not fly and just sat shivering in my hands. So I took her into the house, wrapped her in an old, little scrap of fuzzy rug and put it in a bowl. A couple hours later, she was dried off and warmed up, so I took the bowl outside, unwrapped the rug, and away she went.

July 1991. [I was feeling very blue after my grandma's death and a dear friend and I broke ties.] I walked outside onto the front porch to look at the night, the stars, peace. But a moment later I saw a big glowing fire in the south, toward Ormsby. I went inside and told my parents and sister to come out and look. Next thing I know, we are in the car driving toward the fire to see what it is. I felt like we were intruding on someone's loss, their pain, by going. But it turns out to be a practice fire, so we go home, and my mood shifts. When we got home, I watched the fireflies in the road ditch. Little flashes of light punctuating the darkness like ground-level stars. I stayed outside for a long time watching the stars and the night. I listened to the steady, serene chirp of crickets, the soft wind in the trees, and low buzz of the hog house fans in the distance. I felt at peace. I feel at peace. I feel strength that I will be fine.

Tomorrow I will probably be watching the rain fall again and watching my brothers and my dad waiting impatiently to work the ground. Watching the rain replenish the Earth and everything flourishing, except the crops because they are either not in the ground yet, with it being too wet, or drowning shortly after coming up. In the coming weeks, all I have to do is remember the fire and the stars and I'll remember that I'm going to be fine. Life goes on.

June 2016. Sitting on the cool cement front porch, I watch the stars emerge and let my senses absorb the farm nightlife. There are a few fireflies drifting about. Under the bright full moon, they flicker strangely, like trying to track someone moving silently in a strobe light. The air is still warm and humid from the day's heat with just a whisper of south breeze so I breathe deeply, enjoying the freshness and lack of hog smell. It is the type of air that carries sound for extra miles, and I listen to its layers, separating and identifying. There is the deep bass from the wedding music (my cousin, over the river); a broad croaking (likely American bullfrog); a higher-pitch, full-throated trilling (probably a chorus of leopard frogs); the metronome chirp of crickets; and a dog barking, over the hill and seeming far away.

Ruby [cat] finds me and insists I give her my full attention for petting her soft warm fur, shedding handfuls as I stroke her head and back. She suddenly stops, her attention caught by something I do not sense in the softness of the night. She leaves me, padding silently across the gravel, disappearing into shadows. A few minutes later I hear a distinct scratching of claws on wood. Following the sound, I watch her climbing the light pole in front of my father's workshop. She pops onto the metal roof like a grasshopper, claws scraping for traction. She creeps across to where there are tree branches overhanging the roof and disappears into shadow again. Minutes go by as I wonder what the nightlife looks like through her senses. Suddenly there is a loud flutter of wings and leaves as a small form bursts from the tree branches. My eyes track the bird as a dark missile across empty space between the workshop and the large pine tree in the middle of the yard. Moments later three or four more sleeping birds are rudely roused and follow the same startled trajectory as the first, disappearing into safety in the thick pine branches. Ruby soon emerges from the shadows and looks over the edge of the roof as though judging the distance to leap down. The prank is complete, so, she pops back onto the light pole, giving me the impression she has done this many times. She shimmies down halfway and, jumping like a gymnast off the balance beam, she sticks the landing with a soft thump. She then pads back to me, purring loudly, as though to proudly ask if I was watching.

Autumn is a blur of colors and movement, with leaves falling and people and machines racing to harvest hundreds (and now thousands) of acres of crops before the rains begin the cold transition to darkness.

August 1989. Tonight, there was a total eclipse of the moon. It's cool. The shadow just started to cover and move over the moon at about 8:30. Then around 10:10, the moon was completely covered. It hung in the sky like an orange lantern. As I watched it continue to transform, it soon looked like a copper penny that I could reach up and pluck down!

November 1990.
—Cherished Time—
The years have sped by quickly,
and the past is forever
gone,
but the memories of cherished time
remain, held in
the dried petals of that crimson autumn rose.

September 1991. The fields of corn, that during the summer looked like great oceans of green waves rolling in the breeze, have turned stiff as boards and the same dry golden color. The beans of summer that had reached waist height and branched out to erase the rows of dirt between them have now shrunk to half that size. In their dried appearance they look like twigs with their leaves shed.

Tomorrow I move to college. What does my future hold for me? These thoughts rattle around in my head as I listen to the rain. I like listening to raindrops and thunder. It's kind of peaceful because everything is soft and quiet in the rain. I'll be falling asleep listening to raindrops tonight, in my bed, in my room, in my house. Tomorrow it will all change.

Winter is a time of rest, long star-filled nights with a crackling fireplace, cats curled up in haylofts, and warm family gatherings over good food and hot coffee.

December 1986. Grandma Ida makes the best coffee. Everyone calls it Swedish egg coffee, because yes, she mixes an egg into the coffee grounds. I don't understand why, but everyone loves it that way. I like that grandma lives right next door to our house because after church on Sundays, we walk over there for coffee and cookies. She always gives my sister and me lots of cream and sugar in our coffee. That makes it sooo good. I dunk grandma's molasses cookies in my coffee, because it makes them soft like they're just out of the oven. When I was little, I would help grandma make cookies. It was fun. Now I like sitting around the table listening to my aunts and uncles, my parents, sometimes my brothers and sisters-in-law, talking about life and laughing at somebody's story from the week. It helps the long winters go by quicker.

January 1991. When I got home last night, the air was so cold and still that it made my nose hairs stick together! But I was amazed by how bright the Milky Way was when I looked up to the sky, millions and millions of tiny lights. I spun in a circle staring at it. I cupped my mittened hands around my eyes, trying to imagine seeing all those stars from a spaceship window. I wanted to stand there in the dark patch, away from the yard light, staring up at the stars all night, but the cold was too strong, so I went into the warm house to my soft bed and dreamed of stars instead.

When I live in a city, stargazing is one of the things I miss most from my farm life. The larger the city you live in, the fewer stars you can see in the night sky. The dark-sky movement is working to help cities and individuals recognize the value of darkness, to help us overcome our fear of the dark, to help reduce light pollution, and thereby also help us reduce our energy consumption.[1]

One of my favorite memories from childhood is stargazing from the north-facing window of our house, on a cold winter night. From that warm post, I watched the magic of the glowing green Aurora Borealis, the Polar Light, dancing silently across the sky. The coldest winter nights are the most magical. The arctic air means crystal clear sky, and the extreme cold lends a sharpness so the stars look like tiny shards of glass shattered across infinity. I miss being able to see the amazing swath of stars that is the Milky Way. As many great writers have observed, when we gaze at the stars we can recognize just how small and insignificant we are in the universe, and yet, we also feel a sense of wonder that links us to all living creatures on this planet.

Learning to observe nature while growing up on a farm is not as common as it used to be. In the mid-2000s, we entered a new era of human history, with more people living in cities than in rural areas.[2] This trend will likely continue. I argued with a college classmate once that rural experiences were more valuable than growing up in a town or city because not as many people live on farms, and anybody can move to the city and seek employment, but the reverse is not true. He argued, how would you know? Had I ever lived in a city? Actually, I had, and I had thought a lot about the urban/rural divide in that past year after living in progressively larger cities: six months in Mankato, Minnesota, three months in Akita, Japan, and a three-week visit to Seoul, South Korea.

Many people who have lived their entire lives in cities do not have a connection with "the land", as Aldo Leopold describes it in his essay, "The Land Ethic," from *A Sand County Almanac*: "Land, then, is not merely soil; it is a fountain of energy flowing through a circuit of soils, plants, and animals. Food chains are the living channels which conduct energy upward; death and decay return it to the soil. The circuit is not closed; some energy is dissipated in decay, some is added by absorption from the air, some is stored in soils, peats, and long-lived forests; but it is a sustained circuit, like a slowly augmented revolving fund of life" (p 216).

More and more people do not understand that humans are increasingly disconnected from the land. Many city dwellers have little to no understanding of how fruits, vegetables, and grains are grown, nor do they recognize the uncomfortable fact that their hamburger is made of cow meat or that bacon comes from pigs. Since the 1970s, Americans have been spending less time outdoors and interacting with the natural world. Instead, many spend more time indoors enjoying climate-controlled homes and interacting with technology and screens (TV, computer, smartphone). Some scientists argue this is leading to a nature-deficit disorder that can start in childhood.[3]

A child's brain is primed from birth to absorb and learn about the world around them. When children spend the majority of their time indoors, they are more likely to learn to identify characters from Disney cartoons or Pokémon cards rather than flowers and insects. When children spend more time outdoors, they naturally learn to identify different types of plants and animals, as well as observe how the ecology around them functions. When my dad was reminiscing once about his childhood, he talked about learning "where all the small critters lived." Without those direct experiences outdoors, nature-deficit disorder limits our ability to value the world around us. It may not be realistic to move more people back to farms, but we can work on ideas for making our towns and cities more sustainable, resilient, and nature-friendly.

For example, we can protect and create more urban green space, like parks and community gardens.[4] These places draw us outside and foster social and ecological connections. People can learn about the diversity of plants and animals in their neighborhood and how to attract more. Gardens can provide habitat for birds, flowers, and pollinating insects. We can meet old friends there and make new friends. Community gardens, in particular, can help people learn how to grow food, like tasty vegetables. The natural environment is also good for human wellbeing.[5] Time spent in a park or garden has been shown to lower anxiety and blood pressure. All in all, humans thrive when they spend frequent time in natural places.

My aunt once said, "You can move the girl away from the farm, but you can never take the farm out of the girl." This is my heart. Whether living in city or farm, drinking a cuppa tea with scones in England, eating sushi in Japan, watching flamenco dancers in Spain, or listening to howler monkeys in Costa Rica, I learned to observe life and how it changes through the seasons, and this helps me recognize valuable insights for sustainability thinking. I see these insights everywhere I wander across this blue-green planet. And they show me over and over just how similar people around the world are, even though we may not fully understand each other's cultures and worldviews. Birth to youth to adult to old age to death. Spring to summer to autumn to winter. We all live seasonally.

26

Endnotes

1 https://en.wikipedia.org/wiki/Dark-sky_movement (https://perma.cc/FR49-N6ZW)

2 http://www.un.org/en/development/desa/news/population/world-urbanization-prospects-2014.html (https://perma.cc/T8D6-XZQS)

3 https://en.wikipedia.org/wiki/Nature_deficit_disorder (https://perma.cc/P4QR-TGV4)

4 http://www.bodinestreetgarden.org/why-protect-urban-green-space/ (https://perma.cc/6C9G-HGZW)

5 http://www.smithsonianmag.com/science-nature/moving-area-with-more-green-space-can-improve-your-mental-health-years-180949348/?no-ist (https://perma.cc/TH4G-238K)

Spring on the farm is snowmelt, rain showers, the smell and sight of soft new green growth, and everywhere is a feeling of exuberance, from migrating birds to farmers' eagerness in planting seeds.

Spring snow on green ash tree.
Photo credit 2021 Rebecca J. Romsdahl.

Existential Journey

Minnesota River watershed, United States, April 1995

There is a paradox in this world of ours in that familiar aspects are changed by new perspectives. I travel a path on [the Gustavus Adolphus] campus so often that it is becoming akin to an old friend. And just as you learn something new about a friend when you spend time together, so too I find something new along this path each time I traverse it. Nature's intricate details are as wonderful as the depth of friendships.

In the dreary gray of a mid-winter day, each tree seems as unique as every human. They have personalities and characteristics. Some are as tall and stately as an English nobleman, while others are bulbous and crooked like a very old man. There are pine trees who have incredible strength of character built up over years of leaning against wicked north winds. Then there are little maples who seem so frail. Some fear the winter cold so much that they refuse to give up all their leaves to the autumn winds. But these often stand under the protection of great grandmother cottonwood trees whose very branches seem to brush the clouds into wispy trails of cirrus mixed in watercolor blue. These giants lean only slightly in fierce winds and outlive many of our human generations. How do they manage to stand so tall and so strong? When I think of how my own body leans and struggles to stay balanced against gusty winds on this hill, I realize just how expansive the root systems of these stately giants must be for their survival. The grandeur of the trees only increases as I imagine them upside down, picturing their magnificent canopy as a reflection of their elaborate roots.

The full moon casts shadows on the depth of night where all life around me is colored in hues of blue and gray. A world of shadow creatures comes to life around me, animated by the breeze and by my very movements. The silhouettes of the bare branches against the night sky are like paper cutouts; the stars are their winter canopy. The crisp air on such a clear night bites and refreshes my skin and my breath. The crunch of my footsteps over the frozen ground is the only sound I hear until the black ice, so well hidden by the night, snatches a gasp of surprise from my lungs.

The mist of gray that surrounds life on a cloudy wet day is the perfect backdrop for imagining myself across the sea, strolling through a London park or the Irish countryside. This type of teleportation is so much less expensive than airfare and maybe just as satisfying. It makes the gray haze that much softer and sweeter in its enveloping touch. I appreciate foggy days when clouds drop down from the skies to greet me. I enjoy all the changes in the weather just as I revel in every human emotion. After all, the sun's warmth feels that much stronger and its rays shine that much brighter when it has been hidden behind playful clouds for a few days.

The flux between winter's entrancement and spring's attempts to resurrect life reminds me of a seesaw tottering back and forth. The bare ground of dead brown grass, with the remaining scattered leaves of last autumn, is exposed repeatedly between snow showers by those days when spring throws a bit more energy upon the sleeping earth. This year, those warm days have awakened as early as February when they usually sleep until late March. The breezes happily toss the dead leaves about, lifting them high into rising and falling spirals. The uneven terrain is uncovered to prepare for the new season as the winter snows retreat, first into patches of crusty ice and then eventually fading into the ground itself.

On calm evenings, a friend and I stroll through the night, discussing existential questions under star-filled skies. To say that my friend dabbles in philosophical thought is like saying the night sky dabbles in stars. He is on a quest to find God. I am in search of truth, whatever that may be. He and I search for answers to these similar questions, but our sources of inspiration are quite different. He finds provocation in logical theories while I am devoted to nature's stimuli. I think I believe in a creator, but at the same time I wonder if all the elements of creation each have their own spirit. My friend believes he has found God, but he still wants to find logical proof.

The only aspect that he cannot find a philosophic proof for is the predictability of the world. He believes that everything can be explained, at least to the level of knowledge that we now have, and once we find the remaining knowledge we can explain the rest also. However, what we cannot explain is the actual ability to explain and predict everything. This is the point where he feels God fits into the picture. He likes to paraphrase Paul Davies, that at some point in science and in life you have to make a leap of faith. He fears that once he has found a theoretical proof for God's existence, he won't know what to do with his life. I believe that something new, or more likely something related, will capture his interest. My search is not often as focused as his, but it is always at the edge of my thoughts.

I revel in the journey as much as he does, but I am not sure if I want to find all of the truth, at least not right now. He believes all of his theories and proofs will fit together into a "grand theory of everything," describing it as a loop. Everything that happens affects something else. I listen and am reminded of my own way of seeing the world as a series of circular events. His grand theory of everything is my web of life. Every season and year, every dawn and sunset, every birdsong, every tree, everything adds a little piece to the sketch. But I don't know if I ever want to see the entire picture. Maybe I fear disappointment. I am not often consciously searching and contemplating existence. I don't often feel I have the time to focus on it, but yet I am continuously doing so unconsciously. I feel ever-observant for details.

My curiosity is piqued by our different approaches to such similar questions. I want to delve into his thoughts, wander around inside his brain in the same manner that I wander through nature's beautifully constructed web. His search reinforces my own journey through life.

His ideas challenge my contemplations and force them to the surface of my thoughts. A mist lies thick and heavy as we walk into the park one serene evening, and I notice that as we move through it I can no longer detect its presence. As the theories he is describing become a clearer picture in my mind, the mist disappears. I turn back to see if we had only melded into it for a moment, reemerging as we walked away. But just as the ideas became clearer in my understanding, so too the mist cleared before my eyes.

I continue wandering. Caught up in philosophy and entranced by the stars, I was abruptly reminded of life's irregularities. With my eyes mesmerized by the seemingly endless height of the trees, I failed to notice the depression I stepped into with my right foot. The artificial light from the streetlamp clearly showed one of its purposes, but I was not paying attention to its illuminated radius. Such a surprise brought my senses back down to earth with a jolt, which was a bit disappointing but also amusing. That intrusion of solid reality reminded me of other factors I generally try to block out whenever I traverse through nature.

I do not have to go searching in distant places for nature. I feel no need to. I find nature all around me, from my backyard to farm fields, city parks, and protected wilderness areas. I do sometimes try to keep human influences toward my periphery vision. Human constructions are all around us. Sidewalks, roads, litter, artificial lighting, noise from cars, all of these can interrupt my experience with nature. But, as I remind myself, humans are also a part of nature. Grass grows in side-walk cracks. I can walk or ride a bicycle instead of driving a car. And if I focus, the sounds of birdsong in the breeze can sometimes drown out the distant hustle and bustle of city life. My experiences in nature cannot be diminished by human constructs unless I allow them to be. If I do seek anything beyond truth, it is solitude in nature. In quiet moments, attuned to nature, I find my inner peace. But I can find that by rollerblading through a quiet tree-lined neighborhood just as easily as I can find it in the woods. I don't have to be alone in nature with no suggestion of human presence to enjoy the solitude of a place. In life,

I believe people need a blend, one that allows them to find their place in nature but not dominate it, so that nature and people can flourish together.

The glow from the lamps along the sidewalk lends a theatrical appearance to the trees and terrain, coloring them in shades of rose and amber, in stark contrast to the blue and gray hues of the night. The hallway of pines, further up the hill, is also somewhat aglow from the imposing artificial lights nearby. As we move out of the gently infringing radiance and back into the shadows of the night, my eyes return to admiring the sky, and I imagine myself wandering through a philosophical mindscape.

I see the big dipper standing vertical upon its handle in the early evening of this transitional time of year. Later in the night, as I return home, I notice it has slowly fallen upside down. I wonder if the ancient Greeks ever attributed any contents to its ladle. Would it have contained something heavenly or something earthly? My mindscape expands as my eyes sweep across the faint glimmers of the Milky Way.

Millions of intricate snowflakes fall through the calm air, engulfing all sound. These miniature tapestries float breathlessly through the night, settling silently upon the earth. Their touch caresses everything and wraps the world in a thick, satiny, down-like blanket of brilliance. The sky, faintly luminous, is a rosy shade of pinkish orange, and I wonder if I have somehow stepped beyond the looking glass into Alice's Wonderland.

A wintry breeze catches me by surprise and hastens my steps home. But the pine trees seem to want to speak to me as I pass by them, or maybe it is I who wants to stop and communicate with them. Perhaps there are wood sprites speaking through the wind or the playful antics of tree trolls. I have seen many trolls hiding in the gnarled figures and knots of tree trunks. Some trees even seem to have swallowed them whole, like the bulge of a python's full belly. The tiny sprites are rarely seen. But, if you are distracted, they love to catch you off guard. When I inadvertently walk face-first into a low hanging branch or stub my foot and nearly trip over a protruding tree root, I wonder if I have just been caught in the playground of wood sprites. But then my mind usually reaches for fun science facts to distract me from the embarrassing pain in my head or foot. Scientist Fred Pearce tells us that:

> ... trees act like giant water fountains. Their roots capture water from the soil for photosynthesis, and microscopic pores in leaves release unused water as vapor into the air. The process, the arboreal equivalent of sweating, is known as transpiration. In this way, a single mature tree can release hundreds of liters of water a day. With its foliage offering abundant surface area for the exchange, a forest can often deliver more moisture to the air than evaporation from a water body of the same size (pg 1303).

The earliest heralds of spring's arrival are the songbirds who alight between the heights of trees. Walking barefoot is another sure sign of spring's return to campus. As soon as my friends and I can travel the sidewalk without shoes and without fearing frostbite, we deem that winter has finally been beaten. On such a warm, lazy evening, a friend and I were leisurely walking home after dinner when we made two discoveries on another familiar path.

Along the usual concrete trail to our dorm, we heard a subtle, strange sound. This unfamiliar noise was faint enough that many would not take notice, but it was just loud enough to catch the attention of the curious. We heard a distinct, constant snapping. Following the sound, we approached a pine tree, listening and watching for clues. Then, we realized what it was. The pinecones were opening in the warm weather! Each tiny flap on each cone was snapping open to release seeds. The sound was like a chorus of Rice Krispies in milk, a delight to the ears. After marveling, laughing, and listening intently, we continued on our way. As we crossed the street, we squished our toes as deep as we could into the sun-warmed cracks of tar and then watched the depressions disappear. Such a seemingly mundane activity can provide immense delight. Life has so many great and small joys to offer, and I try to appreciate such experiences each day.

Familiar places may not be as familiar as we think they are. I never take the same path twice, in the sense that it is changed each time by my state of mind, my company or lack thereof, and the ever-changing environment in which we live. Nature is my oldest and dearest friend. I turn to her for comfort, inspiration, and clues to my search for knowledge. In return she gives laughter, joy, and companionship. Her characteristics are as intriguing as any human personality. And the more time I spend with her, the more I feel I learn about people as well. Noticing my human friends' unique qualities and differences stimulates my curiosity, opens new worlds, and shows me different pathways on my existential journey through this life.

Cherry blossoms around the Tidal Basin in Washington, DC.
Photo credit 2000 Rebecca J Romsdahl.

Climate Is Culture

Omono River watershed, Japan, April 1992

After the Olympic-length graduation ceremony that marked the end of our orientation week, we were divided into fourteen groups of ten students. With only one American per group, we were free to fly the nest of adult supervision and explore our new city, Akita, in the northern reaches of Honshu, the main island of Japan. We were all first-year students, but I felt so much more mature than my Japanese classmates, who were just four weeks out of high school. I had already completed two-thirds of my first year of college and now I was immersed in a totally new culture on the opposite side of the world from home. I was like a puppy who had just discovered grass - curious, cautious, and near bursting with excitement.

My group chose to find food first. They introduced me to one of the most popular types of Japanese restaurant, a noodle house, and my cultural journey began. Everyone took their shoes off before crawling up onto a small, raised platform and finding a flat pillow to sit on the floor around the table. When the server brought me a huge, steaming bowl of soba noodles topped with veggies, I realized I had no reason to fear going hungry during my study abroad semester. Yum!

During my travels around the world, I have experienced a variety of different cultures and witnessed how closely culture and food are tied to local climates. In Japan, the fleeting cherry blossoms of spring are celebrated with festivals throughout the country. This cultural tradition was transplanted to the United States after the mayor of Tokyo gifted 3,000 cherry trees to one of my favorite cities, Washington DC, in 1912.[1] Cherry trees have an extensive history as heralds of spring, both culturally and climatically. Their lovely pink and white blooms indicate that the long, cold northern winter has passed for another year.

Toward the end of April, the days were becoming sunnier and the chill of early spring was fading. On a particularly lovely Sunday, several friends and I took the train into Akita City to spend the afternoon and evening at the local Sakura (cherry blossom) Festival. I had visited Senshu Park and its historic castle tower earlier with my orientation group, but that day had been cold, gray, and punctuated with rain sprinkles, so we did not spend much time in the park.[2] Today, the sky was a festive robin's egg blue with pink petals as accents, and the wide, paved paths were lined with booths selling assortments of food and trinkets. Each stall had brightly colored signs announcing its specialty, but my Japanese reading was nowhere near good enough to understand what the characters meant.

Senshu Park is adorned with 700 or more cherry trees. Some of these trees are over 100-years old, but many of the Yoshino cherry trees are still young and not very tall, maybe 20-30 feet high. They stretch their branches as wide as they are tall, growing along both sides of walkways and outlining a central grassy quad. Local residents and tourists from around the world gather here each year to celebrate the return of spring.

The joyful tradition of hanami (flower viewing) started centuries ago in appreciation of plum tree blossoms, but soon it became nearly exclusive to sakura. Hanami continues to be wildly popular today. Widespread in Japanese literature, poetry, and art, the cherry blossoms of spring carry layered meanings. Their brief flowering period, about a week in length, is considered a magical moment.

Hanami also provides a window for understanding how most industrial societies relate to nature. They see their modern human relationship with nature through these fleeting moments. It is a rather temporal relationship without necessarily considering long-term consequences. Many people seem to feel a closer relationship with nature as it moves farther away from their daily lives, such as when living

Castle tower in Senshu Park.
Photo credit 1992 Rebecca J Romsdahl

in large, dense cities. For many Japanese people, the flowering of the cherry trees is a metaphor of the ephemeral beauty of human life, as well as being a symbol of hope and renewal. These are significant values in the Shinto religion that dominates Japanese culture. In other words, life is short, so get out and enjoy the flowers. Sakura Festivals are the most celebrated form of hanami in Japan.

We stopped at several booths selling sweet treats. My friends chose several traditional Japanese desserts for me to try.[3] Dorayaki consists of small pancakes like a sandwich. Between the two pancakes is a layer of anko, a mashed, pasty filling made from naturally sweet azuki beans. These were a very common ingredient used to sweeten deserts before sugar was introduced to Japan. My American tastebuds were not impressed. For the next dessert, they chose a different booth that made savory items. One of my friends chatted with the woman behind the counter and then turned and handed me what looked like three white balls of dough skewered on a wooden stick, each glistening with a sticky glaze. Dango is a chewy rice dumpling, and mine were coated in a teriyaki-like sauce. They were unlike anything I had ever eaten, and I loved them! Later in the afternoon, my friends introduced me to green tea ice cream. This sounded like a strange pairing, but it soon became one of my favorite Japanese deserts, especially when stuffed inside frozen mochi, another form of chewy rice dumpling.

As we walked through the park, sakura petals softly floated down from the trees. The day was calm, and this was one of the first days of the festival, so very few petals were loose. The stray petals looked like tiny pink butterflies fluttering around us. Many couples, families, and groups of young people like us were strolling along the paved paths under the cherry trees while others were lounging on picnic blankets.

One of the rules of etiquette in Japan is that you should not eat while walking, so there were always people standing in clusters around the food booths. But I soon noticed several people sitting on blankets who were eating a delightful looking treat. I pointed this out to my friends, and they happily dragged me to another food booth. Being teenagers, we could eat desserts all afternoon, and we did. This one was sakuramochi in honor of the cherry blossoms. It was a gooey, pink blob of chewy rice dumpling, flavored with cherry blossoms, wrapped in a pickled cherry leaf. Very pretty. Unfortunately for me, it was also stuffed with anko. My friends may have tried to warn me of this, but it was lost in translation, so they burst into giggles as I made yucky-face expressions. This would not be the last time they fed me anko-filled dessert. I eventually gained a reluctant appreciation for the flavor, but never chose it for myself.

After dark, the cherry trees became even more magical as strings of lights created a pinkish glow. We sat under a shimmering tree, our hands wrapped around paper bowls filled to the brim with tangy-sauced soba noodles or a snowball-sized sticky rice ball filled with seaweed and fish. The tiny, pink petal butterflies of afternoon had transformed. I now imagined them as confetti-sized paper cranes silently floating around us. The crowds of revelers had thinned and many people had gone home for their evening meal. With the growing dark, peoples' voices grew quieter also, and the castle tower loomed above the softly glowing trees. The scene gave me the feeling of walking through Shakespeare's play *A Midsummer Night's Dream*. I half expected the mischievous sprite Puck to jump out from behind the nearest tree and offer me a love potion.

Today, I can close my eyes and see distant, snowcapped mountains foregrounded by the blooming cherry trees in the park behind the Akita campus. This is one of the images etched in my mind from living in Japan. It always brings me a smile, now more often tinged with bittersweet longing.

Japan's long history and love of cherry trees, along with its geographic stretch over several ecozones, provides science with a treasure of data to study how the climate change crisis is affecting the nation's environment and culture. In Kyoto, records for the timing of Sakura

Festivals go all the way back to the ninth century. A study of these records shows that cherry trees are blooming earlier than they have in the past 1200 years.[4]

As human-caused global heating affects the arrival of spring weather, Sakura Festivals have an uncertain future. Early warm temperatures have become more common, and this prompts the trees to bloom too early. The fragile blossoms are susceptible to cold snaps that can kill the flowers before the festivals. This leaves you with either a sad, sparsely attended festival with no cherry blossoms to admire and celebrate, or with no festival at all, because the costs of holding it will likely be greater than the profit. Either way, local communities lose income and cultural traditions are threatened. As we witness more changes, the cherry blossoms' symbolic representation of life's impermanence becomes a bit darker, showing more vulnerability and perhaps less hope. This is just one example of how climate and culture are intertwined and changing through the climate crisis.

Endnotes

1 https://www.nps.gov/subjects/cherryblossom/history-of-the-cherry-trees.htm (https://perma.cc/8EZF-Y52L)
2 https://www.akita-yulala.jp/en/festival/senshu-park-cherry-blossom-festival (https://perma.cc/66E7-MKRM)
3 https://www.japan-talk.com/jt/new/japanese-desserts (https://perma.cc/3H7S-WQRF)
4 https://www.theguardian.com/world/2021/mar/30/climate-crisis-likely-cause-of-early-cherry-blossom-in-japan (https://perma.cc/8J9Q-9PXQ)

Replica of the famous sign welcoming visitors to the city.
Photo credit 2016 Rebecca J Romsdahl.

Confessions of an Environmentalist

Las Vegas Valley watershed, United States, March 2016

I am not Catholic. I was raised Lutheran, and my partner's Grandma Angel loved to tease me by telling this bit of a story. She was concerned about her grandson dating a Lutheran, so she talked to her priest about it, and he reassured her saying, "Don't worry, Luther was a Catholic, too." With this, it seems I have been adopted by a Catholic grandmother, so I am taking that as creative license and running with it.

Mother Gaia, forgive me for I have sinned.

This has been my eighth trip to Las Vegas for spring break. And I enjoyed it...again, even though I am a self-proclaimed environmentalist and Vegas represents so many environmental sins. I am helpless to resist the colorful bright lights, the cheerful ringing and dinging of slot machines, the happy people everywhere, the decadent food, the plush comfy beds, the relaxing poolside cabanas. This is my partner's "happy place." And the warm desert sun heals my winter-battered soul.

This is where the guilt sets in. Although I am not Catholic, I believe that "Catholic guilt" is real; it was not purged from the Lutheran doctrine along with the saints and transubstantiation.[1] Catholic guilt flows through Lutheranism and was applied liberally in my childhood. Guilt is powerful. It sticks like oil and no matter how hard you try, you cannot rid yourself of it without help. Therefore, during every visit to Las Vegas, I seek help in soothing my guilty environmental soul.

My first visit to Sin City was in 1997. I was a tender, young graduate student working on my master's degree. My partner and I were poor as church mice, living in an apartment in downtown Lansing, Michigan, between the train tracks and the hospital emergency room.

I am still not sure how we learned to sleep through the train horns and the ambulance sirens. We joked about how safe our neighborhood was, with the hospital right there and the police driving by regularly to keep a close eye on the crack-house across the street. Overall, we were happy, at least when we weren't stressed about schoolwork and lack of money. When his parents offered to take the whole family to Las Vegas over winter break, we jumped at the invitation to escape from reality for a few days.

December 1997. I had fun visiting the odd electric light-polluted mecca in the desert, the lights, the noise, the masses of tourists, the extravagance of everything!

During our many visits over the years, I have always been very aware of this idea of Las Vegas as a mecca of extravagance. I sometimes waver on the edge of feeling guilty that I am contributing to the environmental unsustainability of this desert city before I simply let go and enjoy being engulfed by the spectacle and excess. After all, the city gets its water and electricity from the Hoover Dam and reservoir; that seems sustainable and resilient, so it helps soften my guilt. We toured the massive facility on our second visit to Vegas, and I still marvel at that large body of water every time we fly over it. When full, it is the largest reservoir in the United States.

I have often referred to Las Vegas as the "temple to capitalism" because of the unbelievable amount of money that flows through the casinos. Nevada gaming revenue first reached $1 billion in 1974; now Las Vegas itself often records $1 billion in revenue in a single month! There are luxury shopping malls linked directly to or often within the casinos, so gamblers and non-gamblers alike have plenty of choices for where to spend their money. Everything is tailored to help you feel good and spend money. Many of the casinos even have a signature feel-good scent that is pumped through their air vents, which envelops you and pulls you into the lovely experience as soon as you open a door

Fountain and circular escalator in the Caesars Palace shopping center.
Photo credit 2016 Rebecca J Romsdahl.

from the outer world. Strolling through the casinos and their shopping centers is like living in the Matrix, everyone seems happily engaged in a shared dream world. Nobody wants to see reality or think about it.

When visiting Las Vegas, I check reality at the airport as though it were nothing more than luggage. I choose to look away from my use of water in the desert, my wasted leftovers at restaurants, and my participation in the enormous environmental footprint that is the Las Vegas Strip, in the same way I try to look away from the people experiencing homelessness who populate the sidewalks between casinos.[2] But these bits of reality creep into my thoughts, so I try to ease my guilt. At best though, I try to not overfill my plate at the buffet, and I buy a bottle of water from a veteran who lost his legs. Notions of sustainability and equality are tucked safely away in that reality I left at the airport, where I will pick it up on the way home.

I marvel at how Las Vegas has changed over the years. One evening, we caught a taxi from the Venetian back to the Luxor. During the 10-minute ride, our driver told us he first moved to the city in 1974. During his 42 years of living in Vegas, he has seen significant changes. He was one of the friendliest drivers we have encountered and he regaled us with a quick story of numbers. When he arrived, the Las Vegas metro area population was around 300,000 people, with 8.6 million tourists visiting that year. In 2016, the greater metro area has ballooned to over 1.9 million residents and its entertainment industry has exploded to over 42 million tourists per year. These are such big numbers that it takes a bit of comparison to put them into meaningful context. I went to high school in a town with roughly 4,000 residents. The Venetian/Palazzo complex in Las Vegas is currently the second largest hotel in the world with 7,117 rooms! Every person in my hometown could have their own room in a single hotel in Las Vegas and there would still be enough space for another 3,000 visitors. The size, the extravagance, the demand for resources, it boggles my mind.

I have observed changes as well. In 2016, there were new billboards all around the city promoting water conservation. Lake Mead, the Hoover Dam reservoir, has been shrinking substantially. Due to drought and increasing demands for water, it has not been at full capacity since 1983. This means the Lake Sakakawea reservoir in North Dakota is now the largest in the country. While flying over Lake Mead these past few years, it is easy to see how the water level continues to drop because there are bands of lighter colored rock above the surface of the lake, like rings around a dirty bathtub as the water drains out. Water conservation messages are now common in every hotel room where we have stayed in Las Vegas over the past five years.

Another part of reality that Las Vegas does not want me to think about is how much impact tourism has on natural resources. In a news article, Ken Miller reports that each year a "typical hotel room of the tens of thousands on the Strip goes through 180 rolls of toilet paper (most of which is unrecyclable, for, ahem, obvious reasons), 641 king sheets, 979 pillow cases and 750 bath towels, requiring 7,513 gallons of water for washing."[3] I like to think the messages on the bathroom cards help tourists change their behaviors and conserve water, but the hotel staff do not always help the process. Even when I follow the instructions on the card and hang my towel for reuse, I find it replaced with a clean one later that day. The only strategy that prevents many hotel staff around the globe from thwarting my attempts to alleviate some environmental guilt is to leave the "do not disturb" sign on my door.

At least there are some things that cause me a little less guilt while visiting Las Vegas than they did in the past. My consumption of bottled water is one. I learned during my first trip to Vegas that water fountains, the kind you can drink from, are as rare as water can be in the desert. Toting around a refillable water bottle is pointless and staying hydrated in the desert is essential. That left me with no choice but to buy bottled water, which was crushing to my environmental soul. But a few years ago, I learned that the Vegas casinos are considered recycling superstars, and they are working to reduce their environmental footprint, which also translates into reducing their operating costs. MGM Resorts, one of the largest hotel companies in the world, even has a Sustainability Manager.

The recycling business and the sustainability ethic behind it only arrived on the Las Vegas Strip in the early 1990s, when the owner of R.C. Farms negotiated a deal to help several casinos with asset recovery. Ken Miller explains this as "all the salvageable stuff people throw away at hotels, from glasses and dishes to silverware and coffee mugs." In return, R.C. Farms wanted all the recyclable waste from those properties, such as cardboard, aluminum cans, plastics, and kitchen grease, not to mention the discarded food for the pigs. This partnership proved very successful for both the farm and the casinos.

In 2006, the year after MGM Mirage merged with Mandalay Group, the corporation created an Energy Environmental Services Division, a consolidation of expert resources and all things energy. Five focus areas were created: energy management and natural resource conservation, green building, construction design and development, waste management and sustainable supply chain management, and communication and outreach.

The business side of sustainability and resilience has proven to be so successful that southern Nevada's primary waste and recycling company opened a large, brand new recycling facility in November 2015.[4] But overall, sustainability and recycling efforts are mostly kept hidden from the dream world that I stroll through while visiting the Las Vegas casinos. Like the occasional glitch in the Matrix, however, there are occasional hints of an alternate reality, such as the sign on small trash bins at the Luxor telling me that recyclables get sorted out of the comingled trash. These token messages bring me momentary smiles as they break through the dream fog. I tuck them away in a pocket in the back of my mind, like little slips of paper from happy fortune cookies, so I can reflect on them later when I am reunited with my reality baggage.

Although the Las Vegas casinos are working hard to reduce their environmental footprint, there is much more work to be done. On just the subject of recycling, the residents of Clark County (where Las Vegas is located) still sent 90% of their trash in 2014 to be buried in the seemingly endless desert.[5] This begs the ultimate question: how do we reduce our consumption of resources, especially plastics, so we do not produce all that waste to begin with? I continue to ponder that, but not while I'm enjoying Las Vegas.

On March 19, 2016, my partner and I were out with friends, walking between casinos, when I noticed that it was unusually dark and many of the streetlights were turned off. We thought it was just timing related to the hourly volcano show outside the Mirage casino, but we soon noticed that many lights were dim or off. When we asked our taxi driver, we learned that Las Vegas was participating for the seventh year in Earth Hour. This is a global event where cities, institutions, and individuals raise awareness about climate change by turning off their electric lights for one hour on a designated night. In my studies of sustainability and resilience, this is what critics refer to as a symbolic "feel-good measure" versus activities that do actual good, such as the casinos diverting 50% of their trash into recycling. I understand the critics' arguments that these small symbolic gestures do not help move society toward measurable goals, but I also understand how Las Vegas may be trying to alleviate some of its own environmental guilt.

We can all benefit by acknowledging when we feel bad about how the natural world is being damaged. This is our ecological grief.[6] We need to forgive ourselves for being stuck in these wasteful systems, then move past our grief and guilt into action. This is how I enjoyed a momentary smile for Earth Hour.

Forgive me Mother Gaia, for I am a sinner. Through my words and deeds, let me help alleviate my and others' guilt, so that we can overcome our apathy and work to be better stewards of our environment.

Amen.

Endnotes

1 https://en.wikipedia.org/wiki/Talk%3ATransmogrification (https://perma.cc/WEX7-7J6K)

2 https://en.wikipedia.org/wiki/Ecological_footprint (https://perma.cc/8P8A-NTK2)

3 https://lasvegasweekly.com/news/2011/may/12/recycling-strips-best-kept-secret/#/0 (https://perma.cc/3TS5-5YHB)

4 http://lasvegassun.com/news/2015/nov/12/new-recycling-facility-doubles-regions-ability-to/ (https://perma.cc/EK7Z-NJXQ)

5 http://lasvegassun.com/news/2014/aug/03/why-southern-nevada-stinks-recycling/ (https://perma.cc/SVV6-F38D)

6 https://theconversation.com/hope-and-mourning-in-the-anthropocene-understanding-ecological-grief-88630 (https://perma.cc/32CA-ZWFA)

Temple of Ramses II, built to show how rich and powerful he was and thus inspire fear in his enemies.
Photo credit 2010 Mick Beltz.

Touring the Gaps between Rich and Poor

Nile River watershed, Egypt, May 2010

The Arab Spring Revolution erupted in Egypt on January 25, 2011.[1] My partner and I were transfixed by the news reports as demonstrators and police clashed in cities across the country. We watched in horror as tear gas and water cannons were used against people in Tahrir Square, the main square in central Cairo. Seven months earlier, we had walked across that square after touring the Egyptian Museum. We stopped at a small café in that square and ate one of the most brilliant, hearty meals we have ever had from a street vendor. The dish was koshari, a staple for Egyptians because it is filling, delicious, and nutritious.[2] It is also a simple meal composed of layers: pasta, lentils, rice, and chickpeas topped with a spicy cumin, garlic tomato sauce, and fried onions. Now we stood in our own kitchen, stunned by the television images. What would happen to the wonderful people we had met? Were our guides, Mamdouh and Robert, safe? Were they taking part in the demonstrations? How would their lives change as the government was overthrown?

The British journalist Jack Shenker has helped me better understand what was happening in Egypt behind the pretty picture presented for tourism. He was living and working in Cairo during the 2011 revolution. In his breathtaking book *The Egyptians: A Radical Story*, he writes about his incredible first-hand experiences observing and being swept up in the protests. Shenker gives perspective on how portrayals of the revolution have been simplified and sanitized to limit discussion as well as limit the potential for its success, especially in regard to how the global economic system is harming people who are not rich or powerful.[3]

Shenker argues that this revolution was not just about who the president of Egypt is or elections. It is not just a civil war about religion or about the supposed "backwardness" of developing countries versus the modernity of Western liberal democracies. As he explains, "In reality, the revolution is about marginalized citizens muscling their way on to the political stage and practicing collective sovereignty over domains that were previously closed to them. The national presidency is one such domain, but there are many others: factories, fields and urban streets, the mineral resources that lie under the desert sand and beneath the seabed, the houses people live in, the food they eat and the water they drink" (pg. 3).

Shenker writes about the struggles of Egyptians in their revolution, but he also helps lift the fog of tear gas to illuminate how something like this is bigger than one event in one country. The domains he highlights are relevant to all of us. This connects deeply with my observations in touring Egypt and other countries, as well as with my research and teaching.

In studying the environment for twenty-some years now, I have learned an age-old lesson that seems cliché. We humans tend to believe that we are special and clever, and that these traits separate us from the rest of nature. But what we tend to ignore is that we live on this planet with all the rest of nature. Thereby everything we do, and everything we need, is part of nature. Nature is our home. If we damage our home, we damage ourselves. We cannot understand the environment without understanding humans. This also means that in order to protect the quality of the environment, we must protect the quality of human lives. In this time of growing gaps between rich and poor people around the world, we neglect human interconnections with the environment at our own peril.[4] But to those people who have all the money and all the power, this can often seem more like a game.

Cairo apartment buildings and side street traffic.
Photo credit 2010 Rebecca J Romsdahl.

Layering Shenker's insights with my reflections and environmental perspective makes me think of the game Jenga with its layers of wood blocks stacked in neatly arranged, opposing rows that form a small tower. With each player's turn, a single block is removed from the tower and placed on the top level. The goal is to see how high you can build the tower while maintaining its balance, as you weaken the core structure, before it collapses. When we visited Egypt in May 2010, we did not realize the government leadership had been playing a huge game of Jenga with the country's economy, social justice, environment, and governance. What we witnessed as tourists were the physical representations of the gaps between the Jenga blocks, real gaps between rich and poor. Every country has these gaps, including the United States. In Egypt, we saw them preserved in ancient artwork, pyramids, and temples. We also saw the gaps in its modern cities, rural towns, and tourist economy.

Nearly any trip to Egypt begins in Cairo. After two hours of sitting on a runway in New York and ten and a half hours of flight time, many of our fellow passengers seemed very happy to be home, clapping and cheering as the pilot welcomed us to Cairo.

Shenker describes how Cairo is built on the Nile Delta, which was once venerated by writers for its wild marshlands. "Now you'll find it hard to pinpoint where the city ends and the countryside begins: the lushness of the Nile's arteries is stippled with apartment blocks and spliced by roads in every direction, and any clear-cut divisions have been long buried under a layer of rebars and asphalt. Here, the urban and rural get lost in one another, with livestock living in doorways and workers camping out in fields" (pg. 34).

The pilot announced that those of us seated on the left side of the plane should look out the windows for a magnificent view. We were thrilled at the sights of ancient and modern Egypt below us. The pyramids of Giza, the Sphinx, the Cairo Tower, the Citadel, the Mena House hotel where the World War II peace accord was signed—seeing such grand monuments from the air was enchanting. Air travel to get there, however, is less enchanting.

Jetlag is taxing on body and mind. Our adventure in Egypt started with a communication mix-up. Our hotel had sent a driver to pick us up at the airport, but we did not know that, so we had asked our tour guide company to send a car. We hazily realized our mistake when we found two people holding signs with our names, waiting outside the arrival gate. The hotel's driver was kind enough to only mildly chastise us and let the tour company's two guys give us a ride (they were younger than him and likely not making as much income). In our sleep-deprived condition, the ride from the airport to the hotel seemed to last forever. It was a little more than 90 minutes to drive 30 miles, and most of that time we spent sitting in bumper-to-bumper traffic on Cairo's Ring Road highway, which circles the center of the city.

Shenker's depiction is perfect: "Nobody loves the Cairo ring road; they only endure it. They sit behind the wheels of private cars and fiddle impatiently with the radio dial, or they perch up in the cabins of lumbering, overweight trucks and bellow their horns, or they slump into passenger seats of half-broken taxis and feel great lakes of sweat expanding slowly, and unstoppably across their backs. . . . Everyone moves at breakneck speed, or they don't move at all. It takes only a few moments for the entire highway to congeal and switch from race-track to traffic clot. This happens every morning and every afternoon, and when it does there is nothing to do but wait" (pg. 241).

Once the traffic finally started moving, I was impressed by the Hollywood-style action scene moving around us and thankfully too jetlagged to be afraid for our safety. The drivers organized themselves into four or five lines of cars on a three-lane road and deftly weaved in and around each other's vehicles with only inches of space. It would make most American drivers sweat bullets, and I soon realized I could never imagine driving there. What we did not recognize at the time were the first examples of Cairo's gaps between rich and poor.

In this city of some 18 million people, it was common to see all sorts of transportation mixed together. Flashy new SUVs, junky 30-year-old cars, small motorbikes with five or six people piled on each one (often whole families, including infants in mothers' arms), tuk-tuks

(three-wheeled motorbikes connected to a covered cart for transporting goods or passengers), and men leading or riding donkeys that were
pulling carts.

At one intersection, with no traffic signal and nobody directing
traffic, we watched a serious game of chicken. The front car in the far-
right lane inched its way into the stream of cross traffic until it broke
the flow with its bumper, preventing the next car from entering the
intersection. Once this first lane was breached, the cars on our street
quickly filled in and that first car on the right slowly inched its way into
the next lane, and then the next lane, until our street filled the intersection with flowing traffic. Then the game of chicken swapped back
to the cars lining the cross street. This appeared to be a normal way of
driving in many intersections.

Shenker describes another notable feature of driving in Cairo,
checkpoints:

> Some are permanent and others are makeshift; you turn a cor-
> ner and suddenly there they are, a line of metal barriers jutting
> across the highway, patrolled by overheated men clutching
> weapons and clad in tan or black. . . . [They] force all vehicles to
> slow down and crawl through a small gap. Faces are scanned;
> some are beckoned over to the side of the road, where ID
> cards are demanded and questions are asked. The air around
> these checkpoints is stale; it smells of state control, of authori-
> ty and obedience. If you look the wrong way, or say the wrong
> thing, or wear the wrong clothes . . . your journey on the ring
> road will come to an end. . . . In 2014, an eighteen-year old
> student was stopped by officers . . . because he was wearing a
> t-shirt with the words 'Nation Without Torture'. He was tak-
> en to a police station, beaten and electrocuted, and thrown in
> jail; at the time [of this writing], he had been held for over 500
> days without any charges filed (p 241).

We encountered checkpoints in many places we traveled around Egypt, even at one of our hotels. On our first touring day in Cairo, we climbed into a car with our driver and guide, Mamdouh, but the tourism police (as we took to calling them) would not let us leave after initially checking our documents. We sat in the car for over 30 minutes while Mamdouh and the officers talked and made phone calls. Our driver grumbled about "too much security, especially for Americans."

At lunch, Mamdouh apologized for the delay in our start and explained that the tourism police keep very close tabs on American tourists, "for safety". Our every stop, when we arrived at and left tourist sites, had to be documented and reported. There was a discrepancy in our paperwork that morning between what the officers had on file and what our guide's itinerary outlined, so it took some time to straighten out the detail. We nervously chuckled about this later, saying that they must be either overly worried that Americans will get kidnapped or that we are all spies.

Shenker also gives an insider's perspective to an innovative, if illegal, feature of Cairo's Ring Road and sums up why these traffic interruptions are significant in Egypt's ongoing revolution:

> Gaps have appeared in the low walls which line the overpass. They are rough and jagged, peering out over huge mounds of sand and dirt that have been banked up underneath the highway to form illicit ramps between the ring road and the communities living in the shadows below. For many decades, the inhabitants of these [informal, unrecognized] communities had been forced to share their environment with the underbelly of the highway, without ever having access to its tarmac. Their homes, cars and shops commingled with giant concrete pillars holding up the road, stanchions of separation that threw daily life into darkness and lent each neighborhood a ceaseless backdrop of rumbles and roars. Now without asking permission, residents have decided to end this isolation and build their own unofficial access points to the ring road;

today their tuk-tuks and pick-ups and family wagons are wob-
bling their way up on to the fast lane at pace, with a cheerful
indifference to formal rules.

The security checkpoints and the informal access ramps
represent two very different understandings of power and
space in revolutionary [and counter-revolutionary] Egypt...
home to both a whirlwind of change and its symbiotic opposite, the struggle to prevent change from materializing at all.
One vision is of public space being back in the hands of its
self-appointed custodians, those who know best how to rule it.
The other [vision] is of people physically remaking their city,
and their country, for themselves (p 242-243).

Only years later, after reading these insights from Shenker's book, did
I realize that it was through traffic and police checkpoints that we first
encountered the political and economic gaps between Egypt's rich and
powerful people and its everyday people.

Our second encounter with gaps between rich and poor presented itself in the form of cultural contradictions interwoven with the lack of
economic and political power. For example, I kept wondering if there
were many Egyptians among the groups of tourists mingling around
us. We saw and heard American, British, French, German, Russian,
Japanese, and Chinese tourists. Were Egyptians enjoying their local
and national parks as well? Our guide Mamdouh said he did not know,
but most of the tourists he encountered were foreigners. He believed
that if Egyptians were wealthy enough to go touring, they went to
Europe or elsewhere. In his experience, most Egyptians did not really
care about the historic monuments because they do not learn about
their heritage. Egyptian schools do not teach the ancient history of
the Pharaohs, mummies, and monuments because it runs counter to
the state religion of Islam. Perhaps this is similar to the controversy

over teaching evolution in science classes in the US, as it runs counter to Christianity. It is sad that so many Egyptians do not know how incredible their heritage is and may only see the monuments as pieces of the tourist economy. This feels like another Jenga piece that the government has removed, creating another gap between rich and poor.

In the US, we are protective of the historic monuments that mark our 250 years of heritage. But I think the perceptions in Egypt run something like this: the desiccating power of the desert has preserved these ancient pyramids, statues, and mummies for thousands of years. A few million tourists every year won't harm them.

The Egyptian sites we toured are so old that it's hard for an American to wrap her head around the historic timeline. We were dumbfounded by the fact that we could climb, sit on, and touch statues and pyramids that are nearly six thousand years old! Every time I traced my finger along the rough edge of a sandstone block shaped by human hands thousands of years ago, a thrill like time travel would run through me.

By contrast, in the US there are strict attempts to keep tourists on designated paths and prevent people from climbing, sitting on, or touching historic artifacts at many sites. However, state parks are always my mental model for the relaxed version of protected places. The historic site of Memphis, which was once the capital city of Egypt, reminded us of a US state park. There was nothing fancy. You just wander around at your leisure, explore the artifacts—such as the enormous stone statue of Ramses II, lying on its back, legs broken off, with its beautifully detailed carving—and wonder about the contradictions between what is protected and why.

US state parks are places where you can touch and climb and sit on things because they are not so old or fragile. My partner and I have both worked as summer season Park Rangers in the US National Park Service, so we understand how tourism is good for the economy and education of visitors, but it can also be damaging. Just through sheer numbers of people, our footsteps wear down paths, unwashed hands rub off paint, curiosity can damage architecture when people enter or climb on structures, and there is always litter left behind.

At the pyramids of Giza, we were awestruck and giddy as children to be in the presence of these famous, ancient treasures. From the airplane window and photos, the pyramids look big, but not huge. They don't compare to modern skyscrapers, for example. But as we walked up to the base of the largest pyramid, it seemed to just keep getting larger. This unusual perspective is hard to anticipate, and you don't recognize it until you are standing in front of the pyramids and seeing how tiny people are walking around next to them. I joined the millions of tourists over the centuries in climbing up on the exposed pyramid blocks to stand on one for perspective. A single sandstone block was as high as my waist! As I stood there with dust on my hands, feeling the desert sun heating the sandstone blocks, looking up at the height and breadth of the pyramid, the thought of people building these monumental structures by hand was staggering.

The realization that these were mausoleums, each for a single person, is such a wide gap between rich and poor that it is hard to imagine. King Tut, who ruled for nine years and was only nineteen years old when he died, was found entombed in a solid gold sarcophagus, inside two additional coffins and three outer boxes, all ornately painted or set with gold and jewels. We saw his coffins, and his many other treasures, on display at the Egyptian Museum in Cairo.

Ancient Egyptians' religious beliefs held that the dead should be buried with all the items of daily life that they would need to be comfortable in the afterlife. So, the pyramids of the kings contained burial chambers filled with gold and jewels, chariots, furniture, miniature carved foods, servants, and soldiers. The walls were covered with elaborate, beautifully painted instructions on how to pass the many tests that would be administered by the gods. All of these riches provide insights into how the kings lived.

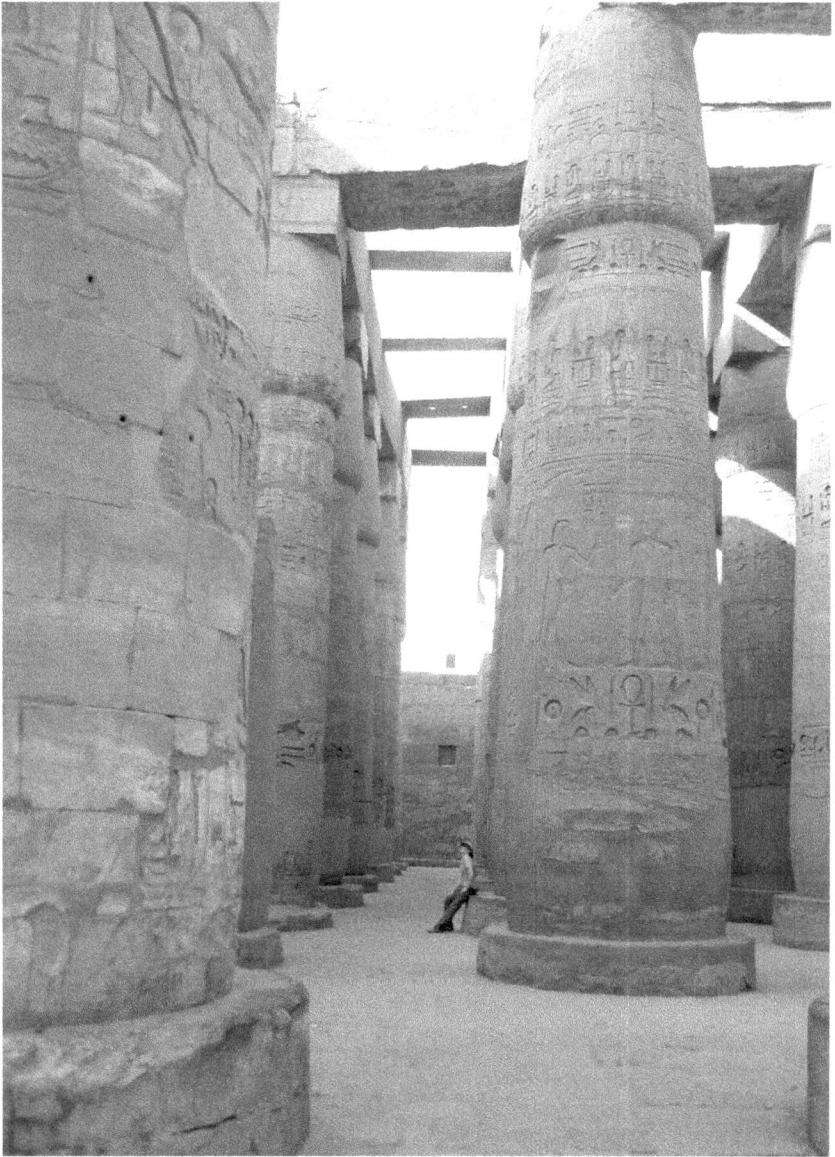

Awe-inspiring temple ruins at Luxor.
Photo credit 2010 Mick Beltz.

When the ancient Greeks found the pyramids of Giza, they assumed that slave labor was used to build them. Greek culture was built on slave labor. This was their worldview, and so it was considered an accurate understanding for centuries. But when the settlement camps surrounding the pyramids were found and closely studied, a different interpretation arose. The people who built the pyramids were most likely the working poor. Farmers and craftsmen were recruited into hard labor during seasonal downtime, such as between planting and harvesting. But they may have viewed this as valuable employment, because the workers would have had housing and meals provided as part of their seasonal labor.

The burial practice for commoners was, of course, much simpler than what the kings received. Wrap the body in a cloth, bury it in the sand, in a cemetery, with some everyday objects and a bit of food. All of this went through my mind as I stood on the pyramid block. When I turned to have my partner take my photo, I laughed to see that he had become entangled with one of the locals trying to sell tourist trinkets: miniature pyramids on keychains, postcards, bookmarks made from papyrus, and small plastic replicas of brightly painted sarcophagi. But it gave me pause to think about how privileged we are compared to the everyday Egyptian, even though we do not fit in the category of wealthy. Walking back to the van, we stopped and bought some papyrus bookmarks from a little girl, to ease our feelings of privileged guilt.

People like us—those wealthy enough to fly around the world and tour other countries—have been rationalizing this guilt for generations. Part of seeking sustainability and resilience ideas while travelling, is coming to a better understanding of privileged guilt and how to compensate for it. My partner and I have an ongoing conversation about these feelings. We struggle sometimes to put these experiences into perspective, trying not to let the guilt cloud our ability to observe the circumstances we encounter. We ask ourselves, how can we help? We try to work with local guides who support local businesses. We bring tourism money into local economies. But does that offset the inequalities that are already present?

The living standards for most Egyptians are much lower than for most people in the United States. Many Egyptians would likely be astounded, and perhaps outraged, at the excessive consumer society Americans live in, especially the amount of disposable waste produced every day. It outrages me when I stop to look at it. But it seemed incredibly arrogant and heartbreaking to try to alleviate our guilt by handing out trinkets like candy or ballpoint pens to children, as many of the tourist guidebooks we read suggested. At different points during our excursions, we observed tourists handing out cash to local Egyptians. Although these were kind and good-hearted gestures, they reminded me of all the uncertainty involved in strategies aimed at trying to alleviate poverty. To me, it seemed more appropriate to thank the guide or family for the tour than to hand them trinkets or a little cash.

There is a deep, multi-layered context of cultural, economic, and political differences between the Global North countries (industrial economies with many privileged middle class and wealthy people) and the Global South countries (developing economies with many people still living in poverty) that I also find hard to express in a brief discussion. But I keep hearing and reading about how our global capitalist system is failing.

When constant economic growth is the number one priority, it comes at the cost of our social and environmental wellbeing. The scholar, Luis Prádanos, sums it up well:[5]

[G]rowth increases inequality and undermines democracy, multiplying the number of social problems that erode human communities. In a nutshell, we have created a dysfunctional economic system that, when it works according to its self-imposed mandate of growing the pace of production and consumption, it destroys the ecological systems upon which it depends. And when it does not grow, it becomes socially unsustainable. In a game with these rules, there is no way to win!

Too many people are unhealthy, unhappy, losing their jobs and their homes, living in poverty, and seeing the natural environment around them polluted and overused. This is an increasingly common sentiment in both privileged countries like the US and in poorer countries like Egypt. We are living in an unsustainable economy.

Jack Shenker explains the situation facing everyday Egyptians: "Since [former President] Mubarak was overthrown, struggles over energy and the environment have been a perpetual feature of [Egypt's ongoing resistance]. Be it against nuclear reactors, chemical plants, power stations or pipelines, popular campaigns have thrown some of Egypt's deep faultiness into focus: the infringement of community rights, the lack of state transparency, the need to shift sovereignty out of the realm of foreign corporations and markets and bring resources under democratic control" (p 344).

The world believes the Egyptian revolution ended with the 2012 presidential elections, with the military takeover in 2013, or when the constitution was amended in 2019 to allow President/General El-Sisi to remain in power until 2030.[6] But Shenker's insider perspective reveals the situation is more complex:

> Opposition protests are focused on far more than the issue of the country's energy mix, or its pollutant level, crucial though those concerns may be. At stake is the fundamental process of decision making in post-Mubarak Egypt, and thus the nature of the [government] itself: in an age of revolution, are Egyptian citizens willing to have choices about their environment made for them? The answer, so far, has been no. The reality is that communities across Egypt have been refusing to allow the state to make decisions for them on virtually every issue of importance since the day the revolution began. [For example,] Egyptians with homes have been fighting off forced evictions; Egyptians without homes . . . have been breaking into the

empty properties of financial speculators and squatting, seizing from the state both land and housing for themselves (p 345).

Examples of how Egyptians continue to fight for their rights can be seen in many ways, from school children up through media and entertainment. After the revolution, children became fascinated with the details of it. At one school, the children (most 9-10 years old) would recreate the fighting they had seen and heard about between the police and activists. In their schoolyard, they were the marchers, rising up against their corrupt headmaster/principal because, among other accused injustices, he refused to allow the children to organize a soccer tournament. One teacher that Shenker interviewed at this school, who had taken part in the marches in Tahrir Square, explained: "The students wanted to know everything, they wanted to know how it felt to have a voice at last. We changed, and they changed with us" (p 20).

In 2012 and again in 2013, the American comedian Jon Stewart, then-host of the late night television program *The Daily Show*, interviewed Bassem Youssef, Egypt's famous political comedian.[7] They discussed the serious role that humor and comedy can play in protesting against unethical government decisions and authoritarian governments. Bassem's story about leaving his successful career as a doctor and becoming a political activist is told in the entertaining, remarkable documentary *Tickling Giants*.[8]

Bassem and his family are now political refugees living in the US. If they returned to Egypt, he would very likely be arrested and tortured for his satirical comedy that pokes fun at the Egyptian government. This is a difficult idea for most Americans to comprehend, but it is a stark reminder that democratic freedoms should not be taken for granted. Bassem now gives speeches around the world about his experience and about how important democracy is to protect.

By protecting democracy, Luis Prádanos explains that we can also protect our ability to change the entwined social, economic, and environmental problems we currently face.

Let's assume that we all agree on some basic facts: first, that the biosphere contains and supports the living systems of the planet; second, that humans are one of the many species embedded in the biosphere and dependent upon its proper functioning; and finally, that an economic system is (or should be) a tool that humans deploy to organize their societies in a functional way.

Based on these commonsense assumptions, the economy is a subsystem of the ecology, not the other way around. Mainstream economics are dysfunctional because they start from the premise that societies and ecosystems must adapt to the market economy. If we begin to organize our priorities according to the biophysical reality rather than the market's demands, it quickly becomes clear that our dominant economic system is absurd because it destroys the ecosystems that are the source of its wealth.[9]

Shenker adds to these insights and pulls back the curtain on our privileged guilt: "Put simply, [the Egyptian revolutionaries] have battled to replace a 'me first' system with an 'all of us' system. In doing so, they have connected the dots of political and economic injustice - at a time in which rampant inequality is compelling many others, in the global north and the global south, to try and do the same. Therein lies the revolution's threat, and its living, giddying possibilities" (p 4).

When the revolution erupted, Egypt's international tourism collapsed into rubble like a pile of Jenga blocks on the floor. Within the first three years, overall tourism revenue dropped 54%. But the impacts on my partner's and my favorite places were devastating. For the city of Luxor and sites outside Cairo such as Memphis, revenue dropped 95%.[10] When we visited Egypt in 2010, we were among fifteen million tourists to enjoy the sites.[11] In 2016, there were only 5.3 million tourists; most of those were from neighboring Arab countries, and they primarily visit the coastal resorts along the Red Sea. By 2019, tourism had rebounded to 13.6 million people. But the Covid-19 pandemic of 2020 severely damaged tourism worldwide. I hope Egypt can rebuild itself beyond relying on an economy of tourism. I found the people of Egypt to be friendly, easy-going, and good-humored. I take hope from Shenker's insights that they are also very resilient.

72

Endnotes

1 http://www.aljazeera.com/news/middlee-
ast/2011/01/201112515334871490.html (https://perma.cc/TS3D-
4QKD)

2 http://kosharirecipe.blogspot.com/search/label/koshari (https://
perma.cc/848A-R76F)

3 https://www.theguardian.com/commentisfree/2019/jan/29/
bill-gates-davos-global-poverty-infographic-neoliberal?C-
MP=Share_iOSApp_Other (https://perma.cc/MZ72-3PDW)

4 https://www.theguardian.com/environment/2020/sep/15/every-
global-target-to-stem-destruction-of-nature-by-2020-missed-un-
report-aoe (https://perma.cc/3PW4-DLPC)

5 https://theconversation.com/an-economy-focused-sole-
ly-on-growth-is-environmentally-and-socially-unsustainable-39761
(https://perma.cc/3HT3-N63F)

6 https://www.cbsnews.com/news/egypt-revolution-january25-tahrir-
square-10-years-later-what-happened/ (https://perma.cc/UC5A-
FHEC)

7 https://en.wikipedia.org/wiki/Bassem_Youssef (https://perma.cc/
Y9VK-LX44)

8 http://www.ticklinggiants.com/ (https://perma.cc/85XP-U3NL)

9 https://theconversation.com/an-economy-focused-sole-
ly-on-growth-is-environmentally-and-socially-unsustainable-39761
(https://perma.cc/3HT3-N63F)

10 https://www.theguardian.com/world/2014/aug/29/egypt-tourism-
revenue-falls-95-percent (https://perma.cc/ZW6S-T93X)

11 http://www.africanews.com/2017/09/19/recovery-of-egyp-
tian-tourism-still-a-mirage-in-luxor/ (https://perma.cc/MD67-
3GFW)

City and residences along the Nile River.
Photo credit 2010 Rebecca J Romsdahl.

The Nile Is Life

Nile River watershed, Egypt, May 2010

Standing in the basket hanging delicately from the bottom of an enormous hot-air balloon, we could see the stark contrast of a bright green ribbon of lush vegetation weaving a path far into the desert. When we commented on this to our guide Robert, he smiled and said, "We say in Egypt that the Nile is life." The Nile is considered the longest river in the world. This lifeblood of North Africa is formed by the merging of its two major tributaries, the White Nile and the Blue Nile. The White Nile forms in the African Great Lakes region, flowing out of Lake Victoria, and is considered to be the headwaters and primary stream of the Nile River.[1] The Blue Nile flows out of Lake Tana, high in the forested mountains of Ethiopia, and it is the source of most of the Nile's water and silt. Similar to the Red River of the North, in North America, the Nile is one of those oddities that flows from south to north.

Author Rosemary Mahoney describes this ancient, unusual, north-flowing river as she first observed it in the modern confines of Cairo: "[W]ide and coffee colored and dumpy, with piles of trash spilling down its eastern bank with the distinct look of having been recently unloaded from a municipal truck. Some of the trash was on fire, sending into the air slender strings of fishy-smelling yellow smoke. This urban strip of river—crowded with powerboats, ferries, tour boats, private yachts; spanned by four or five great bridges; and lined with skyscrapers and luxury hotels—was nearly the very end of the great Nile River. It was understandable then that it looked worn out, congested, and a bit abused" (p 7).

Further north, the Nile Delta, where the river empties into the Mediterranean Sea, is one of the largest river deltas in the world. It stretches 150 miles along the coast and nearly 100 miles deep into the desert to the outskirts of Cairo. For centuries, the Nile Delta has been a rich, fertile landscape of wetlands and agriculture.

To experience the romantic history of the Nile, we embarked on a seven-day sailboat journey. We sailed upstream, traveling south from the city of Luxor to the city of Aswan. In a conversation with our first guide, Mamdouh, he described the sailboat as a dahabiya, the "Rolls Royce" of Nile ships. These dahabiyas are modernized replicas of luxury sailboats first used by European tourists in the early 1900s. They generally have five or six crew cabins, plus four cabins and a suite for tourists. When we arrived to check in, we were surprised to learn that the captain had bumped our reservation up to the suite because we would be joined by a party of four other couples traveling together. We were delighted because the suite gave us a private balcony at the back of the boat, where we enjoyed the centuries-old romance of afternoon tea while watching the changing Nile scenery drift by. Relaxing, refreshing, decadent leisure time.

Some days, the front sail billowed out as the boat slipped smoothly upriver. Other days, the air was still and heavy with a tropical feel, and we were towed by a small tugboat. From our balcony, we would listen to the breaking waves in the small wake and allow this lazy music to transport us out of time while we jotted notes in our journals. I felt immersed in a pleasant daze of pure enjoyment. Every few minutes, one of us would break the trance with a comment about the world drifting by:

- The rise of hills in the near distance seems to plateau into mountains, their sandy, barren dryness such a striking contrast with the lush greenery of bullrushes and palm trees along the shoreline.

- The wailing sound of a call to prayer from the local mosque draws our eyes to its lovely minaret just visible above the palm trees.

- Verdant floating mats of vegetation, some four feet wide, drift by now and again with varieties of birds hunting through them: small, black birds with red and yellow beaks, maybe common moorhens, and pretty long-legged egrets with light blue beaks and feet.

- There are boys swimming, noisy and naked near shore, and more birds where the boys are not.

Eventually, the sound of sparse traffic on the road, paralleling the river, brought our attention back to modernity.

To explore the Nile on her own terms, Rosemary Mahoney took a small fisherman's skiff and rowed up the same section that we were traveling. Her observations came to mind as we idly watched daily life along the shore pass by. "From the luxurious deck of the ship, it struck me one evening that I was looking at an ox, palm trees, sandy banks, mirror-still coves, water jugs on women's heads, pink sails in an archae-ological distance. I saw flamingos and storks, soft colors, an explosive sunset, obelisks and minarets, and now and then a ruined pharaonic temple. I saw no skyscraper and only several buildings that could be truly termed modern. But for a few power lines threading in and out of the tops of palm trees, an occasional plastic water bottle bobbing on the current, a motorized water pump" (p 8). I mostly agreed with her assessment that there is little to be seen in the rural Nile landscape to suggest the complexity of changes that have shaped the modern world in the past two hundred years.

Despite enjoying our romantic sailing journey, we were never far from thinking about the contrasts between rich and poor. As Jack Shenker describes, the Nile itself represents a sadly ironic, but signifi-cant problem for the people of Egypt as a whole:

The country most closely associated with the world's longest river is suffering from an acute shortage of water, and its deficit is only likely to get worse. . . . [T]wo main explanations were usually proffered: population growth and global climate change. Both are relevant. The Delta was once nourished by the water and silt that washed in with Egypt's seasonal floods; since the construction of the High Dam at Aswan in the 1960s those floods have ceased, and in their place a network of irrigation canals has ferried gallons of freshwater from the Nile's two tributary branches across to where it's needed. But increased water use upstream [in other developing nations like Ethiopia, etc.] . . . have taken a toll. Egypt currently has only 700 cubic meters of freshwater per person, well short of the 1,000 cubic meters per person the United Nations believes is the minimum need for water security (p 180).

By contrast, the United States in 2012 had the world's highest water footprint, meaning that each American used around 2,842 cubic meters per person.[2] This is much higher than the world average of 1,385 cubic meters per person. Simply put, Americans use a lot of water in daily life, arguably more than our fair share. This counts everything from how often we wash clothes to how much water it takes to produce the large quantities of meat that many Americans eat every day.

This difference in living standards was well represented as we walked through the village of Esna to view the local ancient temple. For many generations, the temple was lost, buried by flood silt and wind-blown sands. Now, in its rediscovered setting, the excavated section of the temple sits more than 20 feet below ground level. Most of the temple and its grounds cannot be recovered because the modern village is built on top of it all. As we walked through the great hall, admiring the 24 beautifully carved red sandstone columns that hold up the roof as it appears to float above them, each 37 feet tall and 18 feet around, I tried to imagine how much of daily life would seem familiar between now and when the temple was built thousands of years ago.

Although Esna has roughly the same size population (around 50,000) as our home city of Grand Forks, North Dakota, I believe that most Americans would say the people of Esna live in humble poverty. When we visited, the streets were packed dirt. The market vendors had a wide variety of goods (fruits, veggies, beans, clothes, luggage, cloth, even a cobbler for shoes), but the stalls and tables seemed haphazardly constructed and in unsteady condition. There were plastic bags, various wrappers, and other litter strewn about. And many people seemed to show signs of poor health, such as missing teeth or being extremely thin. Our guide Robert laughed in surprise when we told him that our city, where we lived and worked, was the same size as Esna. "What? You have a university in your village?" He shook his head in amazement at such a contrast because he had attended university in the megacity of Cairo, which has a population of around 18 million.

Our dahabiya tied up to shore one afternoon to let a flotilla of hotels (large ships with 75 or more rooms) pass by. We counted 25 cruise boats over a couple of hours before losing track. During our break, we were privileged to tour a nearby family's farm and house. We felt awkward and a bit intrusive to be tramping through their home. I thought of the few times when extended family, or friends of friends, had visited my family's farm to get a tour of the barns, see the animals, and stop in for coffee and cookies. Even as a child, it seemed strange to hear their comments about how they had never been to a farm before and they hadn't known what to expect.

The Egyptian family's mudbrick house had hard-packed dirt floors, a small common living space with a modest television hooked up to satellite dish, a couple of small bedrooms, and a kitchen with a little refrigerator, table, chairs, a five-gallon propane tank fueling their stovetop, and a single electric bulb on a string. The walls were painted bright shades of blue and green, and there were colorful rag rugs scattered here and there on the floor. Several children watched us with smiles and curious eyes. Robert told us there was also sleeping space with mats on the rooftop as we had seen other places, to enjoy the cool air of summer nights.

Outside, the family had a large mudbrick oven and a small, barn-like enclosure attached to the house where they kept several goats and about a dozen chickens and ducks. Robert told us this was an average working-class family. We greeted the smiling women and children by saying "salaam" as one of the women led us through their home. Another guide, Ayman, told us there were four brothers and their families who shared the farm, house, and other outbuildings.

Later that day as we sailed further upstream, we passed another family farm onshore. There was a cow grazing outside a small barn built from concrete blocks, and we could see part of a mudbrick house in the background where children were playing outside. We asked Ayman about the assortment of construction materials that we had been seeing along our trip. He explained that converting the houses and buildings to concrete block structures was a sign of higher wealth and status. But he felt it was an unfortunate decision for families because the concrete buildings are more expensive to build. They are also more expensive to maintain because they do not stay naturally cool like the traditional mudbrick structures, so families have to invest in electric air conditioning. I could not help wondering how much more burdensome this expense might become as the climate crisis continues to increase temperatures and extreme weather events.

The next day, we had a delightful breakfast onshore in a small grove of mango and banana trees on a local farm. The family had an agreement with the tour company that allowed the dahabiyas to tie up there overnight and tourists to receive a brief tour of part of the family's fields and farm life. They showed us their two camels, several donkeys and cows, and sheep. A couple of our travel companions took turns riding one of the donkeys. We declined as we both were recovering from the ill-effects of Tut's trots (a local name for travel sickness, symptoms include stomach cramps, diarrhea, or general gastro-intestinal distress). The farm looked prosperous. I could identify a variety of crops they were growing, including peppers, okra, sugarcane, wheat, alfalfa, and the grove of mango and banana trees also included some tangerine trees. The family rented the tractor and thrasher that we saw

An Egyptian family showing how their waterwheel works.
Photo credit 2010 Rebecca J Romsdahl.

82

in the wheat field for the half day it would take to harvest and process the crop. The farm seemed to have a nice supplemental income from tourists as well. We noticed that another dahabiya had tied up a short distance behind our boat during the night.

During the ancient floods, the Nile River water was likely a muddy brown, the same caramel color of the soil. The Nile we sailed on was a lapis lazuli blue of reflected skies and deep, clear water. While this difference may be more pleasing to the eye, it means the river is not as rich in nutrient-laden silt as it was for centuries before the Aswan High Dam was built. The Dam sits just far enough inside Egypt's southern border to contain Lake Nasser, the reservoir created by the dam. The family showed us their irrigation system, which was made more reliable by the Dam.

The family had a simple system of two cows tethered to a large, iron waterwheel. The cows were led around in a circle to operate the pump. The water drawn out was dumped into a small channel around one to two feet wide from which it could be directed left or right, by removing or replacing mud dikes, into other channels that lined the fields. The water then flooded the field into which it was directed. Some of the crops were planted in high mounded rows. This is an ancient and effective system when the Nile water is plentiful, but in dry years and in a desert climate, it seemed to leave too much water exposed to evaporation. As Shenker describes, this will become more problematic for farming families:

> Climate change and increasing population growth over the coming decades will only make Egypt's water shortage worse. Any rise in temperatures will result in more Nile water evaporating before it ever gets to the Delta region. . . . [T]o make matters even worse, Egypt's northern region [the Delta]—already one of the top three areas on the planet most vulnerable to any rises in global sea levels—is being hit by coastal erosion, enabling the spread of salinity through the fields and damaging soil fertility. Experts . . . predict that wheat and corn yields

could drop by 40-50 percent respectively across the next thirty years, and . . . flooding from the sea could displace millions of Egyptians from one of the most densely populated regions on Earth. Under the Mubarak Government, these facts were used as weapons against the poor; the Government blamed Egypt's ecological problems of massive population, overcrowding, pollution, cars and agricultural chemicals, and rising sea level on the very people who suffer most from these challenges and then used that false environmental concern to legitimize government assaults against marginalized peoples and give priority to government schemes for private wealth development under disguises of social responsibility (p 181).

After a week of sailing the Nile, we landed in the city of Aswan, where our new guide, a young man on summer break from university studying to be a tourist guide, transported us to the final leg of our adventure. The edge of a sandstorm created a hazy view. Our guide hired a taxi ferry, a small powerboat, from the army of them waiting at the docks. The taxi would take us to an island in Lake Nasser, the reservoir created by the Aswan High Dam. There we would tour the Temple of Isis at Philae.

While waiting for the taxi, I kept my back to the sandstorm winds and watched dust devils on the water. My thoughts kept drifting to one idea. The Nile *is* life for Egyptians. The river is the lifeblood of agriculture, which feeds the people. The Aswan High Dam provides electricity and drought management. The Nile provides drinking water to the nation. Whoever has access to the Nile has a better life. Whoever controls decisions about how to use the Nile waters has power over the gaps between rich and poor.

As tiny, cool droplets of water spritzed my cheek, we laughed at the sight of our taxi driver. He was like any other modern teenager in the world today. He was multitasking, smoking a cigarette with one hand, mobile phone in his other hand, and steering the boat with his foot. My partner commented that people are pretty much the same everywhere: "People want their boss to nag them a little less, want to make a little more money, want to have a little more time to laugh and relax, hope for good health and a better future for their kids, and want a safe, healthy place to live." When people recognize that these seemingly simple desires are not within their reach, they become dissatisfied with life, and if circumstances do not improve, they begin to demand change. If changes do not go far enough, people will eventually take actions to create the changes they seek. This is how revolutions are born. This is how Egyptians continue to struggle with their gaps between rich and poor, between powerful and powerless.

November 2017. I recently met an Egyptian student in the US who had been awarded a Fulbright Scholarship to work toward a master's degree. We talked about the 2011 Egyptian revolution. He had traveled three hours from his hometown to participate in some of the Cairo demonstrations. He confirmed much of what I had read and heard in news reports. At first, nobody took the demonstrators seriously, but when they refused to leave Tahrir Square and the police actions became violent, everything shifted and the revolution became real. Many people sacrificed their lives to protest. They demanded recognition of the unfair economy, the corrupt police force and government, and how these injustices have fueled growing gaps between rich and poor people in Egyptian society over the past several decades.

When talking about his experiences during the demonstrations, this young man seemed so American. He was proud to be part of the resistance, and his support for change was unswayed by the setbacks of failed politics thus far. He was confident that positive changes will be made because the people will continue to demand them. I asked if tourism has rebounded (It's a significant part of Egypt's economy that has helped create a modest middle class). "No." He shook his head and his eyes looked troubled, but then he smiled. He asked if I would consider going back to visit Egypt again. Even before the 2011 revolution, we thought ourselves lucky to have enjoyed our tour of Egypt when we did, and we left with a feeling of satisfaction that we had seen all we had hoped to see. I told him we would not likely go back. I asked him if life in Egypt has improved after the revolution and he replied, "No, not enough." With gallows humor, he said that when people challenged the government before the revolution, they would just disappear one day. But now they are arrested as terrorists and jailed as examples of bad behavior.

The fate of everyday Egyptians remains uncertain, and the gaps between rich and poor remain wide.[3]

Endnotes

1 https://en.wikipedia.org/wiki/Nile (https://perma.cc/3X-QR-XMYA)
2 https://www.scientificamerican.com/article/graphic-science-how-much-water-nations-consume/ (https://perma.cc/49ZU-GHH8)
3 https://www.npr.org/2021/05/17/997660501/a-symphony-of-resistance (https://perma.cc/GR2Q-6XFB)

Summer is filled with life: kittens and baby birds, playing in tallgrass, swatting mosquitos, weeding bean fields, the smell of hay in the big red barn, long sunlight hours, and refusing to go to bed because of a desire to enjoy every minute of daylight.

Author commuting to work at the Isle Royale Visitor Center.
Photo credit 1998 Mick Beltz.

Appreciating Small Things

Isle Royale National Park, United States, Lake Superior watershed
June–September 1998

Small and subtle become striking and enchanting when we open ourselves to appreciate the natural world.

    This elusive truth can be found where ever we seek it, and it is the
greatest lesson I learned from my summer living at Isle Royale National Park as an Interpretive Park Ranger. My farmgirl background
provided me with ample experience for exploring and playing in my
new wilderness. My training as a Naturalist/Environmental Educator
at two Nature Centers helped prepare me for communicating ecology
with children and adult visitors. But soon after setting foot onshore, I
realized that the only way to truly appreciate this place was to rouse my
inner child and let her roam free. In wilderness we can reconnect with
our senses. I relearned how to listen, to touch, to see, and to appreciate
the small things we miss when we don't pay attention in the moment.

    I would set off to work each day in full uniform, with my olive
green slacks, button-up collared gray shirt, chocolate brown socks, and
hiking boots, topped off with the silly, yet serious, ranger flat hat. My
commute was a ten-minute walk through sun-dappled forest, including a wood plank foot bridge over a tiny stream, that emerged onto a
sloping hill leading down to a large, sturdy dock on the warm Windigo
Bay of Lake Superior. I believe this is the best commute I will ever
have in my life! But being rekindled by nature's wonders occasionally
made me a few minutes late to work. Fortunately, my supervisor was a
relaxed woman with an easy smile who was very understanding of the
distractions one might encounter on the way to work.

During my commute one morning I was sipping a mug of hot cocoa and eating an apple when suddenly, I heard something. My attention zeroed in on the snap and crack of twigs breaking and brush shifting—it was a foraging female moose just uphill from the forest path I was on. She stopped to watch me as I stood watching her. I believe she heard me munching on my breakfast apple. After several minutes of watching each other chewing, she moved on to continue her breakfast. In my next conscious moment, I realized my feet had carried me to the Visitor Center, while my mind lingered behind in the forest.

After a night of fitful rain showers, lazy clouds of morning mist were draped in open spaces. The woods were pulsing with excitement because the weather had been dry for many weeks. I stopped here and there along the path to stare at the simplicity of waterdrops caught on the leaves of young aspen trees. Their clear, silvery glow was mesmerizing. Minutes passed and I had to tear my eyes away from examining the small liquid beads before I completely lost track of myself and time. Their effect lingered, and the forest seemed to be as aware of my presence as I was of each leaf and droplet. My trance was broken by the plip-plop of falling drops striking the forest floor as a red squirrel jumped from branch to branch above the path. Further down the trail, I paused again, peering into the branches of a ninebark shrub to check on a little gray catbird sitting in her carefully constructed nest. She looked back at me with curious, pensive eyes, ready to take flight at any moment. A couple of weeks later, I was thrilled to visit her nest again and see two pairs of eyes looking back at me from downy-feathered heads, mouths wide open with expectations.

When I hiked along the trail to one of my favorite places in the world, Huginnin Cove, I always stopped to admire a miniature forest. Composed of lichens, mosses, and twinflowers, it grows on top of a large granite boulder—one of many—that was dropped here by a retreating glacier in the last ice age. The quiet tranquility of this place was soothing. Just listen: the lake washes against the rocky shoreline; a soft, cool breeze hums through spruce and fir trees; warbling birdsong echoes out from the woods; a cicada buzz reaches crescendo. I lingered at this lovely rock garden to ponder life, time, and the intricate small wonders of nature.

There is an incredible tenacity in the organisms that find ways to live on this rocky outcrop in the midst of the harsh, cold climate of Lake Superior. Some of the boulders that line the trail are crowned by trees. A few of those trees are old enough that their roots creep over the top and down the sides of the boulders to find the soil. The largest roots are thicker than my arm and have grown smooth bark. Science estimates that it takes 500 years or more to form an inch of new soil.[1] These boulders have watched the changing seasons for thousands of years as wind, snow, ice, and rain lashed and pebbled their surfaces, chipping shallow depressions in their tops. Lichens probably arrived first.[2]

Lichens are composite organisms. They are formed by a partnership between a plant, a fungus, and sometimes a yeast. Their unique nature helps them grow on bare surfaces like rocks, fences, and gravestones. They can dry out and go dormant when there is no moisture, and then spring to life with a breath of fog. Some lichens act like a sponge and soak up 20 times their weight in water. They help erode the rocks and catch dust particles from wind and rain. Some grow flat in mats while others grow upward like plants. One is known as "old man's beard" for how it grows as long tendrils hanging in dense clusters from tree branches. Lichens grow slowly, around one millimeter per year, and they live for a long time—many can live hundreds of years. One Arctic species, called map lichen, has been dated around 8,600 years-old, perhaps the oldest living creature on Earth.

Eventually, mosses join the lichen. They help hold enough moisture and a little bit of soil so that flowers can take root. Tiny pink twinflowers are named for their double, bell-shaped flower heads. They grow on slender, olive-colored stems. Their rounded, smooth and plump, paired leaves are also twins at the base of the stem. Twinflowers are just a few inches tall, yet they tower above the lichens and mosses. I imagine myself as a character in a Dr. Seuss story in this miniature world, straining my neck to look up at twinflowers from the forest floor.

Afternoons on the island are typically uneventful after the boat leaves with the day visitors. But on one of these quiet afternoons, a friend and I watched with bated breath as a mini predator-prey drama unfolded. A bumble bee flew into a spiderweb attached to the outside pane of the Visitor Center window. I did not think the web was occupied until that moment when the spider raced down to secure his dinner. The ensuing struggle is one that I think few people witness because we are generally too busy to notice such a small event, and most people (myself included) don't especially like spiders. The bee fought mightily, throwing her big body back and forth, nearly bouncing off the windowpane, while the spider did all he could to hold the large insect in his harvesting trap. The spider made several attempts to immobilize the bee, trying and trying, to wrap her up with more webbing as the bee tried to sting the spider in return. Suddenly, the bumble-bigness broke free of the sticky web, and we cheered as the bee flew off in a frenzy. We were impressed by the passion of the struggle and felt very privileged to have witnessed it.

Summer evenings on the island are long and leisurely. After supper, I could often be found sitting on the front lawn of our duplex dorm house, engrossed in reading a book. One evening, however, I was being tormented by a small gang of biting houseflies. Before they forced me inside, as if I had sent out a distress call, a pair of shimmering green darner dragonflies came to my rescue. In reality, the dragonflies recognized me as bait. They circled me as they hunted with lightning speed, feeding on my biting tormentors. Time shifted into slow motion as I watched one of the dragonflies catch a fly in its tiny claws and devour it, just inches from my nose! Minutes later, one of those magnificent little dragons landed on my hand, her feet like pinpoints on my skin. She looked at me, tilting her head, considering me with enormous kaleidoscope eyes. I thanked her, wondering what she might say if we could communicate.

Miniature forest of lichen and twinflowers.
Photo credit 2018 Rebecca J Romsdahl.

Living on this island was a dreamlike experience. The days blended into each other like mirages and the weeks flew with the winds. One early-autumn evening, the shifting light of sunset tinted the clouds into shades of pale blue-lavender and pink. The sky began to invert and transform into an alternate reality. There were majestic rays of sapphire streaking into the eastern horizon as though I was watching a blue sun slowly set in a rosy-pink sky. The mind trick was dazzling.

August 1998.
The faint cry of the loon
Rises and vanishes
In the silence of ebony velvet.
The moonless night
Blends into the water.
They reflect each other
And we can touch the stars
Below us.
Their forms flow
Outward
From our fingertips.

July 2018. Twenty years and many adventures later, we return to Isle Royale. Stepping onto the Windigo dock feels like coming home. My teenage nephews help unload our backpacks from the ferry. They are still young, but growing fast, and it is time to introduce a new generation to this enchanting wilderness.

Endnotes

1 https://www.soils.org/about-soils/basics/ (https://web.archive.org/
web/20211022120829/https://www.soils.org/about-soils/basics/)

2 https://en.wikipedia.org/wiki/Lichen (https://perma.cc/4G6J-VY-
HD)

Hiking up toward the scales on the Chilkoot Trail.
Photo credit 1999 Tom Beltz.

Practicing Self-Sufficiency

Chilkoot Trail, Klondike Gold Rush National Historic Site,
United States, Taiya River watershed, August 1999

Rasping glaciers, graceful humpback whales, glistening sea otters,
warm jackets in August, quiet wilderness, pink fireweed flowers, salm-
on leaping up streams, dizzying waterfalls, grizzly bears, crossroads
that dead-end in all four directions, the piercing cry of bald eagles: this
is Alaska.

We arrived in the rain. This was to be expected, given that Juneau
is located in the coastal, temperate rainforest of the Pacific Northwest,
and summer is the rainy season. My partner, his parents, and I were
here to explore. The young woman who served us lunch was from
Wisconsin and was spending her summer waiting tables for tourists
in Alaska. She told us it had been raining for 30 days straight. We had
packed our rain gear, but thankfully, my weather charm worked his
magic. After day two, we had nothing but sunny skies for our two-week
adventure. Our goal was to hike the 33-mile historic Chilkoot Trail.[1]

We were following the footsteps of crazy, adventurous people who
hoped to find a better future for themselves and their families during
the Klondike goldrush.[2] In August 1896, three men found a stunning
pocket of gold where the Yukon and Klondike Rivers merge, setting off
a great and heartbreaking goldrush in the Yukon Territory of Canada.
Over the next two years, thousands of stampeders set off for Alaska
and the Yukon, not knowing that most of the good gold claims had
already been staked. In their wake, they left us with a romanticized,
tragic history of yet another example of human hopefulness dashed by
short-sightedness and folly.

In my personal efforts to overcome short-sightedness, I am always striving to reduce my ecological footprint on the natural world.[3] An ecological footprint is an estimated measure of how much natural resources (water, land, trees, etc.) a person, population, or company is using and how much waste their activities are producing. We can then compare that measure with how much capacity an ecosystem might have to reabsorb that waste.

Backpacking gives me a chance to think, plan, and practice reducing my ecological footprint through self-sufficiency, which leads me to think about connections with sustainability and resilience. Some groups and individuals are very motivated by these ideas as they aim for self-sustainability, implementing practices that allow them to live simpler, smaller, and slower lifestyles. Examples include homesteading, food storage, and living-off-the-(electricity)grid. Self-sufficiency and sustainability go hand-in-hand with the Leave No Trace (LNT) principles of outdoor recreation and education.[4] The LNT principles can be applied anywhere, from national parks to one's backyard, to help minimize negative impacts on the world. They provide the foundation for how I learned backpacking as a recreational activity. When you pause and consider the principles, they are very common sense.

LNT principle: Plan ahead and prepare. When planning a backpacking trip, I start by checking the weather forecasts and thinking about the type of environment where my group and I will be hiking. Should we bring rain gear? Will we need insect repellent? Are we hiking in bear country, and if so, will we need rope to hang up our bags in the trees, or will there be bear-proof boxes at the campsites? We check our tent, boots, water filter pump, and other gear to be sure everything is accounted for and in good working condition. I also make careful lists of food and other items that we will need. And because we must carry all of this on our backs, it forces me to think about what is essential. I don't want to carry any unnecessary weight, but I also don't want to overlook something important like a first-aid kit. This is when I start hearing discussions with my Sustainability Studies students replay in my head.

I ask each class to consider a scenario: if they had only a few minutes to grab a bag and rush out the door to escape a natural disaster, what would they want in their bag? After some discussion, they generally narrow down to a list of common items: clothes, food, phone/tablet/laptop, recharging cables, money, passport, toiletries, medicines, book/notebook, water bottle, and something for emotional comfort, like a childhood teddy bear or a favorite t-shirt. Then I ask how much stuff they brought to outfit their dorm room versus how much of that stuff would they consider essential. Many students bring a lot of stuff to college. For example, our discussions have revealed: desk chairs, reclining chairs, desks, lamps, fans, rugs or carpet, bedding, toiletries, towels, artwork, framed photos and other decorations, books, notebooks and writing supplies, a microwave oven, video game consoles, a television, a mini-refrigerator, laptop computers, cross-country skis or other recreation equipment, dishes, cookware, food, and lots of boxes of clothing. How much of that stuff would they be willing to carry on their backs for the semester? Their reply is usually very similar to the list of essential items for their emergency grab bag. This comparison helps us talk about the differences between the things we want (all the stuff we buy) and the essential things we need (clean air and water, healthy food, good relationships).

The Chilkoot Trail was developed by the Tlingit people as a vital route to move resources and connect communities between the Pacific coast and the forested interior, over a pass in the Coast Mountains. The Chilkoot Pass was also the shortest route for the stampeders to reach the Klondike gold fields in the Yukon Territory. Because the region was so remote and winters so long and severe, the Canadian authorities required every person heading to the gold fields to bring a full year of supplies with them before they were permitted to enter the Yukon Territory, to prevent mass starvation. This soon became known as the "ton-of-goods."[5] For example, the Canadian government calculated that each person required three pounds of food per day, which quickly adds up to over 1,000 pounds of weight. People also needed winter and summer clothing, sturdy boots, tent materials including mosquito nets, and various mining equipment. Imagine planning and preparing to move all of that stuff from a boat on the coast to the scales located at the base of the Chilkoot Pass, then up and over the 3,000 foot pass. This required either multiple trips or hiring Tlingit people to help carry it all. Some stampeders trudged 1,000 miles up and down, up and down, moving 50-80 pounds of supplies each trip over the pass to Lake Bennet where they could load it onto ships.

In her research, author Kathryn Morse chronicles the hardships of the stampeders' journey through the diaries and letters they sent home to family:

> [M]en and women struggled for the words to convey the physical and mental experience of hauling their bodies and their heavy packs and sleds over the coastal mountains to the headwaters of the Yukon River. James Hamil wrote home to Iowa from the Chilkoot in October 1897: 'To go over this trail [one] must wade [a] stream running at the rate of 10 miles per hour and ice cold that runs out from the snow and over Glaciers... One must climb high peaks over jagged rocks down through deep canyons and over mountains of ice which never disappear...and one mile of the climb to the top [of Chilkoot Pass] is almost perpendicular and a portion of this one must crawl on his hands and knees.' (p 4)

All of this and more, multiple times, to move a ton of goods.

For our backpacking trips, my partner and I aim for approximately 10 miles per day and no more than three days on the trail because that is the weight limit of gear and food we are comfortable carrying between the two of us. We each bring a sleeping bag and an inflatable bedroll. Our tent is just big enough for the two of us to sleep in easily, with a little space at our feet. The backpacks get hung from a pole or tree in bear country to keep the food safe. Bears are also interested in any items that have a fragrance, like lip balm or deodorant, so these never go in the tent.

Our kitchen gear includes a hand-operated water filter pump, which makes rest stops at streams very productive. We have two small, nesting cook pots; two titanium sporks; small aluminum plates with a half-inch lip so they can double as shallow bowls; and cups for drinking that also have measurement lines. We also bring a tiny camping stove, that easily fits in a jacket pocket, to cook simple meals and heat water for tea. It has three metal arms that fold out to set a pot onto and the center screws into a small butane fuel canister. Finally, no backpack trip is properly equipped without a multi-tool Swiss army knife.

We have favorite trail foods that get packed on nearly every trip. Granola bars are a go-to snack. Breakfasts are oatmeal, fruit, and Earl Grey tea. We make a trail mix with peanuts, raisins, other dried fruits like bananas, cherries, mango, or coconut, M&Ms, and sometimes a bit of Chex Mix. Tortillas make good sandwich rolls with peanut butter and jelly. They are a bit heavy, but they are durable, especially compared to bread that just gets squished in a backpack. Dinners are often a mix of rice or pasta with black beans or chickpeas. Food wrappers and packaging gets stuffed into a plastic bag, and everything that we carry into the ecosystem gets carried back out.

After a summer spent backpacking across Isle Royale National Park, we learned a lot through trial and error about what gear, clothing, and food works well for our needs. I imagine most of the Klondike gold rush stampeders did not have similar experiences to draw on when planning their expedition. Without reliable news sources and with plenty of misinformation passed along, most stampeders did not have good advice about how to prepare. They would not understand the hardships they were running toward until it was too late. There were murders, suicides, and deaths by hypothermia, avalanche, disease, and starvation. They had little more than word-of-mouth passed on from travelers and the occasional printed advertisement.

Before heading up to the Chilkoot trailhead, we took two boat rides through Glacier Bay National Park, near Gustavus, Alaska. We had hoped to watch whales and see a glacier up close. The whales were rather shy that day, and we only saw a few humped-backs and their large, beautiful tails, which scientists have found to be as individually distinguishable as human faces.

The glacier, in contrast, was surprisingly animated. The leading edge of the ice was noisy with cracking and popping sounds. Many Indigenous peoples around the world consider glaciers to be living entities. I agree with these sentiments. Glaciers are very old beings, some have lived for hundreds of thousands of years. Creaking and groaning, like a slumbering giant slowly waking, crawling out of his mountainous valley bed, slipping and calving pieces of himself; this glacier was falling apart in slow motion right before our eyes.

I don't remember any mention of human-caused climate change while touring Alaska. This might mean that the topic was already being silenced by political agendas or that it was not yet on my active radar. In the 20 years that have passed, the melting rate of glaciers has doubled.[6] This added water has contributed to rising sea levels, over 260 gigatons per year, which can be visualized as flooding the entire country of England in six feet of water for each of the last 20 years.

The next morning, we bicycled around the tiny village of Gustavus, peddling out from the center four-way stop intersection to the end of the pavement in all four directions. Then we stopped for lunch at a kitchen café in the home of a local couple. They told us our salad was picked fresh moments ago, from the greens growing wild in their front yard. Given the remoteness of its geography, having food and other goods transported to Alaska is very expensive, so the need for self-sufficient living is a staple of daily life. Food scraps from preparing our meal would help nourish their compost pile for the backyard garden.

LNT principle: Dispose of waste properly. This is another LNT principle that relates well to sustainability and resilience. In backpacking, this means you carry out what you carried in, which reinforces the principle of good planning. There are no trash bins in the backcountry. This also applies to the sustainability practice of *reduce* what you buy, *reuse* items as much as possible, and *recycle* items that can no longer be used. But this is often challenging. Our society currently relies on a straight-line flow of new resources to make items that too quickly end up in the trash. Instead, we should build a more resilient system that operates like a circular flow of resources, within a set of boundaries.

Think of a doughnut. Economist Kate Raworth created this idea as a new model for a thriving, resilient, sustainable economy: "The Doughnut consists of two concentric rings:[7] a social foundation, to ensure that no one is left falling short on life's essentials, and an ecological ceiling, to ensure that humanity does not collectively overshoot the planetary boundaries that protect Earth's life-supporting systems.[8] Between these two sets of boundaries lies a doughnut-shaped space that is both ecologically safe and socially just: a space in which humanity can thrive." Inside the delicious doughnut, we can build an economy that protects natural systems and human wellbeing. It can also help us focus on the reuse and recycling of materials, so that nothing is considered waste.

We must escape the current economic model that trains us to desire and buy new things constantly. To produce all that new stuff, we have been harvesting and mining natural resources and throwing away disposable items at stunning rates. For example, Americans purchased 50 billion bottles of water in 2018. And that does not count the disposable soda bottles, sports drinks, food containers, and other plastics that are used every day.

Adding to this problem is the myth of recycling.[9] Environmentally minded people feel good putting recyclables into the correct bin and trusting that the system gets it all recycled. But we have slowly come to recognize that this is a myth for plastics. The recycling rate for plastic is only 9% and that is decreasing, not only because of the low recycling rates of individuals. It is mostly because many plastics technically can't be recycled and turned into other products, and for those that can, we don't have enough capacity in current facilities.

This overconsumption behavior is not sustainable. We have created a viciously efficient linear system that turns our natural resources almost directly into trash. At this rate, we are on our way to converting this beautiful Earth into the nightmare trash-filled planet depicted in the Disney film *WALL-E*. To raise awareness of these problems, I have a class assignment that requires students to keep track of all the trash they produce in one week. Many are very surprised by how quickly it adds up because when we put trash in a bin, it is out of sight and out of mind. When you have to keep a record of it for a week, or pack it and carry it around in your backpack, trash suddenly becomes a real thing that you want to minimize as much as possible.

LNT principle: Leave what you find. For those of us who like to ramble through the natural world, it can be very tempting to bring home a little souvenir. A pretty rock, a handful of sand or seashells, some dried flowers—it seems harmless to slip these into your pocket. But if every visitor to a place does that, eventually there will be a noticeable decline or even a disappearance of those resources.

Many stampeders began their trek by setting sail from San Francisco or Seattle for the small port of Skagway, Alaska. We hired the pilot of a six-seat propeller plane to take us from Gustavus to Skagway. He gave us a flyover tour of several local glaciers along the route. To see the slumbering giants from the sky was magnificent. The pilot drew our attention to a dark, frozen river of rock and soil debris trapped in the middle of an ice field, running its length like a painted stripe down the giant's back. Another glacier, upon reaching its edge, was feeding a cascading waterfall that tumbled over a cliff, falling hundreds of feet to splay across a rubble-strewn landslide pile on the valley floor. Once there, the water gathered itself into a stream running into the forest. From inside the plane with our ears covered by headphones, it was like watching a scene in an old-time silent film. The white noise of the plane easily stood in for the missing film projector.

Day one. The Chilkoot Trail starts in coastal temperate rainforest winding its way alongside the Taiya River. Being the height of summer, there were copious waves of pink fireweed lighting up every open meadow space along the river. Keeping the LNT principles in mind, I resisted the alluring idea of picking a few flowers to adorn my hat and instead crouched down for a silly photo with the largest field of fireweed spread out behind me. Leaving the flaming wildflowers, we crossed a series of beaver ponds on raised wood plank footpaths. The skeletons of dead trees saluted us as though they were ranks of soldiers standing guard over the beavers' territory.

LNT principle: Respect wildlife. It can sometimes be tempting to inch a little closer to get a better photo. At the time, you believe you are being careful. But the natural world can be hazardous. I generally translate this LNT principle more broadly than just wildlife. Inching out toward a cliff edge for a better view can result in a fall that ends with a broken leg or even death. Straying too far off the trail can get you lost or a painful case of poison ivy. And getting too close to wildlife can be especially dangerous. The number one injury in US National Parks is people being kicked by deer because they tried to get a perfect photo and they did not respect the fact that these animals are wild creatures, not tame pets.

Within the first hour of hiking, less than five miles from our start, we crossed paths with a couple of women who were making a hasty retreat back to the trailhead. They stopped briefly to warn us that they had encountered a grizzly bear along the trail ahead. Just the sight and sounds of that wild animal going about his business in the woods was such a jolt to their sense of safety that they realized this was not their type of adventure after all. They were done hiking and heading straight back to Skagway. I understand their trepidation. One of my colleagues in the National Park Service was mauled by a grizzly bear when he was a child. The bear ripped through their tent, dragging him and another family member out, attacking them with claws and teeth. They survived. My colleague lost one eye and was left with a limp and deeply gashed scars on face and body. But he embraced his survival as a way to teach about the value of wild animals and space for nature.

Hiking in bear territory is not for the faint of heart. You must learn a few tricks to avoid encounters, like singing and talking while on the trail to alert bears so they can move away from your presence. I will admit that whenever we camp in grizzly country, I do not sleep well. My mind will not relax. At best, it hovers on the edge of sleep, always listening for warning signs of an approaching predator. We had already seen a mother grizzly and two cubs searching for food on the beach of Glacier Bay during our glacier tour. They were beautiful symbols of wild nature, especially as we watched from the safety and distance of the boat deck. But when there is nothing but a few trees and a short running distance between you and a bear, her beauty strikes you with instinctual dread—the type of panic that leaves you frozen like a deer in headlights. The risks can be reduced with careful preparation and vigilance. Because seeing a bear just being a bear in her natural habitat is a heart-fluttering thrill.

Finnegan's Point was the first campground on the Chilkoot, about five miles from the trailhead. We stopped there for lunch. As we wandered around, stretching our backs and enjoying the always wonderful feeling of taking a break from carrying your pack, we found a remarkable view of another glacier, this one set high up in a large mountain saddle. Twenty years later, photos of this same view show the incredible retreat of Irene Glacier, creating a long whitewater river coursing over the exposed, scraped, and deposited rocks beneath it.[10] The stampeders would have also seen this glacier. I wonder how different the landscape appeared in their time. Had many people paused to notice it, or was their attention preoccupied by the rush and stress to move their supplies as quickly as possible along this route?

Relics they left behind are still scattered along the trail. After crossing a suspension bridge over the Taiya River on the way to Pleasant Camp, our stop for the first night, we passed through the ruins of Canyon City. It was a haphazard tent city thrown up to supply the needs of ambitious fools. Today, it is memorialized by the remains of a few building foundations and a modern cabin that holds a variety of artifacts. But my attention was captured by a solitary object. Amidst the greenery of the rainforest sits the carcass of a large cooking stove. Its iron walls and chimney, coated by rust and lichens, were pockmarked with holes. The cooking surface fell into the two large ovens on either side of the central firebox long ago. The skeletal oven doors, open wide but still attached by their rusted hinges, provided a garden platform for lush mounds of emerald moss. The weight of my backpack suddenly seemed so small and insignificant. How many days did it take horses or mules to pull the wagon that transported this oversized, out-of-place appliance into the forest? How many people enjoyed hot meals before this iron relic of civilization was abandoned to be reclaimed by the earth? It strikes me that humans will do very strange things as they attempt to find a purpose and define their success in life. Even after acknowledging that a gold rush by its very nature is not a sustainable activity, thousands of people still marched into this wilderness.

LNT principle: Be considerate of others. Even in the backcountry, we share resources and space with other people and the nature around us. If we pick all the ripe berries we find along a trail, that reduces the food for wild animals and the potential for other hikers to enjoy a few berries tomorrow. This LNT principle can be a good guideline for wrestling with the "challenge of sustainability: meeting the needs of present and future generations while substantially reducing poverty and conserving the planet's life support systems."[11] Humans are social beings, we need to live together in groups. This was originally for survival, but we also have complex emotional and social interactions that shaped our cultures and communities and helped us develop adaptive resilience. Thinking about sustainability can help us remember to be considerate of others in our daily lives and in planning the type of future we want. We must constantly negotiate the challenge of seeking coordination and resilience amongst the three systems of sustainability science: environment, economy, and society.[12] This means that if we constantly strive to safeguard a healthy environment, develop and maintain an economy built on equity and satisfying work, and support a society that values the public good, we will be more likely to live happy, healthy lives.

We were hiking our journey with 23 other adventurers, although everyone set their own pace. This was unusual for us, as our previous experiences had been independent. Even when hiking popular backcountry areas, we had rarely shared our campsites with another group. Hiking and sharing camp with the same group of people for three days gave us a small sense of how the gold rush stampeders may have felt. We traveled the same route together, but each party had their own camp and different preferences, like morning start times.

Having 23 people using a limited number of pit toilets over a 12-hour period translated into overuse at a couple of sites. One was so bad that plugging my nose was not enough to keep out the stench. I could taste the scent of urine as I gagged, taking in short, shallow breaths.

But we also found some helpful aspects of traveling with a group. A fellow hiker approached us one evening and traded a bottle of insect repellent with us for a tube of anti-itch cream. He and my father-in-law had a long discussion about the virtues of head nets versus insect spray by itself. (A decade later, my father-in-law learned that he had a peanut allergy instead of what he thought was severe rash reactions to mosquito and black fly bites. Generally, the only time he ate peanuts was backpacking.) Trying to ignore or escape the relentless, hungry insects could be intense battles. The biting flies and mosquitoes were most bothersome at the campsites, while tiny black flies often swarmed us when we stopped for lunch or rest breaks. I tried to imagine how the stampeders dealt with these issues of daily camp life a hundred years ago, and how they must have suffered in the cold weather that dominates most seasons in these mountains.

Day two. Throughout the morning, the rich forest gave signs of transitioning into high alpine ecology. We had fewer large trees as companions and the trail began to open up, exposing more rocky terrain. As we walked out of Sheep Camp, we suddenly found ourselves in an obvious avalanche chute where the forest had been cleared many times. It was, as always, trying to regrow, as young alder trees were filling the gap.

We stopped for an early lunch and to refill our water bottles before the long, slow climb toward the Chilkoot Pass at just over 3,500 feet. The treeless alpine landscape allowed us to see the steep, boulder-strewn slope ahead of us, and to look down and back, admiring the Taiya River valley that we hiked through. This is part of a deep satisfaction I gain from backpacking through mountain trails, eventually you earn that stunning view, forward and back, of the beautiful landscape you are hiking within. Even at that point, like the stampeders long ago, I did not realize how physically challenging this trail is.

> The trail enters a cul-de-sac, climbing higher and higher. The valley seems to end; a precipitous wall of gray rock, reaching into the sky, seems to head off farther progress, seaming its jagged contour against the sky—a great barrier, uncompromising, forbidding—the Chilkoot Pass

> Quote by Tappan Adney.[13]

Stopping in the boulder field with several other hikers from our group, someone pointed upslope and said "Bear, near the top." All eyes lifted skyward. Slowly, each of us spotted the bizarrely small figure of a grizzly bear making his way over the boulders. Anybody who had not already dropped their pack for a rest stop did so now. Time to watch and wait, to see where the bear was going. None of us really wanted to have a bear encounter amongst the boulders. Over about twenty minutes, the bear slowly picked his way across the difficult terrain and disappeared over the summit of the pass. The anxious among us were chatting about scenarios of what to do if the bear was still in the boulder field when we crossed the summit. The consensus settled on repeating our current "watch and wait" strategy. If the lead hikers spotted the bear nearby when they summited, they would need to decide quickly whether to retreat a safe distance to wait or if they could rest at the summit. Also, if the bear was nearby, they should be considerate and shout a warning to the other hikers below.

We reached "The Scales," an infamous stopping point at the base of the Chilkoot Pass. This was where the stampeders were required to stop and have all their stuff officially weighed and recorded by government officials. As I looked around the barren rocky slope, I found it difficult to believe there was a small tent city here with six restaurants, two hotels, warehouses, and a saloon! It seems impossible. Apparently,

Taking a break before hiking the Golden Stairs to reach the pass (top right). Photo credit 1999 Tom Beltz.

I was not alone in this line of thinking. The landscape was littered with abandoned artifacts, animal bones, preserved wood from boxes, and rusted iron of all sorts. Many eager stampeders stopped here, looked upward at the line of men carrying packs on an often slippery, near vertical rocky incline, and realized with a broken heart that their task seemed unbearable. Some turned around and trudged home. Now we braced ourselves to climb the "Golden Stairs," the steepest section of the trail, rising 1000 feet in about a half-mile distance. At least the day was sunny and dry, and the views were gorgeous.

Crossing the summit pass means you also cross the international border into Canada. This was a unique experience because not only was I hiking a mountain pass, I also had never entered Canada by foot. We stopped at the Parks Canada warden station and were lucky enough to find a ranger on duty, as it is only staffed part-time. He welcomed us to the Yukon Territory and marked our passports with a souvenir stamp commemorating the historic site.

We were elated by our accomplishments so far that day, but we still had a steep downhill hike before we could rest at the appropriately named Happy Camp. It was the opposite of the Golden Stairs—instead of going up, we now had to go down 1000 feet in about a half-mile distance. If we had not realized already, then this side of the pass taught us how truly difficult the journey was for the stampeders. I injured my left knee on the descent. About halfway down, the outer side of my knee began to ache. Within 30 minutes, I was in tears by how much every step hurt. My partner and I stopped for a break. The sole on one of his hiking boots had come loose. He dug out the duct tape and a couple straps from our gear for an emergency repair. A college friend of ours said "duct tape saves lives" when telling us how he once used it for a roadside engine repair to help get his broken car to a mechanic. Since then, we have religiously kept the famous gray tape in our camping gear. My partner also gave me his elastic knee brace to help ease my aching knee. It was not a tight fit, but it provided a placebo of pain relief if nothing else. Our bodies and spirits lifted enough that we were able to walk slowly to the campground.

Author and partner on edge of the lakes region after crossing the Chilkoot
Pass.
Photo credit 1999 Tom Beltz.

After supper, we soaked our feet in the ice-cold stream running parallel with the trail and I placed a bag of that icy water on my knee. My in-laws were also bruised, sore, and covered with badly itching insect bites. But they were hoping to do a little stargazing that night. My partner and I declined to wait for the stars to make their appearance. Early in the evening, we collapsed into our tent and fell away to the deep, dreamless sleep we experience after a long day of hiking in mountain elevations. In the morning, my in-laws reported they had poked their heads outside around 2:00 am only to find the sky still filled with twilight and no stars to appreciate.

Day three. The morning temperatures were appreciably cooler than the previous day. As we slowly descended from the rocky alpine ecosystem, we dropped back below tree line and hiked between open meadow areas with rocky streams and clusters of pine trees across the landscape. By lunchtime, we had entered the lakes region of the Yukon Territory and returned to the boreal forest, which covers a great swath of the middle of Canada. The lakes were a deep azure blue, reflecting the brilliant summer sky. The color on the water looked surreal, as though the lakes were part of a series of old black and white photos touched by a painter's brush.

We hiked the last 16 miles a bit broken and battered. But we had gained a true appreciation for the grit, determination, and strength of body and soul that was possessed by the adventurous people who traversed this route over a hundred years ago to seek their fortunes in the wilderness. We set camp at Bare Loon Lake for our final night among the ghosts of the Klondike gold rush. Listening to lyrical cries from a pair of loons calling to each other on the lake, I fell asleep with a smile.

Day four. There were approximately four miles left to hike that morning before we reached the train station for our return to Skagway. The Lake Bennett area was picturesque, as though it had been manufactured just for "Tour Canada" postcards. The glacier-carved mountains sloped to a narrow focal point just beyond the lake. They had a perfect balance of imposing gray stone above the tree line and the striking green of pines and boreal vegetation down to the lake shore.

The Bennett train station was a shade of red that is dear to my heart. It was the color of a red barn, complete with white trim. I imagine it makes for a lovely winter scene with a snowy white backdrop. Even in summer, the bright red structure stood in sharp contrast to the rich, earthy hues of mountains, forest, and water.

The WPY (White Pass and Yukon Route) train is a heritage railway running from Whitehorse, the capital of Yukon Territory, to the coastal port of Skagway.[14] This narrow-gauge (three foot) railway was started during the early days of the gold rush as a way to help people reach the goldfields. The one-hour-and-forty-minute train ride gave my brain a little time to reflect on the links between sustainability and resilience, the necessary self-sufficiency of the stampeders, and our backpacking LNT experience. If we choose to strive for a future guided by sustainability principles, we will need to borrow some of the fortitude our late nineteenth-century ancestors showed. But a gold-rush mentality is exactly what we want to avoid. We will need to overcome our natural tendencies to run toward short-term ideas and quick-fix schemes. Instead, building a sustainable and resilient future will have more links to the self-sufficiency and careful planning ideas in the LNT principles.

Sustainability and resilience require that we *plan ahead and prepare* because the transition will significantly challenge our current way of life, which is so often dependent on convenience. We need to think and plan long term, beyond our own individual lifespans. The Long Time Project is a good place to start.[15] This project aims to use arts and culture activities to help society develop an emotional connection to future generations and thereby shift our thinking, planning, and decision-making to focus on long-term goals that can benefit all of us.

We face big changes, such as developing an economy that *disposes of waste properly*, or rather, eliminates the concept of waste. We can do this by becoming a Doughnut model instead of a linear model. A Doughnut model would convert the waste from one production system into a useable resource for another system. We also need to create greater *respect for wildlife and for others*. We can do this by rediscovering our love and respect for the natural world around us, and then linking those with our social values and economic system. This includes reducing our impacts on the natural world by recognizing when we have enough stuff. We can pause, reflect a minute before buying something new, and ask ourselves: Do I really need this? Will I use it for a long time? Such reflection links to the LNT principle, *leave what you find*.

The LNT principles also relate to questions of environmental justice.[16] We must consider the needs of everyone by addressing the incredible inequalities that our current economic and social systems are built upon. The LNT principles have not only helped me develop a good hiking ethic, they have also become a good guide for reducing my negative impacts on the world. I like their straightforward simplicity. They feel very common sense, but I also recognize they run counter to the values we see and hear every day on TV and social media. Sometimes I wish that social change was as easy as printing the LNT principles on business cards and slipping one into each person's pocket. But I am an optimist, and the world changes every day. We can plan to be more resilient and build a more sustainable future society. Life is like hiking a trail, it's a journey we take one step at a time.

September 1999. Crossing the North American continent through history and geography in a three-week timeframe was mind boggling. I feel like one of the gold-rush stampeders, but at least we did not have to carry our ton of goods over a mountain pass. In Alaska, we hiked some of the youngest and most rugged terrain on the continent and in the youngest state. Then we visited my family in Minnesota, in the middle of the continent, mid-prairie, and mid-US-statehood timeframe. Now we have unpacked the moving truck and finally nestled into the oldest geology and political geography of the US. The Commonwealth of Virginia, with its red-clay soils washed down from the weathered, rounded Appalachian Mountains, this is our new home. Acquainting oneself with a new landscape will take some time, and I am looking forward to walking new paths.

Endnotes

1 https://en.wikipedia.org/wiki/Chilkoot_Trail (https://perma.cc/
PCN6-4PEX)
2 https://www.nps.gov/klgo/learn/goldrush.htm (https://perma.cc/
CPL8-XESD)
3 https://www.footprintnetwork.org/our-work/ecological-footprint/
(https://perma.cc/L4M7-QEUR)
4 https://lnt.org/why/7-principles/ (https://perma.cc/T3PY-KZKQ)
5 https://www.nps.gov/klgo/learn/historyculture/tonofgoods.htm
(https://perma.cc/LUE7-LQWY)
6 https://www.theguardian.com/environment/2021/apr/28/speed-
at-which-worlds-glaciers-are-melting-has-doubled-in-20-years
(https://perma.cc/P7AY-CL4Q)
7 https://doughnuteconomics.org/about-doughnut-economics
(https://perma.cc/FD8X-674B)
8 https://www.stockholmresilience.org/research/planetary-bound-
aries/planetary-boundaries/about-the-research/the-nine-plane-
tary-boundaries.html (https://perma.cc/9R2A-4TJM)
9 https://www.theguardian.com/environment/2019/aug/17/plas-
tic-recycling-myth-what-really-happens-your-rubbish (https://per-
ma.cc/82UV-92BV)
10 https://www.nps.gov/media/photo/gallery.htm?pg=5038649&id=
FB923B54-1DD8-B71B-0B9355D6FC266351 (https://perma.cc/
G325-5KBP)
11 https://www.pnas.org/content/108/49/19449 (https://perma.cc/
E3X6-9ZY4)
12 https://en.wikipedia.org/wiki/Sustainability (https://perma.
cc/4SJ8-ZAJF)
13 https://www.nps.gov/klgo/learn/historyculture/histor-
ic-chilkoot-trail.htm (https://perma.cc/9VT8-6HPL)
14 https://en.wikipedia.org/wiki/White_Pass_and_Yukon_Route
(https://perma.cc/3QG9-QRAS)
15 https://www.thelongtimeproject.org/ (https://perma.cc/6UAF-
3ACV)
16 https://en.wikipedia.org/wiki/Environmental_justice (https://per-
ma.cc/9BQ6-QMVK)

View of the Spanish landscape from Toledo.
Photo credit 2015 Mick Beltz.

A Taste of Landscape Change

Atlantic watershed, Spain, June 2015

One of the joys of travel is exploring new landscapes and cultures. Another is experiencing old things in a new light. During our tour of Spain, I rediscovered olives. Paired with cheese and ham—I could live happily on such a diet. At nearly every restaurant we visited in Spain, they served a small dish of olives with our drinks. My favorite place, where we ate a tapas dinner, was a local bar in Seville. Dozens of whole legs of cured pork hung from the ceiling and there was nothing in English on the menu. We sat at a cozy streetside table watching the world of tourists walking by. When the waiter returned to check on us, he teased us for eating our cheese and ham with a fork and knife. "No, no, in Spain we eat these with fingers!" We laughed as we tossed aside our silverware. You don't need to tell Americans twice that it's ok to eat with our hands!

Savoring the saltiness of the olives, especially paired with sharp, tangy Manchego (a sheep's milk cheese from La Mancha, Spain) and the enticing flavor of cured ham, was marvelous. Before traveling through southern Spain, I had never stopped to consider the variety of olives eaten in the world, and I did not know how much I could enjoy eating them every day. I had not thought about olive agriculture, nor had I seen an olive orchard or plantation. Therefore, I was enthralled by the view outside our train window as we traversed the Spanish countryside on our way from Madrid to Granada.

After the city quickly disappeared behind us, there were a few small villages with clustered buildings and kids playing soccer in fenced pitches. But mostly the landscape opened ahead of us to varied grassland,

Olive plantation in southern Spain.
Photo credit 2015 Rebecca J Romsdahl.

interspersed with small fields of irrigated crops and the occasional olive tree standing guard at the edge of a town. Then we suddenly entered a new space, as though we had crossed an invisible boundary after the train went over a small hill. In every direction, there was mile after mile of short olive trees, marching across the barren-looking ground. So many questions began to flood my mind. This is obviously mono-crop olive agriculture, isn't it? How old are these trees? Are these large plantations or lots of small orchards? We have only seen a few houses and no villages for many miles, so where are all the people who tend these trees? How do they harvest olives? I don't see any sprinklers or hoses. Do olive trees need to be irrigated? Where did olives originate, are they native to Spain? How long has this landscape been planted with olive trees?

In 1828, the famous American author and ambassador to Spain, Washington Irving, traveled from Seville to Granada by horse with a friend and a local guide. In 2015, we were taking that same journey by train. I was reading Irving's book *Tales of the Alhambra*, and I reread his description of the Spanish countryside:

> Many are apt to picture Spain to their imaginations as a soft southern region, decked out with all the luxuriant charms of voluptuous Italy. On the contrary, though there are exceptions in some of the maritime provinces, yet, for the greater part, it is a stern, melancholy country with rugged mountains and long sweeping plains destitute of trees and indescribably silent and lonesome, partaking of the savage and solitary character of Africa. What adds to this silence and loneliness is the absence of singing-birds, a natural consequence of the want of groves and hedges. The vulture and the eagle are seen wheeling about the mountain cliffs and soaring over the plains, and groups of shy bustards [sic] stalk about the heaths, but the myriads of smaller birds which animate the whole face of other countries

View of the Spanish landscape and city of Granada.
Photo credit 2015 Rebecca J Romsdahl.

are met with in but few provinces in Spain, and in those chiefly among the orchards and gardens which surround the habitations of man.

There is something, too, in the sternly simple features of the Spanish landscape that impresses on the soul a feeling of sublimity. The immense plains of the Castiles and of La Mancha, extending as far as the eye can reach, derive an interest from their very nakedness and immensity, and have something of the solemn grandeur of the ocean. (p 15-16)

From Irving's account, the Spanish countryside has not always been covered in olive trees, so when did they arrive? A few days later, I began to find answers to my questions. As we boarded the train in Granada, we learned that a segment of our journey to Seville would be by bus because of work on the train tracks. On the bus, we found seats on opposite sides of the aisle and settled in for the one-hour drive. My seatmate was a quiet young woman with a smartphone and earbuds. She smiled when I sat down but never said a word to me. My partner settled into his seat and began to read the tourism guidebook we had brought along. His seatmate soon pounced on the opportunity to talk to Americans about his love of Andalusia, Spain, and olives. He was a British-Indian agricultural scientist who worked for a pharmaceutical company in the United Kingdom, and he was on vacation. He told us how he had been visiting the Andalusia region, through which we were traveling, regularly for decades. When we heard his occupation, the conversation ignited. He gave us advice about his favorite places to visit in Seville and answered many of my olive questions.

Many experts believe that the Romans brought olives and olive trees to Spain. The Spanish, in turn, transported olives to the Americas. The agriculture scholar Paul Vossen explains that: "The true origin of the olive is not known but is speculated to be Syria or possibly sub-Saharan Africa. For more than 6000 years, the cultivated olive has developed alongside Mediterranean civilizations and is now commercially produced on more than 23 million acres (9.4 million hectares) in the Mediterranean basin" (p 1093). Some of the oldest and largest olive trees in Spain are estimated to be over 2000 years old, heralding back to the ancient Roman empire!

We wanted to know how olives are harvested. Was it by machine or by hand? Our companion said this varies depending on the size of the trees and orchard. It may still be done by hand, but many farmers use a machine that vibrates each tree, causing the olives to fall onto nets spread on the ground beneath the trees. Harvest takes place in winter, with timing dependent on weather, region, and the type of olives.[1] He said the olive trees will grow just about anywhere across this rocky, sandy landscape; it is ideal for them. Vossen describes the hearty nature of the olive tree that has led to its popularity. It "requires some chilling; tolerates hot, dry conditions; does not like moisture during bloom, and actually produces better with some stress. As a result, olives were traditionally relegated to lands where little else would survive. For thousands of years olives were grown primarily for lamp oil, with little regard for culinary flavor. World production of table olives [for eating, as opposed to olives for oil] is now about 1.5 million tons per year" (p 1093).

We were surprised to learn that in making oil, the whole olive, including the pit, is pressed. Most of the olive presses around Spain are community owned. Many of these communities make local olive oil, but this is not the oil that is sold internationally. Spanish olive oil farms are generally larger and have a higher labor productivity than farms in other European nations.[2] They produce olives that are shipped out and processed by other operators. Spain is the dominant nation in growing olives. It has the highest number of acres planted in olive trees and produces over 5 million tons of olives annually.[3] By comparison, that rivals California's position as number one producer of almonds, with 1.8 million tons grown in 2014.[4]

Our companion also told us to look closely at the base of the olive trees. Some had thick trunks with several branches splitting into smaller stems as they reached skyward. Other trees had thin trunks and seemed to be growing in clusters of three to five trees. He explained how the farmers divide a thick trunk, slicing and separating between the low branches. Each section of the original tree will grow into another individual tree; the dividing process results in the clusters of trees we saw. The purpose of dividing the larger trees is to increase the number of trees, thus increasing the production of olives.

We asked when the landscape became covered in olive trees. He said it began during the fascist regime of Francisco Franco (1939–1978). Urban economic development in the 1960s pushed many farm laborers and other rural residents to work and live in the cities where they could earn higher wages. This great shift of people left many farming regions empty, so the government began consolidating millions of hectares of small farms, effectively creating modern, large, mechanized plantations. Our companion believed the decision to promote olive orchards across the region was very helpful for local farmers and the economy.

With questions of sustainability, resilience, and environmental conservation always on my mind, I wondered how much the rows and rows of trees had changed the landscape. I know a similar pattern in the Midwestern United States, where there is an ocean of corn and soybean fields instead of olive trees. In considering the landscape changes from prairie to monocrop agriculture, I found that Spanish olive plantations and American corn/soybean farms share similar issues. Jose Gómez-Limón and his colleagues have shown that serious environmental problems for olive agriculture include: soil erosion, loss of biodiversity, excess water use, and water pollution from runoff.[5] But recent trends show some environmentally friendly changes taking place with an increase in organic farms and integrated farming practices. Another positive note is that olive trees are very good to help mitigate climate change because their long-life spans can pull carbon dioxide from the atmosphere and keep it locked away in their trunks and branches for hundreds of years.

Unfortunately, the sustainability and resilience of olive plantations across Spain and other parts of Europe are also vulnerable to other threats. A bacterial outbreak threatening olive trees in Italy may result in thousands of olive trees being killed as a strategy to prevent spread of the disease from infected orchards.[6] Experimental treatments are being explored, but it takes time to develop good responses. Sometimes there is no foreseeable remedy. Regional temperature changes in the Mediterranean are likely to increase more than other places due to climate change.[7] And the world wealth gap is encouraging the ornamental sale of some of the oldest living individual trees (1,000 years or more) that families have tended for generations.[8]

When I think about how we have changed landscapes over generations, I sometimes wish I could have been a member of the Lewis and Clark Expedition in 1804, exploring the North American Great Plains. Historian Stephen Ambrose notes how Captain Clark regarded the majestic prairie landscape they encountered in present-day Kansas: "We Camped in the plain, one of the most butifull Plains I ever Saw, open & butifully diversified with hills & vallies all presenting themselves to the river covered with grass and a few scattering trees, a handsom Creek meandering thro" (p 149). I romantically envision a view like that, from horseback, on a hilltop, overlooking waves of saddle-high grasses and flowers, across a landscape as infinite as the ocean. I would love to have been able to see and explore that immense ecosystem.

Throughout the essays in *Tales of the Alhambra*, Irving also describes many of the people he encountered during his journey across the Spanish countryside: a "lonely herdsman armed with blunderbuss...prowling the plain" watching over thunderous bulls destined for the fighting arenas; or the strong, sinewy "muleteer [who] has an inexhaustible stock of songs and ballads, with which to beguile his incessant wayfaring" (p 17-20); and his squire for whom "there is scarce a rock or ruin or broken fountain or lonely glen about which he has not some marvelous story or above all some golden legend, for never was [a] poor devil so munificent in dispensing hidden treasures" (p 103). I have often thought of our friendly bus companion and the wonderful conversation we had. In Irving's time, the Spanish landscape differed significantly compared to now. We must also recognize that personal and cultural values can change our perspectives of landscapes. Prairie landscapes with native biodiversity are often seen as wasteland, while agricultural landscape covered in olive orchards or corn/soybean monocrops might be seen as artificial and destructive. But both can be perceived as valuable and even beautiful by those who support them. We need to work on improving their potential as agroecology landscapes, ones in which the farming of crops is a more holistic process that integrates values for healthy nature and healthy communities.[9]

Now, when I pop an olive in my mouth and slowly enjoy the salty flavor, I see the Spanish countryside and feel the warmth of sunbaked hills spread through me. Irving describes my feeling beautifully: "I have been betrayed unconsciously into a longer disquisition than I had intended on the general features of Spanish traveling, but there is a romance about all the recollections of the Peninsula that is dear to the imagination" (p 20). On this note, I fully agree. There is a romance about my memories of Spain that is now dear to my heart.

128

Endnotes

1 http://www.casaolea.com/blog/olive-harvest-spain (https://perma.cc/WGF4-BEDY)

2 http://ec.europa.eu/agriculture/rica/pdf/Olive_oil%20_report2000_2010.pdf (https://perma.cc/7PKS-CRC6)

3 https://www.worldatlas.com/articles/leading-olive-producing-countries.html (https://perma.cc/8LND-MHSC)

4 http://www.latimes.com/business/la-fi-california-almonds-20140112-story.html (https://perma.cc/N4F8-F6LK)

5 https://doi.org/10.1016/j.landusepol.2011.08.004

6 http://www.nytimes.com/2015/05/12/world/europe/fear-of-ruin-as-disease-takes-hold-of-italys-olive-trees.html?_r=0 (https://perma.cc/6YCR-2AL6)

7 http://www.nature.com/nature/journal/v529/n7587/full/nature16542.html (https://perma.cc/23X9-73T5)

8 http://www.theguardian.com/world/2015/dec/31/spain-ancient-olive-trees-threat-garden-ornaments (https://perma.cc/4NPG-MP-CL)

9 https://en.wikipedia.org/wiki/Agroecology (https://perma.cc/C2GC-AA6P)

Author riding a camel in the Sahara Desert.
Photo credit 2017 Mick Beltz.

Journey to the Sahara

Draa River watershed, Morocco, June 2017

Morocco is known as the place where the sun sets. This country of snow-capped mountains and perfectly sculpted sand dunes forms the northwest corner of the African continent. Morocco is where Africa meets Europe, where cultures and peoples of the two continents have been blending for centuries. As a tourist, this blending seemed a bit like chemistry. Sometimes that chemistry was like sugar and water, where one absorbs the other and the result is a mix of both. Sometimes it was like oil and vinegar, where they mix into a nice combo but never lose their own identity. Other times, it was like a four-spice blend, where you may not be able to identify the original parts without asking, and the result is something new and exciting.

At the start of our journey, we took a train from the Atlantic coastal city of Casablanca, in the north, 150 miles south to the famous city of Marrakesh. All day long, I had the song "Marrakesh Express" by Crosby, Stills & Nash stuck in my head and an ever-present smile on my face.[1] Seeing a new landscape by train is lovely and relaxing. For the first hour, the scene outside my window was dominated by agriculture. There was golden wheat being harvested by small combines and in some places by hand. There were lots of large, round straw bales. A few olive orchards dotted the fields, but the train was going too fast for me to identify many of the vegetables or other lush, green plants in the fields. Overall, the terrain and the agriculture reminded me of southern Spain.

Colorful market stall in Marrakesh.
Photo credit 2017 Rebecca J Romsdahl.

Then something unusual caught my attention. What first looked like just a bunch of wild prickly pear cacti along the train tracks, I soon realized was intentional. People were farming the cacti! There were obvious fields of prickly pear with neatly planted rows. I was further surprised to recognize that in many places, people had planted the cacti as hedgerow borders around their fields. These were four to six-foottall, strong, thick, flowering walls of prickly pear. After asking around, we learned that the red fruit of the cactus is enjoyed for eating. In addition, the French cosmetics industry began incorporating ingredients made from prickly pear cacti almost ten years ago, so many women farmers in Morocco took advantage of this new market demand.[2] Our train was passing through the "cactus capital" of Morocco.

In the middle of the three-hour train ride, the landscape turned to desert. The green farm fields were replaced by rocky terrain interspersed with bare, gravelly ground that seemed swept away across rolling hills. But even in this dry, barren landscape, there were signs of life. Men were working to replace sections of the railway tracks, building new highways, and there were occasional clusters of intended civilization. These were represented by outlines of medium-sized rocks and small piles of building materials that people would eventually transform into houses and other structures. We came to realize that Morocco is a rapidly developing nation with new construction nearly everywhere we looked.

Marrakesh is one of the busiest tourist cities in Africa, and it is a lovely oasis. There are beautiful trees, flowers, and shrubs all around the city. By some estimates, it has 130,000 hectares (over 320,000 acres) of greenery and a Palmeraie with some 180,000 palm trees! Our hotel was located in the walled portion of the old city (the Medina), which is also where you can find the main market. The market was a riot of colorful shops and tourists from around the world. Vendors were selling jewelry, rugs, clothes and shoes, leather goods, silver tea pots and glass cups, camels carved out of wood, fragrant spices, taffy, candies

Snake handler in the Marrakesh market.
Photo credit 2017 Rebecca J Romsdahl.

and cookies, colorful pottery, dried fruits, nuts, fresh-squeezed orange juice (and limeade that will leave your lips puckered for a week), copper wares, huge bundles of fresh mint for tea, and so many other treasures.

But there were some disturbing features about the market as well. After dinner one evening, I was startled by a woman grabbing my arm as we walked by some of the vendors. As I was yanked to a halt, she deftly turned over my arm, exposing my inner wrist where she began to squeeze henna paste, telling me she would draw a good luck tattoo. I was not impressed with being accosted and tried to twist my arm free, without causing a scene, and clearly saying "No, no, no!" She cleverly tricked me by saying, "Ok, I wipe off." This was not her first attempt at a pressure sale. As I relaxed my arm, she started to apply more henna. Her persistence was unshakable until my partner reached over and pinched the tip closed on her henna ink tube. She finally relented, releasing my arm, and we parted ways, each of us cursing the other under their breath. This interaction emphasized our cultural and economic differences. I do not like being seized by strangers, and she was trying to scrape together a meager income from passing tourists. The encounter left me physically and emotionally unsettled for the rest of the night.

I was also saddened at the market by the variety of animals on display or for sale. Tiny monkeys on leashes raced around their handlers, trying to catch the attention of tourists. Too-small cages held tortoises and rare birds. Men opened wicker baskets, spilling out cobras and other snakes, coaxing them to slither across rugs that hinted at long-forgotten colors. When we paused at a distance to watch a swaying cobra and a charmer playing his pipe, another man with snakes draped around his shoulders quickly sidled up to us, asking if we wanted to take a picture with him. I made the mistake of reaching for my camera, and the handler nimbly slid one of the snakes onto my partner's shoulders without asking. He was not pleased. The handler laughed and teased, hoping we would join in his jovial banter. After I snapped a quick couple of photos, my partner indicated his discomfort and asked the man to remove his snake. The handler instead laughed and asked for $20.

Feeling disgruntled by the local customs of coercion, we paid him to take back his snake and we sulked away. At this point, I just wanted to hang out with one of the scrawny, dirty, sleepy, sad-looking little street cats who were watching the world pass by. They were content, sitting unnoticed in the open or happily darting under picnic tables where diners tossed them scraps of chicken kabaabs.

Food is restorative. We bought some almonds to snack on and a limeade to quell our injured pride. With these tasty distractions in our bellies, we strolled through the colorful market stalls to revive our sense of adventure. The June heatwave (106 degrees Fahrenheit) added another layer to the sensory experience of the city. The pavement across the market square shimmered like black water as it radiated the midday heat. We could feel the sweat evaporating off our bodies as though we were walking inside a giant oven, set on broil. The streets throughout the Medina were heavy with scents of potpourri and incense, cardamon, cinnamon, and saffron spices, and the occasional sweetish smell of horse dung or sunbaked trash. After a couple of days exploring Marrakesh, we escaped its urban heat island for a four-day excursion to "Rock the Kasbahs"[3] over the Atlas Mountains and to the edge of the Sahara Desert.[4]

Our driver and guide, Mohamed, was a humble man in his early 30s. He spoke four languages but claimed his English skills were not very good, even as he held fluent conversations with us. He had a laid-back aura and a friendly smile. He took great pride in his work and in his perfectly polished, black Toyota 4Runner. In our four days of travel with him, we learned that he is one of the 40% of Moroccans who self-identify as Berber.[5] The Berber people have lived in Morocco for over 800 years. The name, Berber, came from Greek or Latin and meant "barbarian." Colonial authorities applied the name to many groups of Indigenous peoples who had roamed and settled across north Africa for thousands of years. Berbers call themselves "Imazighen" which translates as "the free." Today, Morocco has the largest population of Imazighen people.

On the first day of our drive, we went off-highway on a red dirt lane to get a historical sense of "the road of a 1,000 kasbahs." This was part of the ancient caravan route used by traders and sultans between Marrakesh and the communities of the Sahara Desert. The section Mohamed drove through showed us that there are still many families who have their homes in the former kasbahs (Moroccan castle or fortress). He pointed out a row of fruit trees, and then stopped and jumped out to pick a few for us. The orchard farmer appeared, they talked briefly, and then the farmer jumped up, grabbing a tree branch, gave it a healthy shake, and small apricots rained to the ground. The farmer and Mohamed gathered them into a small shopping bag. We thanked the farmer and continued our slow, rambling drive along the rutted lane, snacking on the small, sweet, yellow fruits.

That night we stayed at a riad (hotel) that seemed to be carved into a canyon wall. The riad was built to resemble a traditional kasbah. The desert-pink walls and towers were adorned with cut-out accents, arched doorways, and beautifully weathered, dark cedar wood doors. The porter led us up a couple flights of stone stairs and we emerged onto an open-air patio set on multiple levels. It was in the center of the riad with the reception area, guest rooms, restaurant, and small pool all built into the rocky canyon hillside around it. The center of the patio featured a terraced garden, filled with desert flora, accented by a scattering of fragrant rose bushes. The garden created a mini-oasis as it stretched in nearly every direction: we walked under two ivy-covered arches; found potted plants adorning every corner; admired splashes of red and pink on flowering vines climbing iron staircases; and found small pine and cedar trees festooning the highest terrace levels and the hillside outside the riad walls. A maze of steps led up and down to the various guest rooms tucked away on different ledges around the outer walls of the riad. We slept with the windows open to enjoy the cool air of the Atlas Mountains and the lush, intoxicating scents of pine and cedar.

After a beautiful breakfast of pastries with colorful jams and fruits, we continued our driving tour. Not far from the riad, Mohamed began slowly driving back and forth around hairpin turns, slowly climbing up a mountainside. As we gained elevation, he told us that the section of highway we were on was considered one of the most dangerous roads in the world. It led us to an overlook at the top of the Dadès Valley Gorge. The highway was recently rebuilt, with new pavement and strong rock walls as guard rails, so it did not seem dangerous at eye level. When we gazed back down on the sharp turns of the switchbacks, it looked like a huge black snake slithering up the side of the mountain—ominous, impressive, and deadly.

The view from the top of the gorge also let us see the transition we were making from the cool, pine-scented mountains to the dry, rocky landscape of the Sahara Desert. Mohamed directed our attention across the gorge to the rock formations on the opposite mountainside. He told us the rocks were called "monkey fingers" by the local people. The dark, raisin-colored rocks were smooth and rounded by centuries of wind and flowing water. After hearing the name, the rock formations were transformed before my eyes. I could see the shapes of finger pads and creases of joints as if they were fossilized hands from ancient giants.

As we drove through the Sahara's northwest edge, I was surprised by how much life there was in this desert. We saw insects, birds, camels, scrubby plants, clumps of grass, and small trees. Portions of the Sahara were as I expected, barren and as seemingly lifeless as the surface of Mars. But this was a stereotype in my mind, shaped by scenes in movies or television shows that showed nothing but the endless shifting sand dunes of the Sahara. We were amazed by this Mars-scape, a land so tortured by the sun but achingly beautiful in the same breath. There were places where the ground was covered in loose gravel that had been scorched black by the intensity of the sun's rays. Where the gravel was disturbed and turned over, such as by tire tracks, you could see a red path highlighting the original rock color. The desert also exposes secrets from its history. We passed several roadside stands advertising fossils for sale. Millions of years ago, this part of the Sahara Desert was under the waters of an ancient ocean. Centipede-like trilobites and cone-shaped Orthoceras are among the plentiful fossilized creatures uncovered in the sand, like artwork in an open-air gallery.

Over the course of a few days, the Sahara landscape revealed very different scenes. The geologic diversity of this desert was a marvel, with mushroom-colored rocky sand leading toward jagged mountains, flat-topped buttes and sandstone cliffs, and places where black volcanic basalt was broken off jutting hillsides. Smooth, sandy plains stretched for miles, with dead-looking shrubs and clumps of grasses rooted in dry streambeds waiting for rain. In the midst of one of these seemingly empty plains, Mohamed stopped at a tiny abandoned-looking gas station.

We found a very pleasant local man inside and bought a couple small bottles of Coca-Cola from a little vending machine that looked like it belonged on the 1940s film set for Casablanca. Mohamed told us he stopped there regularly with tourists and the clerk opened a guest book for us to sign. We were not the first Americans to enjoy the rest stop that week. A couple from Florida had signed the guest book a few days before us. While we signed the book, Mohamed bought a pint of gourmet honey for his mother. The clerk and his family tended the bees, which make honey from acacia flowers. The sweet thorn acacia, introduced from southern Africa, blooms after a little rain. The tree's flowers look like bright gold pom-poms. As we enjoyed our refreshing sodas under the baking heat of the summer sun, Mohamed swept his arm wide across the scrubby, sandy plain unfolding as far as we could see around us. He described how the winter rains can turn the desert green within days. His eyes brightened as he spoke of the beauty of this transformation, an explosion of color, emphasizing how it only lasts for a few weeks as various flora race through their lifecycles to flower and set seeds before the water disappears again.

Even from the truck window, I could easily trace the wadis, which are low spots and small channels in the sand where water flowed on those few days when rain did fall. Small desert plants grew in thin curvy

lines or small clusters throughout the area where we drove. In one region, four types of trees grew (including acacia and palms) in singles or
groups of twos and threes. Mohamed's response to my sense of wonder
was: "Water is life." So simple and so true. Our planet is a small blue
marble surrounded by the vastness of space. Water is one of the first
things scientists are looking for as they search the universe for other
life. We had heard the phrase "Water is life" in Egypt in regard to the
Nile River, and we heard it again in 2016 as Native American water
protectors protested against the Dakota Access Pipeline and other oil
developments across the United States. The Sahara Desert puts this
phrase into sharp perspective. Without water there is no life.

As we arrived at the Erg Chebbi sand dunes, we experienced more
desert contrasts. We stepped out of the air-conditioned truck as the
leading edge of a storm engulfed us. Red sand swirled in the wind,
stung eyes, coated sinuses, and pumiced exposed skin. In the near distance, a menacing, dark gray wall of clouds reminded me of a prairie
thunderstorm. We suddenly understood the value and purpose of the
long scarves that locals twisted neatly around their head and face. As
my partner fashioned a T-shirt into a bandana to cover his nose and
mouth, I dug a scarf out of my suitcase. It felt strange to be covering
my head and face as though venturing out into a blizzard when the
temperature was actually well above 90 degrees Fahrenheit.

Mounted on our camels, we set off for the Berber camp. I happily
pulled the scarf entirely over my face when the sand blasting wind as-
saulted us in strong gusts as we lumbered up and over the top of each
small dune. We found a bit of shelter from the wind whenever we were
down in a bowl between dunes. There you could see the wind lifting
wispy tails of sand off the ridges of the dunes, creating delicate, curled
tips along the top edges.

Riding a camel is like riding a horse, insofar as you are sitting
astride a tall, four-legged mammal. Beyond that, it is an entirely different affair. Moroccan camels are dromedaries, meaning they have one
hump, which of course means they do not have a nice flat back for a
saddle like a horse. Instead, our camel saddles were a metal framework

with wooden supports that rested on either side of the hump, which was then topped with traditional, thick wool blankets for padding. Camels are also taller than horses, and there are no stirrups on the saddles. Our guide, a smiling teenage boy who was smaller than me, gently but forcefully prodded the beasts to kneel and sit with their legs folded under them so we could mount.

On the front of the saddle is a tall, very solid, T-shaped metal handlebar. When the camel stands up or lurchingly walks downhill, your whole body is pitched forward, and a tight grip on that handlebar is the only thing saving you from flying over the camel's head to land face-first in the sand. No stirrups also means that your bum absorbs all the jarring motion of the camel's steps. At least your knees do not hurt as badly as they do when riding a horse because on a camel you are sitting higher up on the hump, which is thinner than a horse's wide back.

After about 30 minutes, I began to squirm around on the saddle blanket with realization setting in. I was developing bruises on the base points of my pelvis bone, and the ride out in the morning was going to be a sore one! But the long, meandering 90-minute ride was well worth the pain. We even caught a glimpse of a tiny white fennec fox sitting in a small depression in the sand.[6]

Fennec foxes are the smallest members of the Canidae family, which includes wolves and other dog-like carnivores. Fennec foxes have several adaptations that help them live in the hot, dry conditions of the Sahara Desert. Their toe pads are densely covered with hairs, which helps them walk on blisteringly hot, sandy soil. Their kidney functions allow them to live with little access to water. And they have the largest ears in the Canidae family, which allows excess heat to escape their body and helps them to hear prey moving underground. They generally eat insects, birds, and small mammals. If not for its curiosity, I would not have noticed this tiny fennec fox with her straw-colored fur camouflaged well against the sand dunes. Her head popped up out of a depression in the sand. Her huge ears turned toward our little caravan. With her sensitive hearing, we must have sounded like a marching band passing by.

We also had the novel experience of being pelted by raindrops while riding camels in the Sahara. I could not have dreamed of a more bizarre scenario to break my stereotype image of the desert. Unfortunately, that novelty was a trade-off, as we did not have a clear sky for stargazing or to watch the sunset or sunrise. But we trekked out of camp and sat on the dunes, letting the sand pour into our shoes like dry liquid, with hopes that the clouds might clear up for each of those opportunities.

Our Berber camp hosts, two brothers and their cousin, greeted us with hot cups of mint tea. But we were so excited to be in the dunes that instead of sitting down to enjoy "Tea in The Sahara," we drank it like shots and headed out to play in the sand.[7] We climbed the nearest dune and admired the vastness: sand as far as the eye could see. Unless, of course, you turned to look behind the camp at the highway, a few buildings, and some vehicles. But we did not let such a trivial thing as "reality of location" dampen our fun. Despite civilization so close by, we found we could feel completely isolated by simply trekking over the nearest dune and sitting down in its bowl.

The Berber tourism camp was ingenious. The bedroom tents were set up in a large square with the kitchen and dining tents on one side and community space in the center. The ground within this community space, and inside the tents, was covered by brightly colored rag rugs and traditional Moroccan wool rugs that gave the camp a stable, soft floor. There was a common washing area with four sinks and four flush toilets in metal outhouse structures. There was even a shower station if you were inclined to try to wash the sand off yourself.

We shared our desert camping night with four Chinese students who were on vacation from their engineering graduate school studies in Germany. They were excited to chat with two American professors over dinner because we could help answer questions in English, such as "What are the different vegetables in this tagine dish?" We pointed out carrots, potato, zucchini, and yellow summer squash. We laughed at the familiarity of seeing students using smartphones and iPads, even in the middle of the desert.

After dinner, a couple of the students began watching a film on their iPad while lounging on the large cushions around the firepit in the center of the common space. One of our young Berber hosts asked what they were watching. The answer was *Casablanca*, and we chuckled as the Chinese students explained an iconic American film to a young Moroccan who had never heard of it and was surprised to learn it was set in his country.[8] He settled onto a cushion to watch it with them while we grabbed a solar lantern and headed out to the dunes to enjoy some time alone in the desert.

When we dragged our tired bodies out of the tent at 5:15 in the morning, the soft light of dawn was surprisingly bright as it reflected off the disappointing cloud cover. There were a few small breaks in the clouds, so we did see a few bright spots of sunrise, but no hues of pink or lavender, no orange orb, no horizon even. We did get to enjoy tea with a lovely buffet breakfast, and then we mounted our sore bums onto camels and settled into the rhythm of plodding across the sand dunes. The wind arrived on the leading edge of the next storm, and we laughed nervously as thunder rumbled overhead and fat raindrops plastered our shirts against us. I thanked my weather charm for keeping the lightening at bay while we sat tall on the camels, holding tightly to the hefty metal handlebars in front of us.

For our last night of the road trip, we stayed in Mohamed's hometown of Zagora.[9] The city was known as the Moroccan entry point to the famous Sahara caravan road, 52 days by camel or foot to Timbuktu in present day Mali.[10] Camel caravans have crossed the Sahara for centuries, transporting people and trade goods between the Moroccan Atlantic coast all the way to modern Ethiopia and Sudan in east Africa. Cloth, manufactured products, and paper were valuable goods brought inland, while silver, handmade crafts, date fruits, and salt were likely exchanged and sent back to Europe.

Mohamed took us to a local shop that was one of his favorites. He likes to stop there whenever he is home. It had one small room lined with shelves of spices from floor to ceiling, and smelled like walking into a happy kitchen. A second small room was filled with potpourri

View of Zagora city and oasis.
Photo credit 2017 Mick Beltz.

and herbal-infused oils, lotions, and soaps. We bought some Moroccan four-spice, fragrant local cumin, some lovely strands of saffron, and a small brown bag filled with Moroccan mint tea, a beautiful blend of mint and rosemary leaves, anise seeds, tiny lavender flowers, and rose petals.

Zagora is part of an oasis that forms a long ribbon of life between the Sahara Desert and the foothills of the Anti-Atlas Mountains. The oasis is a vast network composed of the Draa River, millions of palm trees that grow along its shores, cultivated crops, and many small cities and towns that have been built over the centuries. From an overlook, we could see boxy kasbah-style buildings made of red sandstone and painted concrete bordering the green sanctuary. The oasis stretched out before us for over 90 miles! To view the contrast of vibrant green against endless desert and red rock buttes was stunning. I had never imagined an oasis could be so large, and I have never seen so many palm trees.

Ten days exploring the northwest edge of the Sahara Desert etched a lasting impression in my mind. The great desert holds unexpected resilience and diversity of life, as well as subtle surprises, if you are willing to explore a little. Going home to the floodplain valley where the Red River of the North meanders, was a shock to my system. The temperature was shivering around 70 degrees Fahrenheit, and the region was awash in summer green. As the verdant landscape passed by our car window, I sat in the passenger seat stunned and marveling at the effect of what many of us normally take for granted, life-giving water.

Endnotes

1 https://en.wikipedia.org/wiki/Marrakesh_Express (https://perma. cc/NT7Z-T3CT)

2 http://news.bbc.co.uk/2/hi/africa/8166905.stm (https://perma.cc/ DFA4-X6X3)

3 https://en.wikipedia.org/wiki/Rock_the_Casbah (https://perma. cc/6VWL-VWA9)

4 https://www.britannica.com/place/Sahara-desert-Africa (https:// perma.cc/TB7X-AAWX)

5 https://en.wikipedia.org/wiki/Berbers (https://perma.cc/KZN6-BTRL)

6 https://en.wikipedia.org/wiki/Fennec_fox (https://perma.cc/ZXF2-6DNP)

7 https://en.wikipedia.org/wiki/Tea_in_the_Sahara (https://perma.cc/ SCR3-KS6V)

8 https://en.wikipedia.org/wiki/Casablanca_(film) (https://perma. cc/5TAS-ZUEQ)

9 https://en.wikipedia.org/wiki/Zagora,_Morocco (https://perma.cc/ DF7Z-J652)

10 https://moroccotravelblog.com/2015/03/30/the-cara-van-routes-of-morocco/ (https://perma.cc/HB6G-2ZHP)

Author standing in the ruins of Midhowe Broch. The distant building
contains Midhowe Chambered Cairn.
Photo credit 2016 Mick Beltz.

Life on the Edge

Orkney Islands, United Kingdom, July 2016

Remote. That is the word that wells up in memory. Isolated bits of emerald-green land tethered where the Atlantic Ocean meets the North Sea. That is where one finds Orkney.[1]

Four of us, friends from graduate school, set out by train from Edinburgh. Our first stop was Inverness, to pick up our rental car and then head north to the top of Scotland. To reach the Orkney Islands, we traveled by plane, trains, car, and ferry, just to get to Kirkwall, the largest city in Orkney. The Shetland Islands lie beyond, so we were not that far off the north coast of Scotland, but it still felt like worlds away from anywhere.

That feeling of remoteness is part of living on an island, and it offers some perspective on resilience planning and sustainability. Living on an island helps you see the relevance of the "Spaceship Earth" metaphor. The term was coined by Richard Buckminster Fuller, an innovative design scientist and architect, who wrote a short book titled: *Operating Manual for Spaceship Earth*. The idea is that our planet is a spaceship where humans and all our fellow creatures live. Therefore, we must be good caretakers of Earth because if we waste our resources or break any systems on the ship, we do not have anywhere else to live. On an island, you see there is a limited amount of land. You gain an appreciation for the interdependence we have with other people. You learn how easily a shortage in resources can occur, so you have to carefully plan for your needs. You are always living life on the edge. The edge of water, the edge of land, often the edge of survival. You must be resilient, resourceful, and adaptable in finding ways to maintain your balance on that edge.

Orkney is an archipelago composed of approximately 70 islands, with people living on 20 of them, and a total population of less than 20,000. The islands were shaped by retreating Scandinavian ice sheets. Many of the islands have tall, steep-sided cliffs on their western coastlines that gently level out over smooth, hilly landscapes down to lovely sandy beaches on the eastern coasts. Although there is evidence of rich forests in the islands' prehistory, early human settlement along with climate shifts resulted in deforestation. Since the Bronze Age (roughly 1500 BC), the islands have been mostly treeless and windswept, with fertile lowland soils allowing some agriculture, mostly for cattle grazing.

Although the islands are located in the far north, their year-round climate is fairly mild, with only a small range of difference between summer and winter temperatures. Average temperatures in winter hover just above freezing, with snow and ice being rare occurrences. Summer temperatures are cool, averaging around 60 degrees Fahrenheit (15 Celsius). This good fortune, which it true for the British Isles overall, is brought by the warm waters of the Gulf Stream. This marine highway is a surface ocean current that flows from the Gulf of Mexico north along the east coast of the United States and across the north Atlantic Ocean, gifting the British Isles, and northern Europe with temperate water, winds, and climate, despite their closeness to the Artic Circle.

The most notable effect of the Orkney latitude is the extreme differences between summer and winter daylight. A day runs 18 hours on the Summer Solstice, when the sun never truly sets. At its lowest, the sun hovers just above the horizon in a twilight that Orcadians call the "simmer dim." In winter, darkness blankets the islands, and they only receive a bleak, often cloudy gray light for a little more than six hours between 9:00 am and 3:30 pm.

In this far north region, I feel a kinship with the people of Scotland and Orkney because of our shared Norwegian heritage. In the late eighth century, the Norse Vikings began to use the islands as base camps for their raids on villages in southern Scandinavia, Scotland, and into continental Europe. The Norse soon settled both the Shetland and Orkney Islands, annexing Orkney in 875 AD. But they weren't the first to live there—people have been living on the Orkney Islands for at least 8,500 years. Localized tribes of people characterize the early settlements of the Neolithic, Bronze, and Iron Ages. Many of their settlements are well preserved on the Orkney Islands because they were constructed of local flagstones and often buried by tidal sands after people abandoned them. They also left great legacies in the form of ancient stone circles, much older than England's famous Stonehenge.

Life on the edge also means that Orcadians have built a culture of resilience and adaptability. Author David Tinch discusses these traits: "What are the characteristics of the Orcadian? We are basically survivors. In spite of having to exist and thrive on an economy based on agriculture in a climate that is far from conducive to it we are still here. Bullied, moulded perhaps even coaxed into being what we are; we have stood the test of time, bent but not broken."[2]

A slender, chestnut-haired, middle-aged man in Kirkwall joined us at the bar one evening. He told us his resilience story as we sipped honey-colored Highland Park whiskey from the famous distillery just up the road. He hailed from a family with a long history in the local fishing industry, but that was no longer a viable career for him. Climate and economic changes, paired with declines in the fish populations, all of which overlapped with more restrictive conservation policies, meant that fishing was not in his future. Drawing on the adaptability of his ancestors, he was quite proud of how he was now teaching himself to be a website designer.

Adaptability is a vital character trait to keep in mind while traveling as well. We had a nail-biting experience on a small ferry over to Rousay Island. The ferry operators were trying to fit an extra car onboard, one that did not have a reservation for that morning. As the friendly man provided instructions and hand signals to move the car a bit further back, to the left, then back more, he said, "Just follow me, don't pay attention to the vehicle." Our rented four-door Nissan crossover had parking cameras and a caution alarm, which was beeping and screaming that we were too close to everything on all sides. We trusted the ferry operators had a good record, since they did this sort of car park Tetris game every day. They did fit the extra car onboard, but we were packed so tightly that opening the doors more than an inch was impossible. We did our best to enjoy the unusual ride: in a car on the deck of a ferry, watching the ocean, feeling sea spray through the car window, and trying not to think about being trapped in a car if the ferry began to sink. We went ashore at Rousay Island without any bumps or scrapes to the car.

In many of the guidebooks about Orkney, Rousay is called the "Egypt of the north" because it has a great number and variety of archeological sites, although only a few of the over 100 sites have been excavated.[3] As we drove the 13-mile loop road around the island, poking ourselves into small holes in the ground to explore chambered cairns (ancient stone crypts within burial mounds), I kept thinking about the idea of a harsh life in a harsh environment. Living on the edge. At our fourth stop, we enjoyed a lovely downhill hike to the coast to tour Midhowe Chambered Cairn and Midhowe Broch. These are part of a large complex of ancient ruins on the edge of Eynhallow Sound, the small body of water we crossed on the ferry from Mainland Orkney.

Midhowe Chambered Cairn is unique for being so well preserved.[4] For further protection, it was enclosed in a steel and stone structure to keep it out of the weather. Being situated on the coast, the structure has a cave-like feel to it, damp and cool with the smell of wet clay. Protecting the cairn from the weather means we can see the original stones and get a sense of how it may have looked when it was first constructed long ago. Most other cairns are still buried under their barrows (grass-covered hills) to protect them from the elements. Some have been topped off with a concrete roof, having lost their original, and then reburied. Instead of walking into Midhowe Chambered Cairn, there are two catwalks elevated on either side of the roofless cairn so you can view it from above. This was a typical stalled cairn, meaning it has a central aisle with standing flagstones that create stalls on either side. Apparently, this reminded people of horse stalls, so the name stuck.

Midhowe Chambered Cairn is also unique for its size. Typical ancient cairns have around four stalls total, while Midhowe Chambered Cairn has 12 along its 77-foot-long passageway. Several of the stalls have ledges, like shelves, where ancient people would have placed the bones of their loved ones. Looking down on the interior is a bit like peering into a miniature version of the many cathedral ruins scattered across Wales, England, and Scotland. There is even a surprising growth of bright green moss that carpets the floor of the cairn, reminiscent of the grassy interiors of the skeletal cathedrals. A footpath surrounds the cairn so one can see it at ground level also. Midhowe was not only a large burial site, but also had a large ceremonial area with space for hundreds of people. Does this hint at the potential size of the surrounding community? Or was this primarily used by a dominant family displaying their wealth?

A short walk along a grassy trail brought us to the ruins of Midhowe Broch, within sight of Midhowe Chambered Cairn. A broch is a stone tower from the Iron Age, and there are many historic examples throughout Scotland. This broch was built on a bit of high ground near the coast, overlooking Eynhallow Sound, between two steep-walled streams. It was situated behind a rock-lined ditch and an earthwork barricade, which you can see the remains of still today. A modern sea wall was built on the coastal side in the 1930s to provide the site with some protection from erosion caused by storms and large waves. The walls of Midhowe Broch ruins stand about 12 feet tall, but they may have originally been 40 feet tall or more, similar to its cousin Mousa Broch in Shetland.[5]

Towers are mostly understood as defensive structures built to protect something. But Midhowe Broch provides a different perspective. The sign at the front of the broch shows an artist's interpretation of

Entrance to Midhowe Broch with flagstone buttresses on left.
Photo credit 2016 Rebecca J Romsdahl.

how the original structure may have looked when people lived there. Building on this interpretation, the Lego toy company created an excellent model of a broch as a home.[6] As a translational ecologist/nature interpreter, I always appreciate when the arts are used to help tell us stories about science and historic places. After reading the signage, my friend suggested that brochs might represent a type of home in the castle complex where the Scottish Princess Merida in the animated Disney film *Brave* lived.[7] This idea caught my imagination because the independent, feisty, redheaded Merida speaks to my inner child.

Although the builders of Midhowe Broch must have been experts in their craft, even the best architects sometimes make mistakes. There are several examples of this tower's individual peculiarities. On the left side of the front entrance, flagstone buttresses form a line of guards to reinforce a section of sagging wall. Experts believe these must have been placed not long after the broch was built.

As we entered the ruins under a large stone lintel, we could see how the exterior walls varied between three and four feet thick. Perhaps the builder of this broch was experimenting. Another unusual feature was how the base, at ground level, had a hollow area, like a hallway between the exterior and interior stone walls. Other brochs have hollow areas higher up in the walls, but not at the base. This may have contributed to the sagging problem with the exterior wall. The experiment did not work as hoped because at some time the hollow area was filled with stone rubble to keep the walls from caving in.

Once inside, the general layout of the ground floor has been remarkably preserved through time. The interior was approximately 28 feet in diameter and partitioned into separate rooms using large, thin pieces of flagstone. Each room had its own fireplace and water tank. These ancient Orcadians were very clever, resourceful people. Water was supplied from a natural spring that flowed up through the rocks. The water was even said to be clear and drinkable during the excavation period in the 1930s. We did not see any obvious sign of the spring, but maybe we did not know where to look or what it should look like.

The artist's interpretation shows that the ground floor of the broch was usually a barn for the family's animals. Walking within the ruins, gravel and sand crunching beneath my hiking boots, I tried to envision a cow, sheep, or horse inhabiting these semi-circular rooms. I could imagine the warmth of animal bodies in the small space. My imagination could also hear the footsteps of Princess Merida and her family going about their daily life on the wooden floor that would have been above my head. The tang of smoke, from cooking and heating the home, would permeate everything. There was easy fishing right outside the door. Farming small crops for food and grazing a few animals seemed possible during the summer months. In its simplicity, the broch could be a good home. But there are many indications that this was also a harsh life on the edge. With no luxury for windows, the interior of this home would always be dark, even during the long days of simmer dim.

A broch tower may have been built as a home and perhaps as a symbol of status and power. Bronze jewelry and pieces of Roman pottery were found in the ruins of Midhowe Broch, indicating a wealthy family had lived there at some time. But many experts continue to argue that these towers were originally built as defensive structures. What did they need to defend against? Midhowe Broch is one of at least nine identified brochs that stood guard around Eynhallow Sound. Did neighboring groups of people in the Orkney Islands fight each other at times? We know that the Vikings raided and eventually took control of the islands. Did the earlier Iron Age people living around Eynhallow Sound have past experiences with similar attacks and thus fear raiders from outside the Orkney area?

We can create a variety of stories to debate why people built the brochs and to imagine how they lived in the harsh Orkney climate. But we may never find evidence to help us understand more than that. Orcadians have always lived on the edge, but in our modern era, climate changes are increasing the challenges, bringing rising sea levels and stronger storms to coastal regions around the world. The freshwater from Greenland's melting glaciers threatens the stability of the warm Gulf Stream current. If that current weakens or eventually shuts down, the climate of the British Isles and northern Europe could become much colder than the people and ecology are accustomed to. In Orkney, the changing climate threatens many of the historical sites, exposing them to damaging erosion from wind and waves. And like the fisherman turned website designer, the climate crisis is already prompting complex changes for both people and wildlife.

The day we ventured out to Warwick Head and hiked to the top of the cliff face we were looking for wildlife, hoping to see a pod of orca whales from the edge. But as we approached the top, there was a stark and startling difference between standing near the edge of the cliff and stepping back just a few feet, where the hilltop provided enough shelter from the wind that it seemed like a mild day. The wind off the North Sea was raw and bone-chilling, churning the dark waters below into whitecaps. We would have no luck seeing orcas in those waves. Despite the fury of that wind, I was drawn into it, over and over again, ducking back to safety every few minutes. I was entranced by the puffins. There was a small colony, tucked into the rock chinks of the cliff wall. Those tiny seabirds, just 10 inches tall, were showing their skills, riding the fierce wind as they dove off ledges into the icy water and returned up to the cliffs.

Puffins spend much of their lives bobbing around the ocean. They only come to land for breeding and raising their young. Warwick Head has a long history as a popular breeding ground for puffins, with great multitudes gathering there in spring to feed their chicks, covering every inch of rock and grass. In days past, the numbers were so large that fishermen claim to have used the sound of the birds' screeching cries to guide their boats back to shore in dense fog. But researchers now fear that puffins may face extinction due to climate changes.[8] Bird counts show declining populations across the British Isles. In 2000, there were 33,000 puffins counted on the southern tip of Shetland, but in 2018 there were only 570. This is heartbreaking. And puffins are not the only seabirds in trouble. Populations of razorbills, kittiwakes, and fulmars, among others, are also disappearing.

Wind tower on an Orkney farm.
Photo credit 2016 Rebecca J Romsdahl.

As the climate crisis causes ocean temperatures to rise, even a single degree has a significant impact. Plankton swim further north to find cooler waters. Plankton are considered the foundation of ocean food pyramids, with many creatures relying on these tiny shrimp-like animals for sustenance. When plankton move north, sand eels—which puffins eat—and other fish follow them. This shifts the entire food web away from the birds' nesting colonies and normal feeding grounds, meaning they are starving to death. Researchers have tracked some puffins needing to travel 10 times farther than they used to, just to find food. Although seabirds are adapted to living on the edge with fierce winds and waves, the wind patterns may also be changing. In 2013, long weeks of strong easterly winds prevented puffins from reaching their food sources, causing thousands to starve, their bodies washing up on shore. Puffins and other seabirds often live 30-35 years. With these relatively long lifespans, their population numbers can withstand a bad breeding year, but not decades of bad years.

The raw power of wind coming off the sea is a force that shapes life in Orkney, not just for sea birds, winds of change are also reshaping Orkney energy and employment opportunities. There may be signs of hope that we can tackle our climate crisis problems. Everywhere we went, we saw wind turbines. Community-owned turbines provide more than local energy for villages. They provide new career paths for young people.[9] Turbines can also provide communities with revenue and residents with a stake in decision-making about local policies. Many Orcadians drive electric vehicles powered by their carbon-free wind energy. They are also testing ferries that use hydrogen fuel produced by local renewable energy. There are so many turbines that Orkney produces more renewable energy than the islands can use.[10] Another hopeful sign is that the renewable energy future is not just focused on wind. There are also experiments testing how well Orkney can capture and use the energy of the ocean waves and tides to avoid or fill the gaps left by intermittent winds.

Orcadians show us, today and throughout their 8000-year history, that we humans are a resilient, adaptable species, especially when we live on the edge. The environmental crises we face today indicate that we are living on a precarious edge indeed. Orkney is leading the revolution toward a carbon-free energy future.[11] Now we need to follow their lead.

Endnotes

1 http://www.orkneyjar.com/orkney/index.html (https://perma.cc/
L8CD-DLWN)

2 http://www.orkneyjar.com/orkney/orcadian.htm (https://perma.cc/
U3TN-DVNR)

3 https://en.wikipedia.org/wiki/Rousay (https://perma.cc/P45H-
R24Z)

4 https://en.wikipedia.org/wiki/Midhowe_Chambered_Cairn
(https://perma.cc/UFV4-9TE5)

5 https://en.wikipedia.org/wiki/Broch_of_Mousa (https://perma.cc/
JC58-EZY4)

6 https://www.bbc.com/news/uk-scotland-highlands-is-
lands-40593010 (https://perma.cc/5QRB-CMG3)

7 https://en.wikipedia.org/wiki/Brave_(2012_film) (https://perma.cc/
X93A-H73V)

8 https://www.dw.com/en/warming-waters-hit-the-iconic-
puffin/a-44090725 (https://perma.cc/SS3Z-ZMLG)

9 http://www.scottishenergynews.com/orkney-islands-gener-
ate-more-than-100-electricity-from-renewables/ (https://perma.cc/
N8DK-SH2V)

10 https://www.theguardian.com/environment/2019/jan/20/or-
kney-northern-powerhouse-electricity-wind-waves-surplus-pow-
er-hydrogen-fuel-cell (https://perma.cc/4ARR-C6RM)

11 https://mitpress.mit.edu/books/energy-end-world (https://perma.
cc/FE64-KMPB)

Galápagos tortoise.
Photo credit 2018 Mick Beltz.

Following Footsteps of Great Scientists

Galápagos Islands, Ecuador, May 2018

> The natural history of this archipelago is very remarkable: it
> seems to be a little world within itself. . .
> —Charles Darwin, Journal and remarks, 1839

Imagine sailing from England across the Atlantic Ocean, all the way to
the bottom of South America, around Cape Horn, and back north to
the equator, stopping along the way to explore unknown shores. And
this was only the first half of the journey. Charles Darwin spent nearly
five years circumnavigating the globe aboard the HMS Beagle. The
mission of this voyage was to chart the coastline of South America and
bring back knowledge about the ocean's physical features, regional climate and weather, geology, and biology. Given the colonial, capitalist
expansion of Europe's wealthy businessmen during that time, the HMS
Beagle's funders were likely hoping to discover some of South America's untapped treasures. These were my thoughts as we flew over broad
blue ocean, 600 miles off the coast of Ecuador toward the Galápagos
Islands.

As a science nerd, I was excited to explore the tiny cluster of islands
that propelled Darwin to develop his theory of natural selection as a
driving force of evolution.[1] Darwin and his shipmates spent five weeks
surveying the Galápagos Islands in 1835, mid-September to mid-Oc-
tober. Like many young adults in their early twenties, Darwin was on a
voyage of self-discovery, though his was somewhat unusual because he
was literally taking a sailing adventure around the world. As we exited

the airport, I felt I was following Darwin's footsteps as a naturalist, eager to spend some time learning about the Galápagos Islands with their curious flora and fauna.

> The day, on which I visited the little craters, was glowing hot, and the scrambling over the rough surface, and through the intricate thickets, was very fatiguing; but I was well repaid by the Cyclopian scene. In my walk I met two large tortoises, each of which must have weighed at least two hundred pounds. One was eating a piece of cactus, and when I approached, it looked at me, and then quietly walked away: the other gave a deep hiss and drew in its head. These huge reptiles, surrounded by the black lava, the leafless shrubs, and large cacti, appeared to my fancy like some antediluvian animals (Darwin, p 456).

The Galápagos Archipelago is a group of 33 named islands among over 125 total small islets and large rocks. They are built by two incredible geologic forces. Like many islands around the world, they are the highest points of giant underwater volcanoes, formed by hotspots where lava seeps through the ocean floor. There are multiple islands in the Galápagos Archipelago because the hotspot of lava pushes through a slowly moving continental plate. As the Nazca Plate slides east toward South America over the hotspot, new islands and islets are formed over hundreds of thousands of years. You can picture it as though the Galápagos Archipelago is on a geologic conveyor belt. The western islands are youngest. In fact, Isabella and Fernandina are still being shaped by volcanic activity, and both islands had volcanic eruptions the year after our visit. Fernandina sits directly over the hotspot.

During our trip, we hiked to the rim of the largest caldera in the Galápagos, which is on Isabella Island. That caldera is the collapsed Sierra Negra volcano, and it forms the tail of Isabella Island. The Sierra Negra caldera was ten miles by nine miles of black, crumbly-looking lava rock at the bottom of what looked like an empty lake basin surrounded by a grassy, scrub-bush landscape. One year later, the volcano awoke and spewed clouds of ash and molten red lava, prompting the evacuation of 50 people; it had been quiet since 2005.[2] Darwin glimpsed the volcanic activity as well:

> We doubled the south-west extremity of Albermarle Island [now Isabella], and the next day were nearly becalmed between it and Narborough Island [now Fernandina]. Both are covered with immense streams of black naked lava; which, having either flowed over the rims of the great caldrons, or having burst forth from the smaller orifices on the flanks, have in their descent spread over miles of the sea-coast. On both of these islands eruptions are known occasionally to take place; and in [Isabella] we saw a small jet of smoke curling from the summit of one of the more lofty craters. In the evening we anchored in Bank's Cove, in [Isabella] Island. When morning came, we found that the harbour in which we were at anchor was formed by a broken-down crater, composed of volcanic sandstone. After breakfast I went out walking. To the southward of this first crater, there was another of similar composition, and beautifully symmetrical. It was elliptic in form; the longer axis being less than a mile, and its depth about 500 feet. The bottom was occupied by a shallow lake, and in its centre a tiny crater formed an islet. The day was overpoweringly hot, and the lake looked clear and blue. I hurried down the cindery slope, and choked with dust eagerly tasted the water—but to my sorrow I found it salt as brine. (Darwin, p 457-458)

As the archipelago of islands creep eastward, they grow older. Crumbling from erosion, the eastern islands silently slip back beneath the ocean surface. Eventually, they are subsumed back into the earth's crust as the Nazca Plate is overtaken by the South American Plate; the Andes Mountains continue to grow from this slow-motion collision.

This collapsed caldera at Vicente Roca point, on the northwest side of Isabella, looks like a wart on the chin of this seahorse-shaped island. Photo credit 2018 Rebecca J Romsdahl.

Darwin observed that even though the islands shared similar geology and climate, many of the animals and plants were entirely endemic to specific islands, meaning they were not found anywhere else in the world. He wondered if these unique species had adapted to certain food sources and microhabitats on each island. Decades after touring the islands, Darwin would use examples of Galápagos finches as evidence for his theory of natural selection.[3]

> A group of finches . . . These birds are the most singular of any in the archipelago. They all agree in many points; namely, in a peculiar structure of their bill, short tails, general form, and in their plumage. The females are gray or brown, but the old cocks jet-black. All the species, excepting two, feed in flocks on the ground, and have very similar habits. It is very remarkable that a nearly perfect gradation of structure in this one group can be traced in the form of the beak, from one exceeding in dimensions that of the largest gros-beak, to another differing but little from that of a warbler (Darwin, p 461-462).

The finches' beaks have evolved over time. These birds, with common ancestors who migrated to the islands long ago, are now at least 15 separate species. Natural selection has helped each finch species find a niche in their habitat and take full advantage of it. Each species has a different beak that evolved for their particular diet. For example, the large ground finch (*Geospiza magnirostris*) has a large beak that acts like a nutcracker to break open big, hard seeds. During drought years, such tough seeds might become the only food source left in their habitat, and large ground finches may be the only species that can eat those. Other finches have fascinating specialties, such as the vampire ground finch (*Geospiza septentrionalis*).[4] The finch is named for its peculiar resourcefulness during times of food scarcity. Vampire ground finches will use their small, sharp beaks to peck into the skin of larger marine birds, such as the blue-footed booby (*Sula nebouxii*). Then they can lap up blood from the wound. The boobies do not seem bothered by these attacks. Scientists think the boobies' acceptance of the little vampires is because the finches often use the same behavior to helpfully pick parasites out of the larger birds' feathers.

Since Darwin made the Galápagos Islands famous, they have served as a living laboratory for science research.[5] As our catamaran sailed past Daphne Major in the distance one day, I used binoculars to try to see the tiny island's steep cliffs and the natural landing spot used by the scientists Peter and Rosemary Grant and their many graduate students. The Grants spent almost their entire 30-year-long careers studying the finches and living on Daphne Major for several months each year.[6] I had a very difficult time following their footsteps because tourists cannot visit Daphne Major and some of the finch species are unique to specific other islands that we did not visit. In addition, many of the finches across the islands are rather drab colored and do not stand out in their habitats, so they are challenging to find.

We did see the medium ground finch (*Geospiza fortis*), which lives on 10 of the islands;[7] we saw one on Isabella. I spotted the bird as he was startled from the path ahead of us. He flew into the grassy scrub brush just off the trail, landing on a skinny tree trunk. The medium ground finches are sexually dimorphic, meaning the males and females look different. This was a male, distinct for his black plumage. His mate would be more sparrow-colored, brown with plenty of lighter streaks. They are not big, just a little less than five inches in length, comparable to an American goldfinch. I was excited to identify one of the medium ground finches because they were the first finch species that the Grants and their students observed evolving in real time. The Grant team's research has shown that times of great stress, such as a multi-year drought, can drive the birds to change their diet and mate across close species, called hybridization. When some of their offspring lived to reproduce, the Grants documented the beak changes becoming established. This means evolution happens at faster rates than we long thought possible!

In addition to being a living laboratory for science, the Galápagos Islands are also a protected Ecuadorian National Park, Marine Preserve, and was the first designated World Heritage site. The protected status given to the Galápagos Islands is both beneficial and challenging. In society, we create laws to protect what we value, which is good. But when a natural area is given protected status, the challenge is that it becomes a magnet for tourism. The increasing numbers of tourists can often overwhelm the country or the local people charged with protecting the area. For me, touring the Galápagos Islands was both incredible and difficult. I wrestled with thoughts about whether our tourism activities were good, because they supported the local economy and the funding for maintaining protection of the islands, or bad, because we were contributing to the problem of more people wanting to move from mainland Ecuador to the Galápagos Islands to join the tourist economy. There was also a bizarre quality about our interactions with nature on and around the islands. It often felt like we were visiting the most amazing zoo imaginable, except the visitors were the ones with limited freedom to roam about. And, of course, nobody is allowed to ride the tortoises anymore.

> I was always amused, when overtaking one of these great monsters as it was quietly pacing along, to see how suddenly, the instant I passed, it would draw in its head and legs, and uttering a deep hiss fall to the ground with a heavy sound, as if struck dead. I frequently got on their backs, and then, upon giving a few raps on the hinder part of the shell, they would rise up and walk away;—but I found it very difficult to keep my balance (Darwin, p 465).

The truly centenarian giant tortoises are the rock stars of the Galápagos Islands; no trip is complete without seeing them. These tortoises are truly massive. The largest recorded examples have been six feet long and weighed over 800 pounds, with the average adult male in the larger species weighing in around 600 pounds. Their size alone brings out the child in us. As Darwin described his own experience, there are also many photos from nineteenth-century records of men sitting on Galápagos tortoises for a ride.[8] This gigantism probably helped the tortoises' ancestors survive the hundreds of miles of floating (they are not very good swimmers) from mainland South America to originally arrive and settle throughout the archipelago. They can survive months without food and fresh water, and they can extend their long necks high enough to breathe while floating around on ocean waves. These characteristics also help them survive the harsh extremes of long droughts in the Galápagos climate.

There remains some disagreement about how many separate species are still living. Scientists have identified at least 11 species; others were hunted to extinction. But in good news, one of the species thought to be extinct for a century was found alive in 2019! Different types of tortoises can be identified by the shape of their shells, helping us to see that different species developed on different islands. There are two distinct shell shapes, saddleback and domed, and there are also some examples of an intermediate shape that has characteristics of both. Several species of saddleback tortoises developed on the smaller islands with dry habitats and less diverse foods and resources. Saddleback tortoises have elongated shells with a distinctive small dip in the middle of their back that looks vaguely like a horse saddle. They are smaller overall than the domed tortoises, but the shape of their shell allows for longer legs and longer necks. This gives the advantage of being able to eat taller vegetation, such as cactus fruits.

Domed tortoises have a rounded, high, bowl-shaped shell. They are the largest tortoises and are better adapted to the higher elevations of the largest Galápagos Islands. Tortoises are ectothermic, meaning cold-blooded. They need to regulate their body temperature using the surrounding environment. If a domed tortoise spends an hour soaking up heat in the sunshine, her larger body can retain more of that heat for a longer time when the misty clouds roll through the humid highlands of the large islands. Recent research has found that many species on the large islands migrate seasonally between the lowland meadows and the highlands. Some tortoises have been recorded traveling up to six miles in two weeks and spreading thousands of seeds in their poop, which benefits the ecology of their habitat.

What I found most fascinating is that no one knows how long these Galápagos tortoises can live, perhaps up to 300 years! Science cannot measure the age of adult tortoises, and the tortoises themselves are not telling us. There are a few examples of Galápagos tortoises that have lived for 100 years in captivity, but that is still considered young. In 1965, a breeding program was started by the Charles Darwin Research Foundation, so we only know the true age of tortoises that have come out of this effort. When our group visited the tortoise breeding center, we witnessed an amusing surprise. A couple of the tortoises were engaged in the ancient act of love, which we heard before we saw them! The male tortoise was very loud and quite rhythmic with his grunting.

> During the breeding season, when the male and female [tortoises] are together, the male utters a hoarse roar or bellowing, which it is said, can be heard at the distance of more than a hundred yards. The female never uses her voice, and the male only at such times; so that when the people hear this noise, they know the two are together (Darwin, p 466).

By appearances alone, some of the other wildlife on the Galápagos Islands looked like they were prehistoric. I love that birds are direct descendants from dinosaurs! I was reminded of the pterodactyls in the film *Jurassic Park* as we watched two of the largest Galápagos seabirds soaring effortlessly above and alongside our boat. The long-winged, long-beaked, long-fork-tailed, black magnificent frigatebirds (*Fregata magnificens*) and the large brown pelicans (*Pelecanus occidentalis*), with their upright heads and plunge-dive method of fishing, both look like they belonged to a long-ago era when dinosaurs still roamed the earth.

Marine iguanas (*Amblyrhynchus cristatus*), found only on the Galápagos Islands, looked like living dinosaurs or miniature dragons.

This lizard is extremely common on all the islands throughout the Archipelago. It lives exclusively on the rocky sea-beaches, and is never found, at least I never saw one, even ten yards inshore. It is a hideous-looking creature, of a dirty black colour, stupid and sluggish in its movements. The usual length of a full-grown one is about a yard, but there are some even four feet long: I have seen a large one which weighed twenty pounds. On the island of Albemarle [now Isabella] they seem to grow to a greater size than on any other. . . . When in the water the animal swims with perfect ease and quickness, by a serpentine movement of its body and flattened tail,—the legs, during this time, being motionless and closely collapsed on its sides. A seaman on board sank one, with a heavy weight attached to it, thinking thus to kill it directly; but when an hour afterwards he drew up the line, the lizard was quite active. Their limbs and strong claws are admirably adapted for crawling over the rugged and fissured masses of lava, which every where form the coast. In such situations, a group of six or seven of these hideous reptiles may oftentimes be seen on the black rocks, a few feet above the surf, basking in the sun with outstretched legs. (Darwin, p 466-467)

They have developed a surprisingly unique vegetarian diet. These iguanas live on land, but they eat algae that only grows underwater. This means they spend a good amount of time in the ocean, using their sharp teeth to scrape their favorite algae off the rocky shorelines. The waters where their algae meals grow are quite cold, so the iguanas must make frequent trips back to shore to bask in the sun, to raise their body temperature again. These unique lizards can dive to surprising depths of 98 feet below the ocean surface, though they spend most of their time diving to and eating at three to sixteen feet for about three minutes per dive. But the extreme divers have been recorded spending 30-60 minutes underwater. Seeing the iguanas all around the coastal areas, warming themselves in the sun, and then watching them dive

Marine iguanas and penguins sunning together.
Photo credit 2018 Mick Beltz.

while we snorkeled was like imagining scenes from a dinosaur documentary. The iguanas have small spikes in a line from the nape of the neck down their back and tail, as well as a crown of bony scales growing on their heads. Overall, they are so very ugly that I found them irresistibly cute.

While seeing the variety of wildlife was marvelous, my most memorable experiences from this trip were linked to the ocean. The Galápagos Islands are remarkable for the unique influences of their ocean currents. They are located on the equator, so we would normally expect them to be tropical, but they are not. The Galápagos Islands sit at the junction of three major ocean currents that shape its peculiar climate: the Humboldt from the south, the Panama from the north, and the Cromwell from the west.

The Humboldt Current is most significant because it brings nutrient-rich waters up the west coast of South America from as far away as the Antarctic Ocean. When it meets the coast near Peru, the current takes a left turn and heads west. Driven by the southeast trade winds, the Humboldt Current is deep, cold water, extending over 980 feet below the surface. When this cold current hits the giant underwater volcanos that make up the Galápagos Islands, it upwells into the surface waters, bringing a bounty of nutritious food sources within it. This attracts schools of diverse fishes, jellyfish, and crustaceans, which in turn provide food for penguins, green sea turtles, and visitors such as dolphins and whales. The Humboldt Current flows through the Galápagos Islands from approximately May to December each year and creates a cooler, drier environment than one would expect at the equator. But when the trade winds shift southward, so does the Humboldt Current. Then the warm season arrives from the north with the Panama Current, but it may or may not be a rainy season depending on the yearly conditions. The Cromwell Current flows in from the eastern Pacific. It is a cool water current and creates a chillier climate on the western island of Fernandina and the west side of Isabella. This creates favorable conditions for whales and dolphins. As we experienced the microclimates created by the interactions between the ocean currents, winds, and the island topographies, I gained a better understanding and appreciation for our watery planet and Darwin's journey.

I also felt I was following Darwin's footsteps in sailing because he suffered terribly from seasickness. Because of this, he spent as much time as he could walking and exploring on land while the ship sailed ahead to pick him up at different locations. During the five-year voyage, Darwin managed to only spend a total of 18 months sailing. He totaled over three years of surveying on land.

> If a person suffer much from sea-sickness, let him weigh it heavily in the balance [before sailing on a long adventure]. I speak from experience: it is no trifling evil which may be cured in a week. If, on the other hand, he takes pleasure in naval tactics, he will assuredly have full scope for his taste. But it must be borne in mind, how large a proportion of the time, during a long voyage, is spent on the water, as compared with the days in harbour. And what are the boasted glories of the illimitable ocean? A tedious waste, a desert of water, as the Arabian calls it. No doubt there are some delightful scenes. A moonlight night, with the clear heavens and the dark glittering sea, and the white sails filled by the soft air of a gently-blowing trade-wind;—a dead calm, with the heaving surface polished like a mirror, and all still, except the occasional flapping of the sails. (Darwin, p 603)

Although I was introduced to the ocean at the age of seven while visiting family in Seattle, I was more captivated by the shells on the beach than with the water. I grew up near the center of the North American continent, so I did not spend much time near the ocean and much less time riding on its waves. I have traveled on ocean ferries for short trips in Alaska, the Orkney Islands north of Scotland, and between Finland and Estonia. But the Galápagos Islands were my first sailing adventure, and it was an emotional and physical challenge to be living on a boat for eight days and nights, eating, sleeping, and bathing while in ocean-motion. To sum up this experience simply, I am not fit for sailing.

The catamaran sailed between islands most nights, which for me was like trying to sleep on a slow-moving rollercoaster. The third night we sailed outside the archipelago and around the top of the largest island, Isabela, which is straight out of a fairytale. Isabela is composed of six volcanos that have formed the island's landmass in the shape of a seahorse! In the open ocean, we traversed over gentle nine-foot swells for five or six hours, which rocked my partner to sleep like a baby, but left me in a cold sweat of simple, instinctual terror. When the catamaran dropped to the bottom of every wave, the whole boat shuddered and sounded like it might break apart, its fiberglass creaking and groaning. The logical part of my brain knew the boat was safe, the crew made this journey every other week, and we would wake to another wonderful day of exploring. But my emotional brain and my reflexes did not believe me, as I lay on my back with arms and legs braced rigid against the mattress. At the bottom of every wave, I involuntarily gasped until I was too exhausted to be conscious. In the morning light, I felt much less silly as we talked to our shipmates over breakfast. They had similar experiences, and my partner was the only person who had slept well!

My medicine for motion sickness was very good at preventing me from turning green and spending the whole trip worshipping a toilet. But it did not alleviate the mild, nagging symptoms of headache and lack of appetite. To ease my stomach and head, most afternoons we enjoyed a gin and tonic for happy hour on the top deck. The endless navy-blue view across the Pacific Ocean surface was enchanting. We even spotted the telltale spray of a whale spout on the horizon one day.

Our guide, Javier, was a fellow after my own heart, a passionate nature interpreter. Javier and the catamaran crew were dedicated to showing us, their 16 guests, all of the extraordinary creatures and places that represent the Galápagos Islands. Every day, they made a grand buffet for breakfast, lunch, and dinner and sent us off on two inflatable Zodiac boats for excursions.

Flightless cormorant drying off on the Zodiac; catamaran in the background. Photo credit 2018 Mick Beltz.

Red-footed booby (brown morph).
Photo credit 2018 Mick Beltz.

Our daily tours were mini adventures. We would: hike to the top of a dormant volcano; go snorkeling with sea turtles and brightly colored tropical fish; visit the breeding center to see little tortoises less than five years old; and marvel at the contradiction of endemic penguins (*Spheniscus mendiculus*) swimming like torpedoes as they hunted small fish in a tropical mangrove forest and sunning themselves on lava rocks with marine iguanas. This is the only place in the world where penguins live north of the equator.

The reason I interpret the Galápagos Islands as having a zoo-like quality is because every place Javier took us, we saw exactly what he told us would be there. And if we could not find what he wanted to show us right away, he always had a second or third location nearby where we would find it. "On this side of the island, we often see flamingos." "We can swim and play with young sea lion pups in this shallow inlet." "This is one of the best places where we find land iguanas." "We will stop in this bay to snorkel and look for sea turtles." "This island is where several different birds are nesting, including the blue-footed and red-footed boobies."

The blue-footed boobies even danced for us![9] My scientific brain understood that the bird was dancing to show off his genetic fitness and attract a cunning female, but this one was putting on such an impressive performance that we felt like his personal audience. Sometimes, it seemed like Javier was a circus ringleader, announcing the next act to delight our inner child.

One afternoon we went snorkeling to look for rarely seen ocean sunfish (*Mola mola*). Javier was able to find us one as soon as we reached the right cove. Sunfish are taller than they are long, and their body is quite flat, like the shape of a short axe head. Sunfish are large, with some reaching 10 feet long and weighing up to 5000 pounds. They are the heaviest bony fish in the world. Although revered in Japan and other cultures, I thought this big, odd fish looked like a well-loved bath toy. It has top and bottom fins and miniature side fins, but it looks like the back half of its body is broken off. With no tail to propel itself through the water, it oddly waggles those top and bottom fins back-and-forth to move forward. Almost as soon as we saw one, he swam away from us with surprising speed! We swam as fast as we could in our flippers, but lost sight of him within a few minutes.

Beyond their size and odd appearance, sunfish are still fairly mysterious in the world of science. But it would be good to know more about them because they have a voracious appetite for jellyfish. This may be very helpful in the near future, as jellyfish are expected to become more prevalent—and perhaps problematic—as the oceans become more acidic due to the climate crisis. *Smithsonian* editor Megan Gambino interviewed marine biologist Tierney Thys to learn what we know about sunfish, which it turns out is not very much.[10]

Thys has been studying and tagging sunfish around the world, hoping to find where they breed and lay eggs. She has found that sunfish are more widespread than formerly thought. On her website (oceansunfish.org), people have reported sightings of sunfish north of the Arctic Circle and all the way south from Chile to Australia. During one trip to the Galápagos Islands, Thys and her colleagues stumbled upon a school of 25 young sunfish in 90-foot-deep waters off Vicente Roca point, which is the collapsed caldera on the chin of seahorse-shaped Isabella Island. Adults swim solitaire, so this was an amazing encounter. The scientists watched, spellbound, as the five-foot-long sunfish enjoyed a spa treatment. They were resting with their heads pointed upward, quietly appreciating the work of juvenile hogfish who were picking parasites off them.

This trip was only my second experience snorkeling, and although I am confident in my swimming abilities, I get a little nervous in the ocean. There are so many unseen and unknown risks, such as muscle cramps, unexpected waves that leave you swallowing saltwater, and shadows or bright sun that obscure your view, leaving you wondering where that sea lion that just shot past might reappear. I was not prepared for so many different types of fish, or so many schools of fish and how fast they flew through their water world. I had not considered that some of these creatures would swim much closer to us than expected or that some of the green sea turtles were as large as a breakfast table!

When suddenly faced with a graceful oncoming, table-sized turtle, learning to quickly backpedal using my arms and legs as fins was as amusing as it was challenging, especially with flippers on my feet.

On one afternoon, Javier said we could go snorkeling to look for sharks in a particular bay. Most people would show some trepidation at this proposal, but not our group. Everyone whooped and away we went. The water was colder than other bays and murky with sand and debris; I was about ready to head back to the Zodiac when my partner and I saw them. Only about six feet away, a large pair of hammerhead sharks passed by us like shadows and left our hearts racing. That brief, thrilling encounter was good enough for me. But my partner snorkeled with others in our group until he encountered another shark. That one passed a little too close for comfort, coming along his side like a car passing through your blind spot. He joined me and another friend in the Zodiac while the rest of our group continued to chase sharks with cameras and GoPro video recorders.

Each day I became more comfortable in the liquid habitat and although this sounds cliché, I was enthralled by the sensations of seeing, hearing, and moving through another world. *The Little Mermaid* story seemed more real after seeing a chocolate chip starfish (*Protoreaster nodosus*) and large schools of golden stingrays (*Rhinoptera steindachneri*) flying beneath us.[11]

The sea lions added to my fantasy tale. Many seemed to have distinct personalities, and one even played a game of chicken with us. In a shallow inlet, a sea lion pup swam straight at my partner as he watched through his snorkel goggles. At the last second, the pup would break away. Then he circled back to his starting point to race in again and again, leaving my partner rolling in hilarious giggles. Another day, a few of our shipmates spotted a group of sleeping hammerhead sharks in the shallows near a beach, so they grabbed their snorkel gear to get a closer look. My partner and I watched a pair of sea lion pups on the shore as they were watching our friends. As our friends got closer to the sharks, the pups became agitated, pacing back and forth and peering into the water with seemingly growing concern. We imagined them saying, "Don't go there!" "Danger, those are sharks!" "Mama says don't wake them, they'll eat you!" After our friends emerged and all was quiet with the sharks, the pups retreated to their corner of the beach to nap in the sun, waiting for their mother to return.

But all is not well for the sea lion pups, penguins, finches, and the other amazing creatures in this incredible island home. As the climate crisis continues to warm the oceans, this will threaten the very fabric of life in Darwin's living laboratory.[12] Recent history shows how dangerous the effects could become. In 1982, warm El Niño waters blocked the upwelling of nutrients from the Humboldt Current for many months, leading to the death of many creatures. Marine iguanas starved, as well as eight out of every ten penguins. Blue-footed boobies, penguins, and other seabirds stopped mating. When fish populations crashed, nearly all the adult male fur seals died. Most of the sea lion pups also starved because their parents could not feed them. Savage storms destroyed entire forests on some islands, and non-native plants, like fast-growing blackberry shrubs, which were already a problem, took advantage of the open space springing up to replace them.

Some animals are showing signs of adapting.[13] Sea lions have revealed they can hunt like wolves. They normally eat small fish individually, but recently a pack of sea lions corralled a massive yellowfin tuna into a cove, where they slaughtered it in the shallow waters and shared the meal. But not all of the flora and fauna will be able to adapt, and many will not be successful in their attempts. I fear that in my lifetime we will lose some of these incredible creatures.

"Among the other most remarkable spectacles which we have beheld, may be ranked the stars of the southern hemisphere . . ." (Darwin, p 606). On one of the last nights of our trip, we traced the footsteps of Darwin and other sailors throughout history as we went to the top deck to look for the Southern Cross constellation. The sky that night was magnificent, clear and dark over the mysterious, inky ocean. This is another reason I wish I did not suffer so easily from seasickness. I would love to sail across the seas, gazing at the stars and experiencing the serenity, the enormity of the sky reflected on the dark waters. We found the Southern Cross easily. Then my partner asked if I wanted to see a surprise. He turned my gaze northward, and there was the Big Dipper. I was so delighted that I spent the next several minutes making myself dizzy, looking from south to north and back again: Southern Cross, Big Dipper, Southern Cross, Big Dipper. . .

> It has been said, that the love of the chase is an inherent delight in man—a relic of an instinctive passion. If so, I am sure the pleasure of living in the open air, with the sky for a roof, and the ground for a table, is part of the same feeling: it is the savage returning to his wild and native habits. I always look back to our boat cruises, and my land journeys, when through unfrequented countries, with a kind of extreme delight, which no scenes of civilization could have created. I do not doubt that every traveller must remember the glowing sense of happiness he experienced, from the simple consciousness of breathing in a foreign clime, where the civilized man has seldom or never trod. (Darwin, p 606)

When we returned home, it took nearly three months for my inner ear balance to recalibrate from seasickness. Eventually, it did not feel like the room was spinning whenever I turned my head too quickly. But even though I was wobbly, this feeling often reminded me of the giddy thrill I had from stargazing that night we crossed the equator and gave me a lingering sense of kinship with Charles Darwin.

184

Endnotes

1 http://darwin-online.org.uk/EditorialIntroductions/Chancellor_Keynes_Galapagos.html (https://perma.cc/NP59-PXL7)

2 https://www.bbc.com/news/world-latin-america-44627725 (https://perma.cc/Y8F5-X4D9)

3 https://en.wikipedia.org/wiki/Darwin%27s_finches (https://perma.cc/4ZH4-KS9X)

4 https://en.wikipedia.org/wiki/Vampire_ground_finch (https://perma.cc/6M2H-NGUX)

5 https://www.darwinfoundation.org/en/research (https://perma.cc/3PHR-W53E)

6 https://www.google.com/books/edition/The_Beak_of_the_Finch/NLdZAwAAQBAJ?hl=en&gbpv=0 (https://perma.cc/LEG2-FU7D)

7 https://en.wikipedia.org/wiki/Medium_ground_finch (https://perma.cc/4SUC-RR6E)

8 https://en.wikipedia.org/wiki/Gal%C3%A1pagos_tortoise#/media/File:RothschildTortoise.png (https://perma.cc/3Q6V-F9WB)

9 https://en.wikipedia.org/wiki/Blue-footed_booby (https://perma.cc/4574-S56M)

10 https://www.smithsonianmag.com/science-nature/unraveling-the-mysteries-of-the-ocean-sunfish-115258763/ (https://perma.cc/8SAR-LWJ3)

11 http://www.happyingalapagos.com/chocolate-chip-starfish-enchanted-islands/ (https://perma.cc/L6WU-3H2L); https://www.galapagosunbound.com/rays-galapagos (https://perma.cc/UY6G-W8UJ)

12 https://whc.unesco.org/en/activities/883/ (https://perma.cc/7Q9Y-YAYE)

13 https://www.nytimes.com/interactive/2018/12/18/climate/galapagos-islands-ocean-warming.html (https://perma.cc/MAT5-6HBS)

Autumn is a blur of colors and movement, with leaves falling and people and machines racing to harvest hundreds (and now thousands) of acres of crops before the rains begin the cold transition to darkness.

Painted lady and monarch butterflies feeding on purple coneflower.
Photo credit 2019 Rebecca J Romsdahl.

Autumn Changes

Red River of the North watershed, United States,
September-October 2019

As the calendar slips toward September in the Mississippi River and
Red River of the North watersheds, I feel a growing sense of tension
in the natural world around me. The days are shortening. The garden
veggies need to be picked daily. A delightful variety of bees and butterflies thrum on goldenrod and coneflowers. The wind shifts more
often to the north. Birds hurry their last fledglings out of the nest and
into the sky. The squirrels and mice are busy building food stores. The
tension permeates me, disrupting my sense of self, leaving me feeling
antsy. I find it difficult to sit still, impossible to calm my nerves. I feel an
urgent need to do things, to prepare for transition. Change is in the air.

As nighttime temperatures dip closer and closer to freezing, the
birds gather in larger numbers, but not as many as in years past. On
the farm, more tension builds like an electric current in the air. Perhaps
this is how it feels just before a lightning strike? Suddenly we explode
into harvest time. There is so much work to be done that everyone
is recruited to help. Teenagers, spouses, great-grandparents, anyone
who can drive a truck is called to transfer somebody from one field
to another; haul a full load of beans to the elevator; deliver lunch to a
hungry crew; or run to town for an engine replacement part.

Bright gold leaves fall gracefully in the background as a combine
eats up corn stalks and strips corn kernels off the ears. This engineering marvel then pours out the separated kernels into a truck driving
slowly next to it. The race is on to complete all the autumn tasks before

the first snowfall, because you never know if that will be the one that stays until spring. Everyone—trees, plants, animals, insects, farmers—is rushing to the finish line.

My family farm is located on the former territory of the Lakota people, and it is an example of change. I believe change is the only constant in life. Stewardship over land changes hands and rivers change landscapes. And of course the seasons change, and with them we grow another year older and hopefully wiser. My family farm has changed hands three times in my life, from my grandfather to my father, to my brother, to my nephew. On dark days, I wonder if enough farmers in the American Midwest will be able to change enough of their practices, in the short time ahead of us to adapt to the climate crisis, or if we are on the edge of another farm bankruptcy crisis like in the 1980s.

The climate crisis is changing farming already. Spring planting in 2018 and 2019 was significantly delayed by rainstorms and cool temperatures that did not help the mud dry. Low spots in fields were repeatedly drowned out and only some were eventually filled in with cover crops. The damage from these back-to-back wet spring conditions was so great, from Minnesota south through Iowa and east into Illinois and Indiana, that it could easily be seen from space.[1] Satellite images of this region show expanses of green fields in June of 2018, while images from the same week, one year later, are shades of dull, lifeless brown. Farmers are already feeling stressed by all the challenges and uncertainty normally associated with their profession, from weather variability to fickle market prices.[2] But these periods of extreme weather changes (from wet, cold spring to years-long droughts), and the struggles they cause, are forecast to become the new normal for farm families across the American Midwest.

Farmers around the world are trapped in a terrible loop. Envision the symbol of the snake eating its own tail. As the 1970s Green Revolution boomed in the following decades, possibly saving millions of people globally from starvation, farming became another industrial business. Farmers who did not adopt the new model of "more" (more chemicals, more acreage, more animals, more debt) were soon eaten up by larger farm businesses and agricultural corporations. The sad irony from the industry model and the great increase in yields it produced is that the success came with a great cost that has now come to haunt us. One quarter of all greenhouse gas emissions worldwide comes from food production and the agricultural industry. Chemical fertilizers that have increased crop yields for decades can evaporate and become nitrous oxide, which is 300 times more potent as a greenhouse gas than carbon dioxide.

As I write this, harvest season in the Red River Valley is sitting idle. Farmers' agitation grows with every rainstorm. We went from a summer of drought to now a record-breaking September with over 15 inches of rain in less than six weeks.

While I continue to enjoy the remaining harvest of a few tomatoes, eggplants, beets, beans, and zucchini from my little backyard garden, I can't help but think of a recent interview with author Amanda Little. She says: "Climate change is becoming something we can taste." For example, drought conditions will change the consistency of fruits, which will make it more difficult to process them into our favorite dried fruit snacks. As climate change intensifies wildfires, the smoke can be absorbed by wine grapes and lead to a smokey flavor in the wine. Most people across the globe will experience climate change as a kitchen table issue. As climate changes put more stress on plants this will change the flavor of foods and is likely to reduce some of the nutritional values. Our current agriculture industry is also not built for resilience to the kind of disruptions that society is already experiencing. We saw this during the first year of the COVID-19 pandemic when restaurants, schools, and stadiums closed. Existing supply chains were not able to shift to get the food where it was needed at food banks and to people staying at home. This led to milk dumped down drains, and fruits and vegetables given away, converted into livestock feed, plowed back into the ground, or left in piles to rot.[3] In Little's book, *The Fate of Food: What We'll Eat in a Bigger, Hotter, Smarter World*, she discusses the impacts of global crop yields that may decline 2–6% each decade. We are already seeing impacts on farming from extreme weather that happens more often: longer periods of drought, excess heat, invasive insects and diseases, extreme thunderstorms with hail, sudden "derecho" storms with hurricane force winds—the list can go on. Vanessa Kummer in North Dakota also points out: "The pace of disaster can be dizzying. Earlier this spring, even putting aside the drought, our farm experienced an unusually late frost that killed off 30% of our soybeans just as they were emerging from the soil, requiring us to replant. Within a week, local temperatures boomeranged back to nearly 100 degrees."[4] All of this is already reducing crop yields. In the not-too-distant future, these climate impacts could translate into higher prices for foods and noticeable shortages of foods. Some foods, such as the beloved banana, cocoa for chocolate, or our morning cup of coffee could disappear from our tables as climate change increases disease threats or makes weather conditions impossible to grow certain plants.

Farmers are very good at adapting.[5] They play high stakes gambling with weather, pests, and global markets every year. Many are experimenting with new strategies to cut down their use of diesel fuel and fertilizers (both contribute to greenhouse gas emissions), such as leaving some fields planted in cover crops for a year and using minimum-tillage practices. Seamus McGraw explores how farmers struggle with climate change impacts and how they are adapting: "As I've traveled around the country . . . I've seen it again and again, that deep, in-your-bones understanding that things are changing, carved into the brows of farmers. . . . But there was something else there as well—a sense of responsibility, a belief that if they work hard enough, farm smart enough, have enough faith in themselves and their abilities that have been handed down from generation to generation, they can survive" (p 112). Farmers can transition to new agriculture strategies and a growing number want to. More farmers like Vanessa Kummer, are recognizing that the climate crisis is already here and sustainability is important for a farmer's budget and for a healthy environment. But farmers also need to feel that they have support and are not alone in these struggles. They want to thrive, not just survive. To get more farmers on board, we need more incentives to help farmers shift into working within the natural ecology of their land, instead of doubling down on trying to engineer technical solutions like more drainage tiling, which seems to be a losing battle in areas like the northern Mississippi River watershed.

Every time I have driven to visit my family in the past couple years, I have seen the Minnesota River and many of its tributaries swollen out of their banks. Is this the new normal? Some low spots in fields appear to have been beautifully transformed back to a native ecosystem of prairie potholes, complete with redwing blackbirds singing their buzzsaw melody, families of ducks and geese, occasional swans, and frog choruses. I asked my father if it might be time to give some space back to the prairie, at least the potholes. His resigned response pointed directly to the paradox we face in the climate crisis: "Well, it seems unlikely. Farmers can't make money on that." How do we change the incentives of our global economic system so that we value the natural world in ways that are not entirely based on monetary value? How do we recognize that allowing more prairie potholes to form and thrive will improve agriculture? More potholes would provide space for more water storage (the rivers can't take any more, they are overfull). Prairie potholes also filter that water and provide habitat for wildlife, including many creatures we enjoy, like songbirds, and other creatures we might overlook, like frogs that eat mosquito pests.

Paul Wapner recognizes how such a change in economics requires a change in our collective perspective: "When we open ourselves to wildness [those things beyond human control and comprehension], when we stop fighting and invite more of it into our lives, we extend moral consideration to these other beings and realms. . . . We see them not as enemies or mere objects of exploitation but rather as fellow humans, kin creatures, intrinsically valuable beings, and life-supporting ecosystems" (p 120). I fear that without this type of ethical extension, we will not be able to manage the global environmental problems we have created, especially the climate crisis.

For sustainable and resilient farms we also need political and policy changes to make farming more equitable. Currently, large food corporations, like Kraft Heinz, Conagra, Delmonte, and Tyson have significant power and influence over elected officials' decision-making.[6] They lobby Congressmembers to argue that any changes to laws and budgets continue to benefit their profits. For example, in 2020, large food corporations spent $175 million on political contributions. Additionally, a small number of large corporations own so much of the production process of the food system that farmers have very limited options for selling their products and sharing in those profits. As one example, the merger of the Kraft and Heinz companies means that 25% of all cheese sold in the US is made by this new mega corporation.

As a farmgirl, I am gravely concerned about what the future holds for my family of farmers and what new agriculture strategies are needed to feed nine billion humans. As a fellow scientist, I relate to Jane Zelikova when she says: "I am both fascinated and shocked by how rapidly climate change is disrupting ecological relationships that evolved over millennia. But science also reminds me that we are not powerless. We can slow and perhaps even halt some climate change with some human ingenuity and courage, and some help from the invisible multitude under our soil-covered shoes. We can help save ourselves, and the planet we depend on, if we're willing to play in the dirt" (p 288).

Strategies for healing and protecting soil are often grouped under the term "regenerative agriculture," and Gabe Brown has been working with this to improve his land since the 1990s.[7] His book, *Dirt to Soil: One Family's Journey into Regenerative Agriculture*, describes his experiences as a North Dakota rancher and farmer learning to heal the ecology of his land. He focuses on five principles for soil health: limited tillage and chemicals, always keep soil covered, strive for diverse plants and animals, maintain living roots in soil as long as possible, and integrate animals. For thousands of years, humans have plowed and tilled soil, converting grasslands and forests into agricultural fields, roads, parking lots, and cities. And we have been losing soil that entire time. Soil is the Earth's skin, and tilling it is like running a knife through it. Tilling the soil exposes it to being carried away by wind and water. Tilling also threatens the tiny organisms, microbes, that are the living components of soil. Now it is time to reverse those losses and help the Earth heal. Widely adopting no-till farming wherever possible can help preserve and rebuild soil. Additionally, Zelikova discusses how to bring back soil, we must feed the microbes, the "wee beasties" that live under our feet in healthy soils. Brown highlights that a good way to do that is to increase the diversity of crops we plant. Diverse plant communities deliver a greater variety of nutrients, including carbon, into the soil through their roots, feeding the billions of microbes living there. Healthy microbes, in turn, transform and store more carbon. If we provide good incentives to farmers to practice regenerative agriculture, they can help rebuild healthy soil, putting carbon back into the ground where it belongs.

Change is never easy, but farmers are masters of adaptation. We have good strategies to transform farming and the food system. As good starting points we should: extend our ethical perspective to value the natural world beyond economics, transition to regenerative agriculture, and make necessary changes in the political system. These changes can build sustainability and resilience in the land and in the future of farming.

> *October 2019. As the weeks slip into autumn, I am reminded how much I love the changing color palette in the prairie and along its edges. The brilliant red of staghorn sumac, the golden leaves of cottonwood, walnut, and birch, the fading shades of green, and the grasses turning bronze, copper, and orange. I try to be outside as much as possible because change is in the air. Any day can bring the first snowfall that announces winter and stays with us until March. As the climate changes, so does the landscape. Its inhabitants will also need to change, or we will disappear.*

188

Endnotes

1 https://www.washingtonpost.com/business/2019/07/02/midwestern-farmers-struggles-with-extreme-weather-are-visible-space/?utm_term=.a809788951c7 (https://perma.cc/8473-MX57)
2 https://www.bnnbloomberg.ca/crazy-midwest-weather-spurs-hardest-year-ever-for-u-s-farmers-1.1307967 (https://perma.cc/YNP8-GQMT)
3 https://www.cnn.com/2020/06/08/perspectives/cabot-dairy-farmers-pandemic/index.html (https://perma.cc/8TZ7-SJUS)
4 https://www.cnn.com/2021/07/08/opinions/farmers-climate-change-fight-support-kummer/index.html (https://perma.cc/K2WM-WDSS)
5 https://www.goodreads.com/book/show/23367627-betting-the-farm-on-a-drought (https://perma.cc/45AZ-YQYY)
6 https://www.theguardian.com/environment/ng-interactive/2021/jul/14/food-monopoly-meals-profits-data-investigation (https://perma.cc/M4DV-YJY3)
7 https://www.theguardian.com/food/2021/jul/18/sustainable-isnt-a-thing-why-regenerative-agriculture-is-foods-latest-buzzword (https://perma.cc/AP8Z-QZUQ)

Sheep farm in the Lake District in northwest England.
Photo credit 2013 Rebecca J Romsdahl.

Autumn Two
Considering Greenspace

River Lune watershed, United Kingdom, September – October 2013

Walking, shuffling, and stomping through piles of dry leaves is joyful. The crackly sound fills me with a childish delight. My usual enjoyment of leaf-tramping was significantly dampened, however, when we lived in England for a half-year because it is often too wet to find crinkly, dry leaves. But this disappointment was tempered by the fact that we would have some greenery throughout the winter since the climate is not so cold and the grass lives on. Do people realize how important greenspace is in our daily lives? Greenspace occupies my mental space more and more as autumn leaves increasingly blanket the ground with splashes of color and then curl up into wonderful crinkly brown paper-like piles. When living in an urban environment, surrounded by brick, stone, concrete, and metal, I am very aware of the lack of greenspace.

In the mid-1800s, earnest naturalists in the United States began a discussion about protecting nature from ourselves, specifically from our shortsighted decisions. These early conversations led to the creation of National Parks, Forests, and Wilderness areas, but these large, protected greenspaces left humans out of the picture. In 1962, Rachel Carson wrenched us back into view. With her famous book Silent Spring, criticizing the use of chemical pesticides as a safe practice, she reminded us that everything is connected. Since then, people have been talking about the need to recognize human interdependence with nature.

This discussion introduced the notion of connecting greenspaces. The first serious attempts in the US emerged from the 1970s deep ecology movement,[1] which values all living things equally, and the activities of groups such as the Wildlands Project and Yukon to Yellowstone,[2] which are working to restore large natural areas of North America to support animals that need a lot of space to migrate, like bison herds. The biggest idea for pulling this all together is E.O. Wilson's Half Earth proposal.[3] Supporters argue that we need to restore large, connected greenspaces across at least half the Earth's landscape, and they are mapping out strategies.[4] All of this may sound like a utopian fantasy, but there are examples of people working to reconnect large greenspaces.[5] Places where land is no longer used for industrial scale farming or logging in North America, Europe, and China are being rewilded by the plants, insects, and animals who used to live there, and often assisted by the people who find joy in them.

Considering cultural ideas about landscape aesthetics and actual greenspaces between the UK and the US has opened my eyes to some noteworthy similarities and differences. The two countries have obvious differences in amount of land. The US has such an abundance of land that it has shaped our cultural perspective. Many feel like our land and resources are infinite. There is a cultural preference that "bigger is better"—big houses, big cars, big sprawling suburbs, big yards, big farms, and big parks. An island nation like the UK, by contrast, has fundamental limits on space for new development, so protecting the rural landscape may result in losing urban greenspace.

The British pastoral countryside is a source of great national pride and has even been awarded the high status of a World Heritage Site in the famous Lake District in northwest England, not far from where we lived. The picturesque landscape with grazing sheep is protected as a heartwarming view of farm life. But some argue that this is a deceptive view of misplaced government subsidies protecting a farming model that is no longer cost effective and is damaging ecosystem health. The famous nineteenth-century environmental advocate John Muir called sheep "hoofed locusts" as he observed their ability to eat everything across a landscape. Interestingly, Muir and his family had immigrated to the US from Scotland. His naturalist observations condemning sheep grazing in the Sierra Nevada mountains of California helped his arguments to protect the Yosemite Valley region, which later became the second US National Park.

Echoing Muir's disdain for sheep, the environmental activist and Guardian news columnist George Monbiot tried in vain to slay the serene myth:

> The Lake District's new designation is based on a fairytale with great cultural power. For 3,000 years this story has presented sheep farming as the seat of innocence and purity; an Arcadian refuge from the corruption of the city, an idyll in perfect harmony with the natural world. The reality couldn't be more different. . . . Sheep, by nibbling out tree seedlings and other edible species, are a fully automated system for ecological destruction. They cleanse the land of almost all wildlife. In the UK they occupy some 4 [million] hectares of our uplands. Compare this to the built environment (houses, factories, offices, roads, railways, airports, even parks and gardens) that covers 1.7 [million] hectares. Yet this vast area, which is roughly equivalent to all our arable land, produces around 1.2% of our food (probably a good deal less, as the figure includes lamb from lowland farms). Our infertile uplands, including most of our national parks, would be better used to protect and restore the wonders of the living world. If we are to spend £3 [billion] a year of public money, it should be deployed for ecological restoration rather than destruction. But the cultural power of this [sheep] industry is so great that hardly anyone dares challenge it.[6]

The argument swirls around a question. What is culturally/socially valuable enough to be given protection? The British are famous for their sheep-dotted countryside and their love of walking. Wherever you go, there are lots of paths and guides for taking a nice walk. Nearly every scenic landscape, overlook, historic site, park, or bird sanctuary we toured involved a walk through a sheep pasture.

There is also a growing recognition that wildlife and their habitats are threatened by human encroachments, such as expanding cities and agricultural practices. In the **Howgill Fells** area of Yorkshire Dales National Park, we can see signs of changing attitudes that both Muir and Monbiot would appreciate.[7] Sheep grazing has dominated these hills for more than a century. But over the past decade, wildflower meadows have been replacing some of the sheep meadows, and they are being actively managed to benefit wildlife, with noticeable results. Red squirrels, voles, and birds such as grouse and owls are making a reappearance. Environmental groups are partnering with sheep farmers to introduce hundreds of acres of native trees, including hawthorn, rowan, willow, and birch. These efforts to rewild the landscape involve fencing off areas for the new trees to protect them from sheep and working with the government to develop a policy that will pay farmers for providing ecosystem services. For example, the new tree enclosures help slow the rainfall flowing downhill, thus reducing flood risks in small streams. By helping farmers transition from sheep grazing to new ways of managing their lands, these partnerships will begin restoring ecological processes across the landscape and increase the diversity of plants and animals. Essentially, restoring good ecological health to the landscapes damaged by 'hooved locusts.'

In late October, we took a daytrip north to the Lake District National Park, which borders the Yorkshire Dales National Park. To get a better sense of this landscape, we trekked 20 minutes uphill to Orrest Head overlook. It was high season for autumn tree colors, but on a wet, gray, overcast day, they were subdued as though we stood behind a tinted-glass window. Despite the dreary weather, the view from 784 feet above sea level was worthy of appreciation. The surrounding landscape was a mix of sheep farms, forested hillsides, and the little tourist town of Bowness on the shore of Windermere, the largest lake in the park.

To complete the lovely three-mile circuit, we headed downhill through a sheep paddock enclosed by three-foot-tall drystone walls. The path continued along a single-track paved road and past several charming houses built from the same dark slate rocks as the paddock walls. Then we were off into a wooded area with tiny streams trickling down the rocky path under our feet. In some sections, the ground was so saturated that it was like walking on a sponge. Oddly, these spots did not appear that wet until you stepped on them and then the water gushed forth. Happily dressed in our waterproof hiking boots, we tramped along the spongy trail chatting amiably as the sogginess of the woods muffled our voices. We stopped at a footbridge that was just big enough for the two of us and fell silent. The small but fierce whitewater creek rushing under our feet created a further dampening effect, blocking out the sounds of nearby street traffic and the voices of people behind us on the trail. For those few minutes, we were alone in a bubble of imagined wilderness. Reluctantly leaving the creek, we soon found ourselves exiting the trees and walking back amongst the village houses and shops of Bowness.

The inclusion of towns within the borders of UK National Parks is unavoidable and even then, these parks are much smaller in acreage than their cousins in the US. The Yellowstone and Yosemite National Parks are huge swaths of land with sparse human development and little or no private property within their borders. But, regardless of size and human settlements, parks are important greenspaces because they provide refuge for biodiversity at small and large scales.

My thinking on this has been expanded by Emma Marris' book *Rambunctious Garden*. She discusses how human relationships with the natural world change over time and space.[8] Marris argues that we need to change our attitudes about what is worthy to protect. Should we continue to focus most of our efforts on "untrammeled nature," as described in the US Wilderness Act? No. She discusses why it is time to shift our focus away from trying to preserve nature only in a pristine, museum-like state and instead embrace all the nature around us, even in cities. She suggests this shift can become a "hybrid of wild

Paved-over front gardens add parking spaces to Lancaster homes.
Photo credit 2013 Rebecca J Romsdahl.

nature and human management." This would mean that even sheep farms, city parks, and the yards around our homes could be managed as sanctuaries for nature.

American and British cultures both value the beauty and personal enjoyment of a green yard, but they are a bit obsessed with the idea of perfectly manicured lawns. This topic surfaced often in my research interviews with local government planners across the UK. I was talking with them to learn how local governments were planning to adapt to climate changes. In urban residential areas of the UK, it is common to have row houses with very small yards. Even in neighborhoods with individual homes and yards, there is often not much open area for greenspace. Instead, many planners emphasize protecting large, open greenspace outside cities, like the sheep-dotted countryside. In my research interviews, local government planners also described a problematic trend in the UK, which once pointed out, I started seeing everywhere. More and more homeowners are putting tarmac, or pavement, over their front yard to add parking space for more cars.

Another British trend seems completely retro, and not in a good way. Some people are installing artificial grass for their lawns, called **plastic gardens**.[9] Awareness and concern about the climate crisis, threats to wildlife, and the damaging amount of plastic pollution in our lives has been increasing. But apparently, not everyone is concerned yet. The reasons people give for **wanting fake lawns** are often centered on that common social pressure problem: keeping up with the Joneses.[10] If your neighbor has a perfectly manicured, green yard, you feel embarrassed if your lawn does not look the same. Then add in the economic pressure of long workdays. Many people lack the time and desire to do the mowing, fertilizing, weeding, reseeding, and general care necessary to create and maintain a flawless looking lawn. I can sympathize with that. After working a long day, I like to grab a beer and sit quietly in the yard, enjoying the birdsong and the silliness of squirrel antics, rather than doing yard maintenance. But even fake lawns are not maintenance free. People have replaced mowing with vacuuming, and they still need to remove colonizing moss, dead leaves, and other debris brought in on the winds. A fake lawn is like carpet. In time, it will get a crushed, worn-out look to it. Rain will not refresh it. Eventually it will need to be pulled up, carted off to the landfill, and replaced. Again, which is not environmentally friendly in the slightest. A fake lawn also destroys habitat for many insects, birds, and small animals.

Having grown up on a farm, I see value in Marris' argument for rambunctious gardens. Manicured lawns look fake to me. Our farm yard was a mix of grasses and small plants, whatever would grow in a given area. When I see a patch of white clover flowers in a lawn, I find it lovely. I think dandelions are beautiful. Expressing these opinions often gets me eye-rolls and scornful laughter. But so-called "weeds," like dandelions provide sources of food for pollinating insects in spring before other plants are flowering. Dandelions also provide joy to children who are learning to value the natural world through playing outdoors.

Converting front yards into parking space and replacing backyards with plastic gardens represent significant losses of greenspace in urban areas where it is already sparse. This is also a growing problem in the face of the climate crisis. Both practices create more hard-packed surface area, meaning that rain cannot soak through it. As the climate changes, extreme rainstorms will become more common in the UK. In several of my research interviews, people commented that this is already happening. They have seen "once in 200-year storm events" now happening in two out of the past five years. The increasing amount of pavement in urban areas in the UK means there is less greenspace where that excess rainwater can be absorbed and slowly filter through soil layers, nourishing soil-dwelling critters, and eventually join up with small streams. More pavement means the rain rushes straight into Victorian-era stormwater systems, which do not have much capacity, or straight into small streams, which also cannot hold that much water in a single event. Some of my interview participants referred to this problem as "overdevelopment," and it leads to overland flooding during heavy rainstorms. One local government official shared an example of how lack of community planning allowed an apartment developer to

Author's pollinator garden.
Photo credit 2018 Rebecca J Romsdahl.

build directly on top of a small stream, encasing it within a concrete channel running under the building. Not surprisingly, that neighborhood has suffered many overland flooding events since then.

Many cities in the US also struggle against the tide of increasing pavement, but some are changing direction by adding parks along streams to reduce flooding, making space for community gardens, or using xeriscaping in desert regions. In my home ecosystem, residents in states from Texas to North Dakota, are recreating patches of native prairie and planting pollinator gardens. I have joined this effort to help give space back to nature by cultivating several pockets in my own flowerbeds. Seeing hummingbirds and even a rare, endangered rusty patched bumblebee visit my flowers is delightful. Against the backdrop of a manicured lawn, these **"pocket prairies"** stand tall and rowdy.[11]

Early spring clusters of prairie smoke (*Geum triflorum*) transform
as soft pink buds bloom, an illusion of ground fog,
drifting across the prairie.
Summery green clumps of prairie dropseed (*Sporobolus heterolepis*) mix
with long plumes of switchgrass (*Panicum virgatum*).
Riotous pinks, purples, orange, and gold,
the mingling of coneflowers (*Echinacea purpurea*),
bergamot (*Monarda fistulosa*),
blazing star (*Liatris pycnostachya*),
milkweeds (*Asclepias syriaca* or *Asclepias tuberosa*),
goldenrods (*Solidago*),
and black-eyed Susan (*Rudbeckia hirta*).
The garden hums—
wild bees, monarch butterflies (*Danaus plexippus*),
painted lady butterflies (*Vanessa cardui*),
damselflies (*Zygoptera*), and dragonflies (*Anisoptera*).
Wings sing.
Nights fill with crickets' (*Gryllidae*) songs.
Summer transitions to autumn,
silvery blades of little bluestem (*Schizachyrium scoparium*) blush red.

Suddenly, tiny white asters (*Symphyotrichum pilosum*) appear
like stars sprinkled amidst
beautiful chaos.

Rewilding sheep meadows and planting pocket prairies give us more than just gorgeous greenspace, they also provide valuable ecosystem services, meaning we don't often recognize the free benefits nature provides to us. The roots of plants pull carbon out of the air and lock it into the soil, creating a rich, dark, organic mass that is black gold. This lush soil and all those roots provide habitat for many types of insects and microorganisms. Together, this creates a healthy ecosystem that filters pollutants out of rainwater and provides natural flood protection by slowing the flow of rainwater toward streams and rivers.

In my research interviews, I learned that on top of individual homeowner decisions, local governments across the UK have faced **extreme budget cuts**, and some have had to choose between maintaining greenspace or providing essential services.[12] Governments at every level, in every country, are constantly negotiating that fundamental question. What do we value? What do we prioritize in our decision-making and funding? I often present this to my students as a forward-looking question: What do we want our future to look like?

Do we want our future to go the way of plastic gardens or pocket prairies? As concerns increase about the climate crisis and threats to ecosystems, there is a growing worldwide call for rewilding. And rewilding experiments, such as those with the Howgill Fells sheep farmers, are gaining more support. But in the back of my mind, I hear the concerns and questions of science experts and environmental activists. Are these efforts moving fast enough and at large enough scales to counter the tide of negative trends? We don't know. So, I tell my students to keep the baton moving forward because the race is still being run. We haven't lost, yet.

202

Endnotes

1 https://en.wikipedia.org/wiki/Deep_ecology (https://perma.cc/F5YB-TP67)
2 Wildlands Project: https://wildlandsnetwork.org/ (https://perma.cc/QJQ5-NXEN); Yukon to Yellowstone:https://y2y.net/about/vision-mission/frequently-asked-questions/ (https://perma.cc/9BU6-KX9Z)
3 https://www.smithsonianmag.com/science-nature/can-world-really-set-aside-half-planet-wildlife-180952379/ (https://perma.cc/6UST-XWWQ)
4 https://theconversation.com/3-global-conditions-and-a-map-for-saving-nature-and-using-it-wisely-124063 (https://perma.cc/5U86-3EB5)
5 https://science.sciencemag.org/content/364/6447/1226 (https://perma.cc/8NJZ-4NSL)
6 https://www.theguardian.com/commentisfree/2017/jul/11/lake-district-world-heritage-site-sheep (https://perma.cc/559H-V5M9)
7 https://www.theguardian.com/environment/2020/oct/30/un-managing-the-land-the-hill-farmers-helping-to-rewild-britain-aoe (https://perma.cc/9GWW-RWK7)
8 https://www.emmamarris.com/writing (https://perma.cc/GQD4-KMLT)
9 https://www.theguardian.com/cities/2019/aug/02/turf-it-out-is-it-time-to-say-goodbye-to-artificial-grass (https://perma.cc/JQ2Q-8U87)
10 https://www.bbc.co.uk/programmes/m0009jl4 (https://perma.cc/G5DA-MJ4T)
11 https://www.sciencefriday.com/segments/turning-flood-water-into-freshwater/ (https://perma.cc/H6V6-875Q)
12 http://www.theguardian.com/environment/2013/nov/19/england-parks-spending-cuts (https://perma.cc/QHR3-V8X6)

A glimpse of Skyline Drive from the crest of Frazier Discovery Trail.
Photo credit 2000 Rebecca J Romsdahl.

Worthless Lands or Crown Jewels?

Shenandoah National Park, United States, Chesapeake Bay watershed. October 2000

Rounding another bend on Skyline Drive, my imagination conjures a tale where I am driving along the back of an ancient dragon who has been asleep for so long that his body has been hidden by the forests that cover the mountains. The only parts of the dragon visible now are some of the spikes that run in a line down his back. Skyline Drive requires you to slow down because it is a very curvy highway. Admiring the rocky wall jutting out of the ground and driving safely at the same time requires my full attention, and it is tiring. Today I am off-duty and seeking a little solitude to recharge my soul. This is my second summer season as an Interpretive Ranger with the US National Park Service and the second park I have worked at. As the scenic road is laid out, I am driving atop the spine of a section of the Blue Ridge Mountains through the state of Virginia.

In geologic terms, these mountains are as old as my imagined dragon. The basement rocks, the foundation of the Blue Ridge, formed more than a billion years ago.[1] But thanks to tectonic upheavals and erosion, we can see and touch some of this ancient history today. I pull off at one of my favorite spots, Mary's Rock Tunnel overlook, to contemplate the dragon's spiky back. The lumpy, rounded granite exposed above the tunnel entrance and the boulders that seem to have rolled off toward the edge of the mountain slope suggest the dragon has been restless. As I daydream of a slumbering beast guarding a treasure of jewels, a memory from one of my graduate courses jumps to mind suddenly—the worthless lands argument—and I ponder if it actually fits the story of Shenandoah National Park.

Driving a bit further, I stop at Hazel Mountain overlook. Looking east, I take in the gorgeous view across the rolling mountain tops blanketing the dragon's back in a patchwork quilt of gold, orange, and scarlet leaves, while my mind is wandering through the philosophy and cultural values that created our National Parks. The US National Parks are sometimes called America's Crown Jewels because we do not have a royal family, historic castles, or centuries-old gothic cathedrals. The lack of historic works of art and architecture was a sore spot for the founding generation of Americans, akin to an inferiority complex in our national identity for decades.

This anxiety of the early 1800s overlapped with a growing concern for protecting natural scenic beauty and wonders from the rapid expansion of cities and the Industrial Revolution. Niagara Falls was one of the most beautiful natural wonders known in the United States at the time. But it was not protected from private enterprise and had become a national embarrassment. European visitors compared it to a carnival scene with its hucksters, booths, and trinket vendors. Early American conservationists (who we would now call environmentalists) saw this national identity crisis as an opportunity. The government was just purchasing, or conquering, the vast western territories in the mid-1840s, which would stretch the national boundaries from the Atlantic coast to the Pacific coast. Against this backdrop, the conservationists started a discussion with national leaders and promoted the unique idea of national parks as "America's Scenic Wonders," beautiful enough to compete with Europe's greatest art and architecture. But they recognized that crafting an argument to protect places of natural beauty would not stand on its own merits. They would need to convince Congress that these parks would not interfere with farming, ranching, logging, mining, and building, the march of progress from sea to shining sea. This is why they developed the worthless lands argument.

Historian Alfred Runte traced the beginnings of the worthless lands argument to a speech in Congress. In 1864, Senator John Conness gave voice to the argument, which became the standard, unwritten rule for creating national parks, as he introduced Yosemite to Congress: "I will state to the Senate that this bill proposes to make a grant of certain premises located in the Sierra Nevada Mountains, in the State of California, that are for all public purposes worthless, but which constitute, perhaps, some of the greatest wonders of the world" (p 48-49).

Back in the car again, I decide to hike to a spot that has been recommended as one of the best views in Shenandoah, Hawksbill Mountain summit. I park at the trailhead and get out to stretch a bit, feeling like a cat waking from a nap in the sun. After a few minutes of walking down the trail, my muscles begin to relax, and I realize just how badly I needed a day to myself with no work, no responsibilities, no timetable.

I like to discuss with my students how Yellowstone National Park might not have been created if geothermal vents had been recognized as a valuable energy source in 1872. But Shenandoah National Park is a different example of this idea to protect scenic landscapes that are considered worthless for economic purposes. The boundaries of the park mostly follow the contours of the mountain range spine with spindly fingers stretching down to protect some of the rivers that have cascading waterfalls. Overall, the area is not well suited for farming, city development, or mining, and some of the land was mismanaged in logging. But the region had long-established families of **mountain people** who farmed, logged, hunted, and lived comfortably for generations, until economies shifted much of their lifestyles away from the mountains.[2] Before Europeans spread out in these mountains many Native American peoples lived and passed through the region including, the Iroquois Six Nations tribe, the Catawbas, the Delaware, the Cherokees, and the Shawnee people. Shenandoah—the park, the river, and the valley—all take their name from a **Native American Chief** of the **Oneida people**.[3]

Throughout the history of creating our National Parks, Native Americans were living in many of the territories that were set aside as crown jewels. Ojibwe author and historian **David Treuer** reminds us that the parks and Native American reservations were being created simultaneously.[4] He notes how the Oglala Lakota spiritual leader Black Elk described darkly that the United States "made little islands for us and other little islands for the four-leggeds, and always these islands are becoming smaller." Native Americans were killed and pushed out of lands that were designated as National Parks. The beautiful landscapes we chose to protect were shaped by Native peoples for millennia, but their relationships with the land, their management skills, and their knowledge were not recognized. The people were erased, and this allowed the crown jewels myth to be created. As Treuer says, the US National Parks "offer Americans the thrill of looking back over their shoulder at a world without humans or technology. Many visit them to find something that exists outside or beyond us, to experience an awesome sense of scale, to contemplate our smallness and our ephemerality." I am guilty of this pleasure.

After a short but invigorating 1.7 miles hiking uphill, I am sitting on a rock ledge at Hawksbill Mountain summit and my soul feels renewed. This is the highest peak in the park at 4,051 feet, and it provides a sweeping view west over the Shenandoah Valley. But on this warm autumn day, the valley is partially hidden by puffy clouds, as if the dragon is breathing smoky plumes in his slumber. Looking down on the clouds enhances the philosophic frame of mind I have had all afternoon. Every few minutes, I catch a glimpse through the clouds of the checkerboard fields and farmsteads on the valley floor. On the western edge, peaks in the Massanutten Ridge, and another ridge beyond, rise gracefully out of the cloudbank as it slowly purls and flows through the valley.

We are nearing peak visitor season in the park, but weekdays are still quiet. There are no namesake hawks at the summit today. But I do get to watch a pair of young peregrine falcons testing their wings, and I am enthralled by their aerial games for an hour. I also enjoy being

Sea of clouds in Bacon Hollow.
Photo credit 2000 Rebecca J Romsdahl.

incognito in my civi-clothes. Pretending I am just another visitor, I enjoy chatting with a woman from New York State. She tells me all about the falcons that live in her neighborhood. We exchange goodbyes and a chuckle about the nature of hiking in Shenandoah National Park—you only hike up or down, back and forth to Skyline Drive.

Although early conservationists were hoping to create a US National Park in the Appalachian Mountains of Virginia and had a proposal submitted to Congress as early as 1901, this landscape was still viewed as too valuable for resource use and population expansion.[5] The unwritten standard of the worthless lands argument was so strong that in 1926, when conservationists selected the area of land they wanted to promote for creating Shenandoah National Park, they also developed a **myth**.[6] They concocted a story that the land had been overused and abused by local populations and now was virtually worthless for continued logging and farming. This myth also helped the argument for using eminent domain to remove the remaining mountain people who lived within the boundaries of the proposed park. The truth is closer to the idea that those who lobbied for the creation of Shenandoah National Park had cherry-picked an area of the Blue Ridge Mountains that had indeed been used for farming, logging, and charcoal production in the past, but had recovered so well that it was in beautiful ecological condition in the 1920s.

This legacy can still be seen in the splendor of Shenandoah National Park around me today, but I feel unsettled by the myths and argument that created our national treasures. The parks are more than worthless lands, and even though most visitors only want convenient views of the highlights, the parks are also much more than jewels to be protected in museum-like settings. The US National Parks are living landscapes. By the time my feet return to the black pavement of Skyline Drive, however, I am doubting the conviction of my opinion. The construction of this road damaged the natural landscape more than the generations of people living here before the park was established, and since Skyline Drive is the only way most visitors see this park, the damage is ongoing—car exhaust equals visitors.

The National Park Service safeguards an idea, that scenic beauty and wildness can and should be protected for public enjoyment. Now I am dreading the upcoming peak season weekends when thousands of cars, carrying thousands more visitors, will soon arrive daily. As the National Park Service seeks to stay relevant and increase visitor numbers, the parks themselves feel more like museums with narrow halls, crowded by visitors vying to get a good picture of the famous crown jewels. Not wanting my day to end on this melancholy note, I hatch a new plan. I will drive down to Big Meadows, grab some picnic goodies, meet my partner after his shift ends, and entice him to join me in hiking to the Stony Man Trail overlook to watch the sunset.

Endnotes

1 https://www.nps.gov/shen/learn/nature/geology.htm (https://perma.cc/DQL9-ASFQ)
2 https://www.nps.gov/articles/mountain-settlements.htm (https://perma.cc/YW33-QV6C)
3 https://en.wikipedia.org/wiki/Skenandoa (https://perma.cc/2E-BL-S6DV); https://www.oneidaindiannation.com/chiefshenendoah/ (https://perma.cc/G2G3-QEDF)
4 https://www.theatlantic.com/magazine/archive/2021/05/return-the-national-parks-to-the-tribes/618395/ (https://perma.cc/6C6N-B8F3)
5 https://en.wikipedia.org/wiki/Shenandoah_National_Park (https://perma.cc/HW9C-ZTBB)
6 https://www.nps.gov/shen/learn/historyculture/abused_landscape.htm (https://perma.cc/7ECE-DSH5)

Lovely row houses along a canal in Amsterdam, with a swan.
Photo credit 2018 Mick Beltz.

Can Sustainable and Resilient Cities Improve Our Relationship with Nature?

Amstel River watershed, The Netherlands, November 2018

March 2006. Exiting the electric tram, I took two steps away from the door. Ding-ding! Hearing the bell, I glanced to my right and dazedly took a large step backward onto the curb as my partner simultaneously pulled me out of the path of several speedy bicyclists. This was my introduction to the incredible network of public transit, bicycling, and walking that makes Amsterdam a very sustainable city. Shaking the fog from my brain, I reconsidered jetlag—definitely more dangerous than I remembered it being.

November 2018. Over a decade later, we have returned to the Netherlands. A steady, gentle, autumn rain chilled us quickly and made the day feel colder than the temperature might suggest. Amsterdam felt bigger, but also more ethnically and culturally diverse, which enhances its appeal. We walked to our favorite pancake house and found it still thriving. Sitting by the fire helped dry our jeans, soaked from thigh to ankles. Eating crepe-like, savory pancakes with gooey slices of gouda cheese and topped with a drizzle of molasses restored warmth to body and soul.

In 2015, we crossed a threshold. For the first time in the history of our species, **more humans lived in urban areas** than in rural ones, and this trend is projected to continue through at least the end of the twenty-first century.[1] Not all cities are growing, some are shrinking as people move to different cities. But the overall pattern shows more humans shifting to city living. I look at this trend and see an incredible opportunity. We can carefully plan for this growth. The idea of thoughtfully designed cities, or **urban planning**, is very old, with evidence found in ancient Egypt and even earlier settlements in Mesopotamia.[2] This long history shows that we can develop sustainable, resilient cities. Outside of these dense human habitats, we can then work to restore and rewild large, interconnected areas of protected landscapes for non-human nature to flourish.

But can cities improve our relationship with the natural world? I recently read an essay entitled "From bottleneck to breakthrough."[3] It suggests this utopian idea just might be feasible over time, and it gives me hope. Sanderson and coauthors describe how we are currently in a bottleneck point in time wherein humans are placing many great pressures on the natural environment. They propose that long-lasting conservation success is possible if human actions, discussions, and planning continue their current trajectory along three paths: 1) the human population stabilizes and begins to decrease; 2) extreme poverty is alleviated; and 3) the majority of people and institutions act on a shared belief that it is in our best interest to care for, rather than destroy, the natural systems of life on Earth. They argue that these goals might be accomplished through the social dynamics of cities.

As a farmgirl, I have never really liked cities, especially large ones. I see them as concrete valleys with too many people, noisy vehicles driving too fast or stuck in bumper-to-bumper traffic, choking exhaust fumes—overall, just too stressful. And yet, I fell in love with Amsterdam.

It is nonsensical. Amsterdam's dense, bustling urban population is over 1.3 million. Cities chew up natural habitats and spit out brick, concrete, and metal. Amsterdam and the entire country of the Netherlands is built directly on top of the Amstel River. The natural landscape of a delta, composed of two branches of the Amstel River, has been transformed, channeled and contained. We used to call this progress, and some still think this way. I cannot change the past, so I try to appreciate the present. In the Netherlands, canals of water flow everywhere, alongside brilliant blocks of colorful red and yellow tulip fields, through pastures of dairy cows, parallel with cars zipping along

Bicycles parked on a canal bridge in Amsterdam.
Photo credit 2006 Rebecca J Romsdahl.

highways, even under airport runways, as Amsterdam's Schiphol Airport sits below sea level. The whole country seems to float on the slow current of the Amstel River as it seeps into the North Sea.

But this is part of Amsterdam's allure. It is a water city, and this has required very careful planning. The canals provide form and function to the city. The city was built from west to east, with the canals giving the old central city its half-moon shape. Amsterdam has over **60 miles of canals**, 90 islands, and at least 1,500 bridges.[4] The canals shape the layout of the streets and thus the layout of districts for commercial and residential developments. They have always been used for transportation of goods and people, but nowadays they are used more often for houseboats, recreation, and tourism.

Like many cities in Europe, Amsterdam is a walkable city. Modern urban planning, with a focus on resilience, health, and sustainability, seeks to enhance city life for walking and bicycling. Strolling along the central city canals in summer gives you a perfect perspective from which to experience the historic, romantic character of Amsterdam. Pedestrians bustle about their daily lives, easily walking the narrow sidewalks of narrow streets and sidestepping out of the path of tiny Smart cars and bicyclists. Charming seventeenth-century row houses, built in warm, earthy hues of brick and stone, line the canal streets on both sides. Some are still homes, others are welcoming bed and breakfasts, and others are a hybrid of shops on the ground level and residences above. I can imagine being one of the locals, walking or bicycling, to get some groceries for supper.

Amsterdam is also a **bicycle city**.[5] Estimates suggest that there are more bicycles than residents in the city, with an average of two bikes per household. Nearly 70% of all trips to work and school are done by bicycle. Regardless of age or income, people bike everywhere and in every type of weather. Amsterdam's city planning focuses on bicycles and electric trams as the primary forms of transportation, making this one of the most sustainability friendly cities in the world. Transportation is cheap, efficient, quiet, and clean, and the city is always working to improve bicycle safety.

There are several key factors that shape Amsterdam's bicycle culture. To create a bike-centric urban transportation network, city planners needed to actively discourage car ownership. Driving a car is quite inconvenient due to limited parking, expensive taxes and parking fees, and the designation of many bicycle-only streets. Historically narrow streets also help this effort. On larger shared streets, there are separate, elevated bicycle tracks, not just painted lanes on the road next to car lanes. This adds a significant layer of safety for bicyclists. Other streets have been completely converted to bicycle lanes and sidewalks except for a grass-covered center lane where the tram tracks run. Streets open to cars employ every type of traffic-calming strategy available, including speed bumps and tables, textured pavement, and raised intersections where bicycles can cross. There are also separate bicycle traffic signals at intersections, which improves safety and lowers a cyclist's stress at busy crossings with car traffic. Amsterdam's long-term goal is to become a car-free city.

Amsterdam is one of many cities working with a popular non-governmental organization called ICLEI – Local Governments for Sustainability. ICLEI is helping cities around the world develop in more environmentally friendly ways. They have a **five pathways** plan that focuses on: 1) lowering air pollution and emissions while creating new economic opportunities; 2) nature-based developments to protect and enhance biodiversity in urban areas; 3) circular development that increases recyclable, shareable, and replenishing resources; 4) building resilience to anticipate, prevent, absorb, and recover better from stressors and shocks, such as rapid economic, social, and environmental changes; and 5) equitable and people-centered development to address poverty and build more inclusive, just, livable communities.[6]

Amsterdam's increasing ethnic diversity provides opportunities for different parts of the city to develop their own unique character, and city government has allowed experiments in locally led initiatives. Two examples show how abandoned land and buildings can be reclaimed to benefit residents. Through an art and urban design community partnership project, one district that has many immigrants from rural areas of Morocco and Turkey now has a community-designed chicken coop inside a new park that was created by reclaiming an unused, derelict city block.[7] Another neighborhood had a situation with many children going to school too sleepy to learn. The problem was that many families who live in small homes would let visiting relatives stay in the children's bedrooms, thus disrupting their sleep. The community partnership project developed a simple, clever solution. They converted a vacant apartment building into a guesthouse maintained and run by community members where people can stay for a small fee.

To learn more about how Amsterdam has changed in the past decade, we chose a hotel in a different part of the city than we had stayed at in the past. This gave us a chance to walk through new neighborhoods and discover new experiences. After touring a special museum exhibit of the famous British street artist Banksy, we meandered back to our hotel and happened upon a vegetarian burger shop. Being a self-described "vergetarian" (on the verge of being vegetarian, meaning I try to eat most meals meat-free), I am always excited to find new vegetarian and vegan restaurants. The menu had several enticing options to try: a classic mushroom burger, crispy falafel with tzatziki sauce, a burger made from lentils and beetroot. I chose the chickpea and carrot burger with a zesty creamy chipotle sauce and a side of crispy zucchini fries, which did not disappoint.

Strolling through the Vondelpark after enjoying the grand paintings of the Dutch Masters at the Rijksmuseum, we stopped to watch a little girl crouching down and staring eye-to-eye with a large goose sitting peacefully on a grassy bank. The staring contest lasted several long moments before the girl popped up and the goose gave a startled honk! Despite the many parks in Amsterdam, if I lived there, I would always long for more greenspace. That is the farmgirl in me. Amsterdam has a forest park covering over 2,000 acres, which is 20 times larger than New York City's Central Park.[8] We heard it is a unique combination of park, woodland, water, and nature, in order to be environmentally and people friendly. But there is never enough time to see everything during a single visit; we had to save that one for next time.

April 2020. As the human population is being ravaged by the Covid-19 global pandemic, forward thinkers in Amsterdam are plotting an expansion of the city's sustainability efforts for the future. **Amsterdam is the first** city in the world to adopt Kate Raworth's Doughnut Economics model as a tool to assist their public policy decisions, especially to help increase resilience.[9] City planners will consider how to keep all projects within natural boundaries (the doughnut glaze) while also finding ways to improve social equity issues, such as reducing gaps between the rich and the poor (bringing everyone into the doughnut ring). The global economic crisis that has arisen out of Covid-19 lockdowns is forcing governments at all levels to recognize that they need to care about how **society and the natural environment** are integrated, in everything from healthcare, jobs, and housing to climate change and access to food.[10]

Amsterdam's leaders are combining doughnut economics with principles of a circular economy, wherein the goal is to reduce, reuse, and recycle materials across consumer goods, manufacturing, building materials, and food. In an article for *Time*, Ciara Nugent found that the city is **applying this in big and small ways**.[11] One way is through infrastructure projects, such as building a new neighborhood that will not produce any greenhouse gas emissions and will prioritize affordable social housing and access to nature. Another example: During a Covid-19 lockdown, city leaders realized that thousands of residents did not have home computers, meaning they would not be able to socialize with friends and family online, or work from home, and children would not be able to attend school remotely. Rather than buy new machines, which would be expensive and contribute to electronic waste, they arranged a donation and collection of used laptops, contracted a company to refurbish them, and distributed over 3,000 to residents who needed them.

Amsterdam residents are also contributing to changes that increase sustainability and resilience. One community began using parking spaces to host outdoor dinners between neighbors, so they could help each other cope with the Covid-19 pandemic. They eventually persuaded city officials to convert many of those spaces into permanent community gardens.

The Covid-19 pandemic is forcing us to confront our unsustainable modern society and pushing government leaders to ask how they can help communities become more resilient. Kate Raworth starts by asking this simple question: "How can our city be a home to thriving people in a thriving place, while respecting the wellbeing of all people and the health of the whole planet?" Because the pandemic is forcing us to change so many aspects of our lives, it has the potential to inspire and accelerate transformational changes. Examples of such changes include: shifting some city streets from car traffic to bicycles, pedestrians, and restaurant tables; allowing more flexible work schedules and work from home that reduce transportation demands; and encouraging people to spend more time outdoors, which can increase their appreciation of the natural environment.

Amsterdam gives me hope for the future of human habitats. With local governments and active residents leading the way, we might just be able to plan and develop healthy cities. I envision human habitats that are more resilient to the increasing shocks of climate crisis and that move us closer to sustainability by being more socially and economically equitable, as well as by allowing us to reconnect with the natural world.

Endnotes

1 https://ourworldindata.org/grapher/urban-vs-rural-majority (https://perma.cc/W8KK-ATKH)
2 https://en.wikipedia.org/wiki/Urban_planning (https://perma.cc/EZ6R-Y4N5)
3 https://doi.org/10.1093/biosci/biy039
4 https://en.wikipedia.org/wiki/Canals_of_Amsterdam (https://perma.cc/Q7N4-FR4E)
5 https://www.bloomberg.com/news/articles/2017-10-31/5-reasons-why-amsterdam-works-so-well-for-bikes (https://perma.cc/3RHX-CTAX)
6 https://iclei.org/en/our_approach.html (https://perma.cc/9P42-L4VP)
7 https://www.theguardian.com/cities/2014/may/19/how-art-chickens-revived-amsterdam-kolenkitbuurt-cascoland (https://perma.cc/626J-XKXN)
8 https://www.amsterdam.nl/en/policy/policy-green-space/policy-forest/ (https://perma.cc/QZ2Y-M9YG)
9 https://www.kateraworth.com/2020/04/08/amsterdam-city-doughnut/ (https://perma.cc/9774-UNAM)
10 https://www.iisd.org/articles/covid-19-and-planetary-health-how-pandemic-could-pave-way-green-recovery (https://perma.cc/P5W4-BH8T)
11 https://time.com/5930093/amsterdam-doughnut-economics/ (https://perma.cc/4M6Y-UYYU)

Winter is a time of rest, long star-filled nights with a crackling fire-place, cats curled up in haylofts, and warm family gatherings over good food and hot coffee.

Farmhouse and outbuildings in northern England.
Photo credit 2013 Rebecca J Romsdahl.

Winter One
Beer, Community, and Sustainability

River Lune watershed, United Kingdom, November 2013

In July 2013, my partner and I overpacked our bags and flew across the pond to live in the United Kingdom for seven months as part of my US-UK Fulbright Scholar Award.

One of the aspects of British life that we most enjoyed is pub culture. Beer has been an important part of British life for a long time. There is evidence of beer making on the island prior to the arrival of the Romans in 43 AD. During the Middle Ages, drinking water was a sure way to get sick. Because of poor sanitary practices, water was polluted with cholera, dysentery, and other nasty diseases. Beer was one of the safest things you could drink because in the process of making it, the water is boiled, which kills the germs swirling in it.

In American English, you might say we became "bar flies" while living in Lancaster, England. But that term has a bit of a negative stigma. In the UK, going out to a pub (short for a public house, alehouse, or tavern) is not necessarily just about drinking beer. It's also about socializing. In the United States, day drinking is often frowned upon; you should at least wait until happy hour. But in the UK, pubs have long been places to socialize over a pint, even for a business meeting. In the UK, everybody seems to have "a local," meaning a pub close to home which they visit regularly to get a bite to eat, catch up on neighborhood gossip, and relax with friends.

During our travels, we found the best equivalent place to get a Denny's- or Perkins-style breakfast is at a British chain of pubs called Wetherspoons, which are everywhere. The major difference from their American counterparts is that you can get a beer for breakfast. Some

British pub sign.
Photo credit 2013 Rebecca J Romsdahl.

British people compare Wetherspoons to Starbucks or McDonalds, condemning the "Starbucks-ification" of British pubs. The criticism is that Wetherspoons is buying up local pubs and turning them into cookie cutter pubs, making them all look the same and have the same menu.

While British pub culture is definitely about beer, there is also much more involved. First, there are the great names of pubs, which can often tell you a bit of history about the city or neighborhood. There are some excellent examples in our adopted city of Lancaster.[1] There are pubs named for tradecrafts, such as the Boot & Shoe and The Bobbin. The only operational bobbin manufacturer left in the UK, from the early industrial revolution timeframe, is just north of Lancaster in the Lake District.[2] I heard a rumor that it may start making wooden bobbins again for sustainability markets. Then there are pubs named for pieces of history or myth. The Pendle Witch pub conjures the infamous, terrible witch trials held in Lancaster in 1612.[3] The George & Dragon pub honors the story of Saint George slaying a dragon in Libya.[4] Last but not least, The Friary pub is a converted eighteenth-century church, which seems sacrilegious, but it's a really lovely conversion.

Second, pub culture provides a variety of entertainment. There is the usual music scene, similar to American bars, where you can hear bands or soloists playing blues, jazz, folk, pop, and rock. But there are also unique finds such as an ukulele club or a Q&A lecture by an engineer working to design a robot magician! Other interesting activities we have heard about or stopped to see include book clubs and character readings. There was a quirky evening at Ye Olde John O'Gaunt pub when a group of people were playacting as Admiral Lord Nelson and friends from British history. Above all the other entertainment, we became regular fans of Quiz Night. You can find this trivia game happening at a British pub nearly any night of the week. We were delighted when one of the questions was about American culture because it usually meant we could score a few guaranteed points. People would often take notice of our American accents and beg us to share our answer. Occasionally, someone succeeded by promising to buy us a pint.

Interestingly, a British pint is larger in volume than an American pint. The difference is 95 milliliters (which is a little less than a half cup) The British Imperial Pint holds 20 imperial fluid ounces (568 ml) while the American Pint holds 16 fluid ounces (473 ml). This is one of the inconsistencies of both the US and the UK not using the metric system. The UK uses it more often, such as displaying the temperature in Celsius, but the US has flatly refused the metric system.

Third, pub culture provides a welcoming and relaxed setting for a nice lunch or dinner, especially on a damp, chilly winters day. Steak and ale pie became my new favorite comfort food. There are entertaining activities centered around pub food as well. Some pubs have special menus for different days. On curry night or fish night, you can get a meal and a pint of beer for a reduced price. For example, on a special menu night you might spend £6 ($9.60) total when normally you would pay £3 for the pint and £8 for the food. We also attended two delicious beer pairing dinners at a local pub. The chefs created a meal where each of three courses was paired with an appropriate beer. For example, a stout beer complements a chocolate strawberry tart by adding a roasted, malty, almost coffee note to the sweetness of the dessert. These pairing dinners were sponsored by a local brewery and featured three of their beers.

Last, but not least, there is of course the beer. But this is not just any beer, it is **British cask ale.**[5] In my humble opinion, this is the best type of beer. The cask ale is different from your average Budweiser or Coors because it is a living product. This means the fermenting yeast is not filtered out, so it continues to condition the ale even after delivery to the pub. This gives the beer a richer, fuller flavor. But it also has a short shelf life of just a few days, so drink up!

The enjoyable beer pairing dinners got me thinking about the **resurgence of British cask ale.**[6] Many of the breweries are small and craft small quantities, similar to the growth of American microbreweries.

Lancaster market square.
Photo credit 2013 Rebecca J Romsdahl.

Both have grown in parallel with the local food movement, which emphasizes enjoyment of foods grown and produced in the local community. This movement was the catalyst behind a resurgence of farmers markets that popped up all over the US in the mid-2000s. This push seems to have started a little earlier in the UK with the return of farmers markets starting in the late 1990s.

The revival of cask ales as local products is emphasized by the **Campaign for Real Ale (CAMRA)**.[7] This British organization has been lobbying the government since the 1970s to support pub culture. "CAMRA . . . is an independent, voluntary organisation campaigning for real ale, community pubs and consumer rights." The group has over 192,000 members across the world and has been described as the most successful consumer campaign in Europe. CAMRA supports well-run pubs as centers for community life in rural and urban areas, and it believes their continued existence plays a critical social role in British culture. CAMRA also supports pubs as the only place where you can drink a real ale (also known as cask-conditioned beer or cask ale). CAMRA highlights that there are over 5,500 different styles now produced across the UK. By supporting community pubs and small breweries that use local ingredients to produce a rich variety of unique beers, British cask ales are another way we can enjoy the local food movement.

Although I was raised in the meat and potatoes farm culture of the American Midwest, my taste buds have expanded through my travels and I can be enticed to try just about anything. When we found out about my Fulbright award, nearly everyone I talked to had a similar sentiment toward British food. Their opinions can be summarized as such: "Britain, wow! London is great and enjoy the pretty countryside, but too bad you will have to eat British food for six months. Nobody visits Britain for the food." Because of this, I did not have high hopes about British cuisine. The thought was depressing; over the years, I have greatly enjoyed trying new foods in different countries around the world.

As a college exchange student, I spent a semester in Japan, where I learned that food can be both delicious and beautiful plates of artwork. In Egypt, I savored the blend of Middle Eastern and Mediterranean spices. While visiting Finland, I discovered a new part of my Scandinavian heritage—reindeer is probably the most delicious meat I have ever tasted. Growing up in the center of the North American continent, I did not have a lot of exposure to seafood. But a visit to Costa Rica introduced me to the mouthwatering flavors of local, fresh-caught seafood including swordfish, squid, and shrimp.

My first Thanksgiving spent outside the US was in the UK, and food was on my mind that week. I found myself comparing British and American foods. There are classic British dishes, such as a savory Yorkshire pudding, which is a popover pastry often served with a beef stew or used as a bread bowl for the stew; Welsh pasties, which are a pocket pastry filled with seasoned, minced meat and onion; the adopted and adapted Indian spicy curries; and of course, Scottish haggis, which I quite enjoyed when it was used as a filling in a meat pie. We rarely found turkey, that quintessential Thanksgiving bird native to North America, in grocery stores or on menus except as a special item for Christmas dinners. An unexpected surprise was the variety and wonderful flavors of British cheeses. Many are historic, locally made cheeses named for the city or region where they were developed. One of my favorites was Yorkshire Wensleydale, with a cheddar-like taste and moist crumbly texture. Some Wensleydale varieties have cranberries mixed in. I feel like Pavlov's dog, my mouth watering, just thinking about a nice wedge and a handful of crackers to put it on.

During Thanksgiving week, I also spent a good amount of time thinking about local food and sustainability. We enjoyed delicious fruits, veggies, meats, pastries, and street vendor lunches from the Lancaster farmers market on Wednesdays and Saturdays. Although farmers markets in the UK began to reappear in the 1990s, the market square as a physical space for farmers to sell their foods has been a significant part of British life for centuries. It faded somewhat with the rise of supermarkets and large grocery chain stores. But the local food movement has emerged in response to a backlash against large-scale commercialization of food and catalyzed the recovery of busy market squares. The local food movement emphasizes production and use of foods and craft from local sources with three goals: reducing the miles that food travels from field to plate; supporting local small businesses; and helping to build resilient, sustainable food systems, meaning farming and production that more easily adapt to challenges and have fewer impacts on the environment, for example, less chemical pesticides, and more use of cover crops.

I believe the local food movement has had significant benefits for British cuisine. All across the UK, we found restaurants and pubs advertising that they use locally produced ingredients for their menus. Locally grown foods have given British chefs much more to brag about. If you don't believe in the added value of local foods, I encourage you to try the tomato test. Buy a regular tomato from the grocery store, get a locally grown tomato from a garden, and then compare how they taste. The locally grown tomato will have a rich flavor because it has ripened on the vine, while the grocery store tomato will taste a bit like damp cardboard because it was likely picked green to keep it fresh while traveling and therefore it ripened on a truck.

Demand for locally grown foods also supports local farmers. This has led to wonderful partnerships between restaurants and small farms across the UK, and in the US as well. I believe the global food market has also brought benefits because I do enjoy some fresh veggies in winter (in the UK, they often come from hot-houses in Spain and the Netherlands). But I am also trying to eat more seasonally, for example, by avoiding strawberries and other foods outside of their local harvest seasons. I sometimes wonder if we could feed everyone on the planet with locally grown foods. There may be too many people living in places where it is impossible to grow foods year-round or specific foods. The global food market can help with that, as well as when local crops are destroyed by storms, drought, etc. But we can be more resilient by using more locally grown foods to supplement the larger global food market, provide local employment, and promote regional pride. Many parts of the UK and the US are proving that these local food networks can be revived.

We found that British food is delicious, especially if you enjoy a hearty dish with meat, potatoes, and veggies. But it is also more than just sticky-toffee pudding, meat pies, and fish and chips with mushy peas. We found street vendors who create wonderful variations of Greek and Indian dishes for the British palette. We spent a weekend in Belfast and relished the Northern Irish influences of cabbage, fish soups, and Guinness beer in an Irish stew. We spent a few quiet days in Edinburgh, Scotland and enjoyed local whiskies with steamed mussels, deep-fried haggis balls, and neeps and tatties (mashed turnips and potatoes). The local food movement has invigorated British cuisine, and the food tastes even better knowing that the restaurant is part of a sustainable food partnership that benefits local farmers and businesses.

236

Endnotes

1 http://en.wikipedia.org/wiki/Lancaster,_Lancashire (https://perma.cc/Q7VV-62PF)

2 https://www.english-heritage.org.uk/visit/places/stott-park-bobbin-mill/history/ (https://perma.cc/HVE6-7YAR)

3 http://www.pendlewitches.co.uk/ (https://perma.cc/3Z84-FE7M)

4 http://en.wikipedia.org/wiki/Saint_George_and_the_Dragon (https://perma.cc/NGG4-PHBF)

5 https://camra.org.uk/learn-discover/the-basics/what-is-live-beer/ (https://web.archive.org/web/20210203054852/https://camra.org.uk/learn-discover/the-basics/what-is-live-beer/)

6 http://www.independent.co.uk/life-style/food-and-drink/features/cask-ale-ancient-and-modern-1928602.html (https://perma.cc/8YNL-64FR)

7 https://camra.org.uk/ (https://web.archive.org/web/20211029194226/https://camra.org.uk/)

Many Americans have stuffed closets.
Photo credit 2021 Rebecca J Romsdahl.

Rethinking My American Lifestyle

Red River of the North watershed, United States, December 2014

You think too much. This critique has been pointed out in relation to my major life decisions and probably some of my daily decisions as well. Generally, I don't find this problematic. I believe the average American would benefit from slowing down more often and thinking about the broader implications of their daily decisions. For example, how much water is used to make a pair of blue jeans? Roughly 1,800 gallons is needed to grow and process the cotton required for making one pair of jeans. That means I have over 12,000 gallons of virtual water sitting on the shelf in my closet—and that's just my jeans.

Thinking about the amount of natural resources used to make the things most Americans buy every year leaves me depressed with environmental guilt, especially because the average amount of time we use items before discarding them is only **six months**.[1] (The farmgirl in me is especially disturbed by this waste, since my grandparents and parents who lived through the Great Depression taught me to sew up holes in shirts, use cloth napkins, and wash and reuse Ziploc sandwich bags.) But this is not something most companies want us to think about. If we slow down to ask questions, we might rethink our lifestyle and the impacts it has on people and the natural environment. Our modern American lifestyle encourages us to buy more stuff, drive our cars everywhere, and enjoy the conveniences of all it has to offer. The bigger problem is that we are not alone. The global economy has spread this convenience-focused lifestyle worldwide. But some of us (including

---

An earlier version of this essay was first published in the *North Dakota Quarterly*, Vol. 80, No. 2 (2014).

myself and many others in Global North countries) have more power, more wealth, and more privilege than other people. As scholar Paul Wapner points out, we "are more responsible for wrecking the planet's organic infrastructure than others. We may do so unintentionally; as resource-rich participants in a capitalist economy and globalized consumerist culture driven by corporate interests, it is often hard to do otherwise" (p 108).

What if we asked questions about the effects of our convenience-focused lifestyle? As a thought experiment, consider all the different products one can choose from in popular warehouse-sized grocery stores. The sheer number of choices can be overwhelming. Each of those items requires water and other resources to produce them, trees and petroleum for the paper and plastic packaging, and gas to transport them, all of which is making Earth's health poorer. Do I really need fresh strawberries in January, which requires them to be shipped to North Dakota from Mexico or South America? Instead of increasing my ecological footprint, could I use frozen strawberries that were grown in California last summer? If we don't ask questions about what resources are used, it is easy to overlook how the conveniences of our lifestyle—like fresh fruit in winter, another pair of jeans, and disposable plastic containers—have consequences on the natural world.

As an environmentalist, one of the choices I have made is to be a conscientious, reflective consumer, meaning I try to slow down and think about the effects of my choices. Can I find environmentally friendly choices in my shopping? I look for products with characteristics like less plastic packaging, grown or produced locally, ecologically nontoxic ingredients, made from recycled materials, etc.

I recently found myself frustrated by the amount of time I spent at the grocery store just trying to select the dozen or so items on my shopping list. Which type of bread do I want? This seems like a simple question. But looking at the multiple shelves full of bread choices was mind numbing. Do I want white, whole-grain, wheat, rye, multi-grain, sourdough? A small or large loaf? A local brand? One made with organic ingredients? After reading many labels, I picked a wheat bread made by a regional company. During this particular grocery store trip, I began to consider just how much my convenience-focused American lifestyle was interrupted by thinking about sustainability while living overseas and experimenting with a slower, smaller lifestyle.

Living in the United Kingdom for half a year as a Fulbright Scholar was an incredible experience in my career, and it was also an opportunity to try a completely different lifestyle without the risk of full commitment. I call it a non-American lifestyle because it had so many qualities that are contrary to what most of us think of as the average American lifestyle, but primarily it was slower and smaller. Living smaller is tied to living slower. Some people also link these under the idea of living simpler. Occupying a smaller living space, reflecting on what I need, reducing the amount of stuff I buy and use, walking and using public transit—these were activities that allowed me to slow down and step back from some of the stress in our modern lifestyle.

The city of Lancaster is the place my partner and I called home during my Fulbright semester. It is a modest-sized city, with a population of roughly 50,000. We found a small, sparsely furnished flat (apartment), to rent. It seemed like the perfect size for my experiment in smaller, slower living. The flat felt like two dorm rooms pushed together, with the kitchen and the living room together in a single space. Almost everything we needed was within arm's reach, except for a kitchen table and chairs. Sitting on the floor and using the coffee table for meals felt very Japanese in style, which brought back fond memories of my college semester there. Living in this smaller space for half a year was insightful, both for learning about British culture and for thinking about sustainability.

Home laundry is a surprising activity where American and British cultures clash, and the differences are relevant for sustainability. In our flat, we had the convenience of a washing machine, but it was oddly located in the kitchen where an American would expect to find the dishwasher. Laundry became a near daily activity. The washing machine was small, only holding about two pairs of jeans and three shirts at maximum capacity. This saves on water use, but it takes extra time.

The wash cycle also required a bit of extra planning. Despite the machine being small, when it hit the spin cycle it sounded like a jet plane taking off. We tried to only run it whenever we were out of the flat.

Another surprise was that the machine was a **combo washer-dryer**.[2] We could never figure out how the dryer component worked. The buttons on the machine were labeled with Chinese characters and even Google was no help in finding instructions. Even if we had found the instructions, we learned from friends that these dryers never really dry the laundry. Thus, we became a bit more British in our daily lives. We used the second bedroom as the space for line drying our laundry. But this was a baffling cultural difference to us. While an estimated 85% of American homes have a tumble dryer, only a little more than 50% of British homes do. Britain has a damp, chilly northern climate, and it seems to rain nearly every day. To line dry our laundry, we quickly found that additional help was required in the form of a six-inch-tall fan and a small dehumidifier. We kept asking ourselves why British people would not want soft, tumble-dried socks and underpants.

I began asking this to some of my new friends on campus, and I also brought up the question with some of the local government officials in my research interviews. I was examining how local governments were planning for climate changes, and energy consumption was a big topic of discussion. Generally, their first reaction was a matter-of-fact reply: "It's just the way we do laundry here." But some people reflected a little deeper. Space is probably the most common challenge. British flats and most houses are quite a bit smaller than their average American counterparts. A tumble dryer is seen as an unnecessary luxury expense that would take up prime space. Our two-bedroom flat in Lancaster did not have any unused space. It was approximately 700 square feet, which felt a bit small on rainy winter days with both of us working at home and no desk or table to sit at. By contrast, the US Census Bureau shows the average American home size has increased by more than 1,000 square feet since the 1970s (from 1,660 in 1973 to 2,679 in 2013). At home, our house is around 2,000 square feet, and the laundry machines have their own room with space to line dry and iron our clothes.

Energy is another challenge. Americans demand cheap energy to maintain convenience-focused lifestyles (big homes, big appliances, big cars, etc.), and because it is inexpensive, I don't usually think about how much energy I use. But in the UK, electricity and gas utility fees can be expensive and seem to always be increasing. For our flat, we found our utility bills were about 30% more expensive than an American apartment of the same size. A tumble dryer uses a lot of electricity that many British people can't or don't want to pay for. From a sustainability and resilience perspective, line drying your laundry is better for the planet because most of the world's electricity is still produced using fossil fuels, which contribute to the climate crisis and are subject to extreme changes in pricing on the global market.

Line drying is also better for your clothes. Tumble dryers damage your laundry. All that gray fluff that collects in the lint trap is physical evidence of the fibers lost. Research shows that just 20 dryer cycles can strip away 50% of clothing durability. If our clothes don't last as long, we replace them more often, which contributes to the culture of overconsumption.

In my memory, the mall culture of the 1980s brought us this culture of overconsumption, where we buy new items every week and fill our houses with stuff we don't need and don't use. Shopping was marketed as a recreational pastime with friends and family. But these were usually stressful experiences—crowded parking lots, crowded stores, everybody in a rush and only looking out for themselves. This, plus a focus on low prices (which often translates into low quality and/or disposable products), lets us see some of the waste, overconsumption, and environmental problems in our modern American lifestyle. If we keep producing and buying new stuff and then throwing it in the trash, we will run out of the raw materials (trees, metals, water, sand, etc.) to make it all.

Too often we buy things because they are cheap and we believe the advertising that says it will impress others and make us happy. We buy things regardless of the numerous scientific studies showing that shopping is stressful and that buying things does not actually bring happiness. We buy things regardless of personal experiences where we see the stressed-out parent with the screaming child in a store. We buy things regardless of the frustration or guilt we might feel over the tons of cheap, broken products we throw in the trash each year. We buy things regardless of all of this, continuing to believe that it will make us happy.

We could walk to shops for the goods and services we wanted from our flat in Lancaster— groceries, restaurants, public transportation, cinema, and a twice-weekly farmers market were all accessible. As an environmental scholar, I was pleased by the opportunity this gave me to try a slower lifestyle. I walked to the bus station several days each week, which then took me to the university campus or any number of nearby cities. The train station was also an easy walk from our flat. I was happy to read a book while the train took me to new places. We would often get tickets to visit Edinburgh on a Saturday morning and return that evening. We could get connections to almost anywhere in England, Scotland, or Wales to conduct interviews for my research project or just to get away for a weekend. There was also a direct train to the Manchester Airport, which gave us access to world.

In contrast, Americans have a car culture, and many tend to get a bit obsessed with their vehicles, often treating them like an extension of their personal space. Americans put stickers on their cars that tell other drivers how many kids and pets are in the family, whether they support a particular political candidate, or to share their religious preferences. I spent my high school weekends with friends driving a loop around our small, rural town to pass the time. This probably sounds boring, and it was, but it was part of our car culture. We did not have a mall, the internet, or more than one film at the movie theater. Driving then lost its recreational appeal when we lived in the Washington DC area, where traffic is congested nearly all day long.

According to the 2010 US Census, 80% of Americans live in urban areas (populations of 50,000 and over). I am one of those people, however, this does not mean I live in a dense urban area or that I can access my work, shopping, or entertainment options by walking. I live in a residential community of single-family homes in a midsize, Midwestern city where the closest shopping option is a gas station convenience store approximately one mile from my house. There is a public bus system, but it is not as convenient as driving myself. There are bicycle paths, but the northern climate means the streets and paths are covered in snow and ice for half of the year. I primarily drive wherever I want to go. Although I live in a predominantly rural state, I do not live far away from stores where I can buy whatever I need. For example, my grocery store and the summer farmers market are both less than five miles from my house.

But while living in Lancaster, I greatly enjoyed the freedom of not having a car. That may sound counterintuitive to the many Americans who live in wide-open rural places and sprawling suburbs because a car gives you the freedom to go where you want, when you want. But owning a car is a complex responsibility that often feels burdensome to me. You must keep up with payments, insurance, parking permits, license tags, and maintenance, and you are always spending money on fuel, oil changes, tires, etc. There is also environmental guilt from contributing to greenhouse gas emissions because fossil fuels are needed to run a car. I found a great weight lifted from my shoulders when I did not have a car. I needed to learn to be patient sometimes when waiting for a bus or sitting on a stopped train, but these seemed like small inconveniences when compared to all the responsibilities involved in owning a car.

In Lancaster, I quickly adjusted to the flexibility of walking instead of driving. I could pop out to pick up a few groceries without the expense and hassle involved in driving and finding parking. I learned to limit my shopping excursions to what I could carry home in a backpack or a couple of cloth bags. Above the practical adjustments, however, I learned to enjoy the slower lifestyle of living by walking. Walking allowed me time to admire the medieval stone architecture that dominates the Lancaster city center and to develop a sense of community with the people around me. A couple of local vendors at the farmers market began to recognize me when I stopped at their carts each week. One was the pie guy. His family baked meat pies, which were slightly smaller than a potpie and filled with minced meat and a dab of locally made cheese. He brought the delicious pies into Lancaster each Wednesday to sell at the farmers market. We often chatted about the weather and compared life between the UK and US while I chose a few pies to take home.

I also enjoyed the opportunity to observe the residents of Lancaster going about their daily lives with me. On rainy days there were so many baby buggies being pushed around by tired-looking parents. They caught my attention because the buggies were all equipped with clear, plastic rain covers. I also noticed that Wellies (Wellington rainboots) were a fashion statement. Young people wore them in bright colors of red, yellow, and purple, or in bold patterns, like leopard spots. Older folks wore dark, practical looking Wellies in traditional hunter green or plain brown. I would not have noticed these fun cultural differences had I been driving. Walking gave me very different perspectives from my car-centric American lifestyle.

Another adjustment in my slower, smaller lifestyle was adapting to a smaller collection of clothes and household items. There were a surprising number of charity shops around Lancaster where people donated and bought secondhand clothes, and the charity shops always had several pairs of Wellies in their window displays. While walking around the city center, I often stopped in these shops to look for useful items.

In our sparsely furnished two-bedroom flat, we had one large wardrobe to share. This was plenty of storage because we had a limited amount of clothes: two medium-sized suitcases of summer/autumn items and one box of winter clothes that was shipped to us. It did not feel challenging while we traveled during the summer months because we stayed in hotels, and the fewer suitcases we had to haul up and down steep, old staircases, the happier we were. When we settled into our flat, however, I felt fashion-limited for a few weeks. And as the cooler autumn weather arrived, our box of winter clothes was held up in customs for several weeks. We edged closer and closer to buying some sweaters and jackets. Once I had access to my winter clothes, however,

I adjusted quickly to my options. I had the following items to get me through the cold months (I sent home most of my summer clothes around Christmas):

- 1 pair rainboots, 6 pairs shoes
- 1 wool coat, 3 jackets, 2 blazers
- 27 shirts (5 long sleeve button-up shirts, 7 long sleeve t-shirts, 10 short sleeve shirts, 5 tank tops)
- 2 sweatshirts, 5 sweaters,
- 6 pairs pants/jeans/dress slacks, 2 pairs sweatpants
- 2 skirts, 1 dress
- Various undergarments, socks, gloves, scarves, hats, etc.

I provide my basic list in order to compare it with what an average female college student listed as clothes in her dorm room (in James Farrel's book *The Nature of College*, p. 39):

- 1 pair slippers, 2 pairs boots, 21 pairs shoes
- 6 jackets, 2 blazers, 1 dress suit, 1 vest
- 76 shirts (short sleeve, long sleeve, tank tops, etc.)
- 7 sweatshirts, 19 sweaters
- 11 pairs pants, 6 pairs sweatpants/pajama pants
- 6 skirts
- Various undergarments, socks, gloves, scarves, hats, etc.

I tried to pack clothes that I could mix and match easily, some favorite pieces, and essentials. When I felt something was missing, I would visit one of the charity shops around Lancaster to see what I could find secondhand instead of buying new clothes. While shopping for secondhand clothes may not be common for the average college student, especially those who have grown up in this age of overconsumption, I found the comparison of the two lists above to be interesting. My small flat and an average dorm room share similar closet/wardrobe space, but my wardrobe was never full while I lived in the UK. In contrast, I remember my college dorm closet and drawers were usually stuffed.

The above lists are misleading, though. They only count the clothes that a student and I took with us for temporary living. The lists do not reflect our cluttered closets at home. Most Americans only wear 20-30% of the clothes they own, and with the **rise of online shopping**, they now buy a new piece of clothing every week.[3] Because most of these clothes are inexpensive and mass-marketed through social media, they have created a culture of disposable fast fashion.

Fast fashion is a strategy that emerged in the late 1990s, wherein high-fashion designs are replicated using mass production, cheaper materials, and low-wage workers.[4] When people get tired of their current clothes, they simply replace them, cheaply and easily. What is shocking is that we are sending most of these clothes to the landfill. Americans on average dispose of 70 pounds of clothing and other textiles (roughly equal to 200 men's t-shirts) per person each year! Fast fashion is another factor contributing to the problems of overconsumption, waste, and **environmental damage**.[5]

The mass production of these clothes uses tons of toxic chemicals to produce vibrant colors and printed patterns, tons of petroleum for synthetic fabric and shipping, and tons of water to grow cotton and produce fabric. Polyester, which is a synthetic fabric made from petroleum, is the most common fabric used in fast fashion, and it increases greenhouse gas emissions and plastics pollution. Every time polyester fabric is washed, it releases tiny microplastics that are so small they easily flow through water treatment facilities and into the natural environment. Microplastics pollution has been found in nearly all lakes, rivers, and oceans that have been tested. It has also been found deposited by rain on mountains and in protected wilderness parks. Alarmingly, microplastics have been found in tap water and even in bottled water. Science is just beginning to examine what potential harm this **microplastics pollution** may cause for human and environmental health.[6]

When I arrived back in the US and unpacked, I was shocked by the overwhelming amount of clothes in just one of my two closets at home. This was a stark realization of how much my attitude had changed. I had become so well-adjusted to having a smaller selection that I forgot the clothes I had at home. Staring into my closets, I made a conscious decision that we would benefit from a deep clean of our storage spaces—closets, laundry room, garage, cupboards, drawers, all of them. By deep clean, I mean sorting out what we actively used and wanted to keep from all that stuff we no longer used, so that we could donate, recycle, or trash items that were broken or no longer useful. In tackling just the first two closets, we filled our large garbage bin and took a full carload of items to donate at the Goodwill Store.

Sadly, much of what is donated to charity shops like Goodwill is no longer wanted or fits in the category of "wish-cycling," when something broken or unrecyclable is donated or put in the recycling bin with the hope that it will be reused or recycled.[7] As author and son of a junkyard owner Adam Minter summarizes: "Most American homes contain very little of value beyond the sentiments of the person who purchased them" (p 4). Many secondhand shops refuse to accept certain donated items, like electronics, because they are so abundant and inexpensive that charity shops cannot sell used versions. These plentiful, cheap options also mean that for too many products—TVs, computer printers, and even clothes washers—it is less expensive to buy a new version than to repair one that is broken. Plus, who has time to sew up the holes in socks? We just buy new socks. Such overproduction and overconsumption are particularly overwhelming when it comes to clothing donations.

Clothing donations from the US and the UK have supported **thriving markets** for secondhand clothes in several African nations since the 1960s.[8] In fact, these two countries lead the world in exporting secondhand clothes. As much as 70% of clothing donated to charity shops in the UK is sent overseas. But the popularity and large scale of fast fashion has overwhelmed the donation system, and the poor quality of the clothes means they are not useful as resale items.

Every day, more than 50 tons of donated clothes are discarded in many African countries. The result has led to disturbing mountains of clothing that overload landfills and pile up outside cities and on beaches.[9] As the clothes decay, these dumps create a toxic chemical soup contributing to microplastics pollution in the ocean and alarming new pollution problems near communities. In Ghana, the methane produced by one such decaying pile spontaneously exploded into flames! Fueled by toxic gasses, the clothes smoldered for over six months, contributing to local air pollution. In an effort to slow the deluge of fast fashion castoffs, some African nations have imposed high import duties and strict inspections on secondhand clothing, which has helped reduce the worst loads from unethical companies.

The positive feelings my partner and I experienced after getting rid of excess clutter in our home initially gave us a great sense of accomplishment and made our living space feel a bit bigger and cleaner. But no transition is perfect; we are immersed in the culture of overconsumption, so there are limits on how much change individuals can accomplish. When we recognize these limits, doubts can creep in. Sometimes when I donate a bag of clothes now, I wonder if I am only contributing to a larger problem of exporting our waste overseas. But it is important to remember that change is a process, and changing one's habits is often a slow process.[10]

While we can't change all the unsustainable aspects of our economy through individual behavior alone, we can start by reflecting on our own decisions. I am working to slow down and ask more questions to simplify my lifestyle. I still enjoy having a variety of clothes and buying new pieces occasionally. But I am also slowly weaning myself away from the overconsumption and conveniences marketed by our modern global economy. There is a lovely consignment shop in my city where I can buy fashionable secondhand clothes that are in good condition. I made a conscious decision to slow my fashion consumption by shopping there first when looking for "new" clothes. Supporting these types of shops promotes small, local businesses, and it is also a more environmentally friendly shopping option. When buying something new, I try to find companies that have sustainability plans in their mission and promote high-quality products over increasing their sales.

Another change we have implemented is to cook more meals at home instead of eating at restaurants or getting food delivered. To improve the benefits of eating at home, I try to be consistent in meal planning by creating a list of ingredients to purchase before going grocery shopping. This helps reduce food waste because I'm less likely to buy things on impulse and then forget to eat them. Combining errands so that I go to several stores near each other in the same trip helps reduce the complexity of the dreaded driving-shopping process. Plus, it saves fuel, which reduces our greenhouse gas emissions.

Overall, I have found some success in making changes, but there are also challenges to negotiate between a slower, smaller lifestyle and the modern American lifestyle. Reflecting on my decisions sometimes leaves me feeling overwhelmed by questions. How can I curb the pressures of the modern American lifestyle of overconsumption, with its convenient online shopping, disposable plastics, and tasty fast food? What new strategies can I try to relieve environmental guilt? Trying to live slower and smaller can sometimes feel isolating because you are disengaging from the "normal" way that most people around you are living. But my partner and I are not alone in these efforts. One New York woman is raising awareness about overconsumption by taking daily "trash walks" and documenting her findings on social media.[11] She has highlighted that some companies purposefully damage products they could not sell rather than donating useful items, like protein bars, toothpaste, or hairbrushes, to people who cannot afford to buy things. Other people are sharing advice and ideas online about living more sustainably, such as strategies for reducing waste in your lifestyle so that nothing goes to the landfill.[12]

While individuals can't change the problems of plastics pollution, overconsumption, and convenience-focused lifestyles alone, we can be part of the solution.[13] As more of us change our habits, we can use our collective voice to push our elected officials to help make changes happen in the larger economic, social, and environmental systems. I encourage my students, friends, family, and everyone to be citizens first and consumers second. Give your elected representatives a call or send them an email to let them know you are concerned about pollution, climate change, or other issues! You can even offer suggestions for how we can become a more sustainable and resilient society.

The lessons I have learned is that the transition is worthwhile, and there are options available to help one adapt and thrive in a slower, smaller lifestyle. You can visit the farmers market, support local businesses, share items with neighbors, join an online group, and find environmentally friendly shopping options. I would also argue that we should bring back some of the practices of past generations. For example, for clothes: try repairing items, using them longer, and buying natural fabrics such as cotton, wool, or Tencel (made from wood fibers).

Sometimes it may be true that I think too much. But despite this and despite the challenges, I have enjoyed making changes in my home and my habits that are more environmentally conscious. Living slower and smaller could benefit all of us—I encourage everyone to give it a try!

Endnotes

1 https://www.storyofstuff.org/wp-content/uploads/2020/01/Storyof-Stuff_AnnotatedScript.pdf (https://perma.cc/E8K2-K5CV)

2 https://qz.com/1034914/it-doesnt-matter-where-brits-keep-their-dryers-the-point-is-they-dont-work/ (https://perma.cc/49UD-UX-WL)

3 https://www.theatlantic.com/magazine/archive/2021/03/ultra-fast-fashion-is-eating-the-world/617794/ (https://perma.cc/YYA8-UYYB)

4 https://en.wikipedia.org/wiki/Fast_fashion (https://perma.cc/NKH7-LGQD)

5 https://www.theguardian.com/fashion/2020/apr/07/fast-fashion-speeding-toward-environmental-disaster-report-warns (https://perma.cc/73H3-2ND5)

6 https://www.scientificamerican.com/article/microplastics-pollution-is-everywhere-is-it-harmful/ (https://perma.cc/52SK-7GG2)

7 https://www.npr.org/2021/05/06/993821945/goodwill-doesnt-want-your-broken-toaster (https://perma.cc/34AV-KNPQ)

8 https://www.npr.org/sections/money/2013/12/10/247362140/the-afterlife-of-american-clothes (https://perma.cc/A9Z9-VDR9)

9 https://www.dailymail.co.uk/news/article-8044313/Shocking-report-reveals-cheap-clothes-resold-end-rotting-Africa.html (https://perma.cc/6B3M-XTND)

10 https://theconversation.com/read-this-before-you-go-sales-shopping-the-environmental-costs-of-fast-fashion-88373 (https://perma.cc/QC3Q-CC3W)

11 https://www.theguardian.com/us-news/2021/aug/07/new-york-city-garbage-trash-walks-anna-sacks?CMP=Share_iOSApp_Other (https://perma.cc/68WF-KNH9)

12 https://www.goingzerowaste.com/zero-waste-1/ (https://perma.cc/5DYZ-LKSW)

13 https://www.npr.org/2021/07/12/1015296355/zero-waste-single-use-plastic-trash-recycle (https://perma.cc/X2NQ-ZNRX)

The author exploring ancient ruins along the Inca Trail.
Photo credit 2016 Mick Beltz.

Reflecting on the Sacred and the Profane

Urubamba River watershed, Peru, January 2016

Breathtaking.

That one word encapsulates so much of my four-day experience hiking the Inca Trail to reach Peru's famed lost city of Machu Picchu.

Breathtaking. The sacred natural beauty was overwhelming. As morning mist rose slowly off the emerald forest toward the peaks of sheer, craggy mountains, I momentarily forgot to breathe.

Breathtaking. The profane mundaneness of climbing another set of knee-bruising Incan stone steps at 10,000 feet above sea level. I stopped again, gasping for breath.

Breathtaking. The mundane exercise of using a public toilet became profane, as I often found feces spattered across most visible surfaces, and I struggled to *not* breathe.

The sacred and the profane. French Sociologist Émile Durkheim introduced this paired concept in his studies of society and religion in the early 1900s.[1] He felt this dichotomy was central to all religions. In his work, the sacred represented the interests of group unity, while the profane was applied to individual concerns. Critics feel that his work was too focused on European Christianity. But this criticism may provide insight about how different spiritual cultures relate to the natural world. Christian ideas of the human-nature relationship are often looked down on because there is a focus on the idea that God gave humans dominance and control over the Earth and other living creatures. But some Christian interpretations seek to soften that idea by emphasizing the role of humans as stewards who are commanded to care for the Earth and its creatures. Both of these fit well with Durkheim's view that religion needs representations that unify the group toward what is sacred and what is above the individual's (daily) concerns.

In contrast, many Indigenous cultures around the world believe that humans and other living creatures are equals or members of a large family. This is called kincentric awareness. As Native American attorney and author Sherri Mitchell describes, "Every plant, tree, and animal carries its own unique wisdom and can teach us how to live harmoniously with one another and in relationship with Mother Earth. . . . In healthy systems, we treat our kin with a greater degree of care, often expressing more gentleness and protectiveness toward them" (p 24). Many Indigenous cultures see representations of the sacred all around them in the natural world. Some refer to Mother Earth, Father Sky, Brother Bear, or Sister Moon. Many creation stories tell how sacred animals formed the Earth.[2]

The Indigenous peoples of the Andes Mountains have a sacred goddess they call Pachamama.[3] She is generous with her gifts and watches over the Earth, life, harvest, farming, crops, and fertility. Incan culture also saw her embodied in the mountains and believed that she could cause earthquakes. In modern times, environmental values and activism across several South American countries are associated with Pachamama, emphasizing the idea that environmental problems arise because humans are taking too much from Mother Earth. The Pachamama Alliance is an organization working with Indigenous people in the Amazon rainforest to protect land and cultural heritage.[4] Ecuador enshrined legal rights for nature in a 2008 constitutional amendment and Bolivia passed the Law of the Rights of Mother Earth: "Mother Earth is a dynamic living system comprising an indivisible community of all living systems and living organisms, interrelated, interdependent and complementary, which share a common destiny. Mother Earth is considered sacred, from the worldviews of nations and peasant indigenous peoples."[5]

Mircea Eliade, a Romanian historian of religion, also explored the contrast between sacred and profane in the 1950s, but his work focuses more on spaces/places. He sought to understand more universal representations of the sacred. Eliade argued that "[humans become] aware of the sacred because it manifests itself, shows itself, as something wholly different from the profane. . . . nature is never only 'natural;' it is always fraught with religious value. . . . The sky directly, 'naturally,' reveals the infinite distance, the transcendence of the deity. The earth too is transparent; it presents itself as universal mother and nurse. . . . The cosmos as a whole is an organism at once real, living, and sacred" (p 11, 116-117). He felt that the "completely profane world, the wholly desacralized cosmos, is a recent discovery in the history of the human spirit" (p 13).

Perhaps many modern humans consider themselves as living in the "desacralized cosmos," that science explains the world and spiritual/religious observations are not important in their lives. Despite how widespread this feeling might be today, I believe that many people, regardless of their spiritual faith or lack thereof, still experience a sense of the sacred when they interact with the natural world. (Though the natural world is likely not as large a part of their daily lives as it was for their ancestors.) If we interpret the sacred to represent those things or places that transcend the humdrum of daily life, this fits well with Eliade's understanding that nature, especially protected places, still reveals the sacred.

We can then interpret the profane as representing everything else, all that is dull and routine: our job, commuting, household tasks, sleeping, paying bills, getting groceries, and on and on. Although I was not thinking about religion while hiking the Inca Trail, I spent a good deal of time contemplating this seemingly simple but very important contrast between the sacred and the profane. I thought about the mundaneness of daily necessities versus those moments when my experience was elevated to the sacred and I forgot to breathe.

The Inca Trail is an ancient highway and communication network covering over 18,000 miles through the incredible landscape of the Andes Mountains and down to the Pacific coast. Most of the trail is paved with granite stones and looks like it is a natural extension grown out of the mountains themselves. The staircases up and down the sheer mountain slopes, and the ruins of cities and palaces that they lead to, are feats of head-shaking wonder. Several times, the lack of oxygen and steepness of the steps meant we had to climb them using both hands and feet! In researching his book, *Turn Right at Machu Picchu*, Mark Adams found that the perfectly carved stonework of Incan architecture is not only beautiful artistically, it was also superbly engineered to be resilient to earthquakes that often shake the Andes region. "The interlocking stones in an Inca wall are said to "dance" during seismic turbulence before falling back into place. When a huge earthquake struck [the Peruvian city of] Cusco in 1950, many Spanish buildings collapsed, revealing the intact Inca walls underneath" (p 36). Saying these ruins are masterpieces of engineering and art sounds so obvious, but when I think about the fact that the Incan ruins—built over centuries until the 1400s—are the same age as many of the Cathedrals we admired in Europe, I am inspired to give sacred praises.

In 2014, the Qhapaq Ñan (the Inca Trail system or Andean Road System) was granted World Heritage status, which essentially elevates it to the sacred.[6] The site of Machu Picchu was designated in 1983.[7] World Heritage status is an incredible honor for any natural and/or cultural area. The sites are evaluated based on ten criteria and must be considered places of "outstanding universal value."[8] This designation, however, is both blessing and curse. Although it opens up opportunities for the home nation to apply for valuable funding to assist with restoration and protection efforts, it also broadcasts to the world that this is a site you should come and see.

As more tourists make the pilgrimage to a "new" sacred place, the profane burdens of people management quickly accumulate. To address some of these problems, the Peruvian government limits the number of people who can be on the Inca Trail each day to 200 hikers plus 300 support crew. The government recently, and reluctantly, limited the number of visitors who can tour Machu Picchu each day to 2000, including those arriving via the Inca Trail. However, our guide talked about how this limit is not strictly enforced. After all, no government wants to refuse easy money or anger tourists by denying them a visit.

We began our 30-mile trek to Machu Picchu on New Year's Day in 2016 with a local support crew consisting of a trail guide, a cook, and seven porters. There were four of us in my group. We were one of the smaller parties among the 500 people setting out on the Inca Trail that day. There were Germans, British, other Americans, and a rather large group of New Zealanders and Aussies. This last group was often amusing. We could hear the young people among them coming up behind us on the trail from a mile away. They were prone to loud singing or playing party games like "Six Degrees of Kevin Bacon." What made me really laugh, as we stood on the side of the trail to let the group pass by when they had a faster pace, were the embarrassed looks and apologies of the New Zealanders, who generally brought up the tail end of the group. Although they were a bit bawdy, the Aussies' happy spirits lifted the mundaneness of hiking for those around them.

Each day revealed small and large moments for sacred appreciation. The southern summer sun felt delicious on my skin, especially considering there was a foot of snow at home and temperatures were probably sinking to -10 degrees Fahrenheit. After our first serious climb in elevation on day one, we entered the cloud forest canopy and stopped for a rest at the edge of a small community.

Each day also held the profane, mundane necessities of life. Many local communities along the early section of the Inca Trail, from Cusco to Machu Picchu, operate small shops, essentially tables lined with goods, where tourists can buy snacks, bottled water, and energy drinks. Tourists also have a choice between paying a Peruvian sol (approximately 30 cents in USD) to use the privately managed toilets or using the government's free toilets. We had used the last of our coins earlier that day, so off I went to the free toilet facilities. Upon entering the first stall, I found a poo-pie staring up at me, like a perfectly coiled snake. All it needed was the goofy big eyes and smiley face to match the emoji on my smartphone.

Reflecting back on this moment, I can't help but think of the children's book *Everyone Poops* by the Japanese author Minna Unchi.[9] This classic picture book explains the fact that all animals poop, including people. It makes comparisons, like elephants make big poops and mice make small poops. It helps children understand the universal truth of this mundane daily activity, why it happens (we all eat food) and the need to keep things clean (showing a child using a toilet and toilet tissue). The illustrations of animal butts and pooping will make a person giggle at any age. This book has undoubtedly helped many parents with the challenging task of toilet training their young children.

Being a farmgirl and an avid backpacker, I have dealt with a variety of poo in a variety of situations, without much concern. I know how to poop in the woods properly by digging a 6-inch deep cathole and burying it afterward. I have used pit toilets in campgrounds, porta potties at roadside rest areas, and confusing high-tech toilets that play music in Japan. I have shoveled shit. And I have accidentally stepped, barefoot, in a cowpie and cat poo. But here, in this particular facility on the Inca Trail, as I tramped from one stall to the next, searching in vain for an acceptable toilet while holding my breath, I quickly realized the limits of my poop experience were going to be profoundly tested! This was the beginning of a profane nightmare that I would have to repeatedly conquer over the next four days.

Let me highlight some factors that lead to this mundane people-poo-management nightmare. There are 500 people each day traveling the Inca Trail from various cultures around the world. Many people suffer travel sickness when eating new foods and altitude sickness at elevations above 7000 feet. Many North Americans and Europeans are not skilled at using **squat toilets** and this is especially problematic during times of digestive distress.[10] A squat toilet is essentially a hole in the floor with a long, shallow bowl in front of it. You squat down over the hole to relieve yourself. This requires a bit of practice and some degree of muscle strength in your legs to support your squat position. Unfortunately, the lack of familiarity with this type of toilet means that many visitors make a mess on themselves and in the facility. Although these public squat toilets had plumbing, it did not often work properly, resulting in either a pile of poop left sitting on the bowl or, if the waterflow flush was too strong, everything getting blasted all around the tiled interior of the stall, leaving streaks on the walls and small puddles of feces mixed with mud on the floor.

Backpacking and remote camping can give financially comfortable people a tiny glimpse into the profane sanitation problems that 4.2 billion people around the world still face in the mundaneness of daily life.[11] In the Caribbean nation of Haiti, some of the poorest men have a sanitation job that is so thankless and unspeakable, it is only done in the middle of the night. They empty the toilet pits of family homes, scooping everything out by hand. In many cases this involves climbing down and standing knee-deep in excrement. Other countries struggle to change unsanitary traditions or habits. In India, many rural residents still practice open air defecation. They feel it is appropriate and natural to have bowel movements in a nearby field, ditch, or behind bushes. This creates dangerous conditions for spreading disease, as flies are drawn to the waste and then to people's homes, and windy days can carry dried feces back into communities as dust. For people who live in many of the unplanned neighborhoods that poverty has built in and around the outskirts of megacities like Rio de Janeiro in Brazil, Lagos in Nigeria, or Dhaka in Bangladesh, there are no city services of the kind many people take for granted. There is no garbage pickup, no plumbing, no sewer system, meaning no water, no toilets, no sanitation.

Flying toilets are a particularly filthy problem in impoverished areas of Nairobi, Kenya. A flying toilet happens when a person poops into a plastic bag, ties it closed, and flings it as far away as possible. These are not practical jokes as the term or practice might suggest, flying toilets are a symptom of multilayered problems. Many people are uncomfortable talking about toilet behaviors and sanitation needs, and in some cultures this may even be a taboo subject. Lack of discussion means the problem is less likely to be acknowledged and fixed, which leads to compounding problems. Flying toilets pile up on flimsy rooftops and in ditches. Exposed to sun and weather, this can lead to worse pollution and disease problems as the plastic bags break down and leak feces when it rains. The immediate problem also can be very personal when unsuspecting persons, going about their mundane daily activities in these overcrowded shantytowns, suddenly get hit by a bag that may explode on contact, covering them with poop, and they have no running water to clean themselves. It is very difficult to imagine living in these conditions, but even in the United States, people in cities like Detroit experience poverty that leaves them unable to pay their utility bills and stuck in a house with no running water.

One evening, I emerged from another Inca Trail campground toilet facility after a particularly profane experience, and my partner commented that the look on my face was a mixture of disgust and horror. I was concentrating on shallow breathing (and *not* through my nose). As he dispensed a large dollop of hand sanitizer gel in each of my quavering palms, I found my voice: "Do you have any Purell for my eyes and my soul?" (Even as I write this, I relive the nightmare—my heartrate increases, my throat tightens, and I feel a knot forming in my stomach. Deep breath. Remember the sacred.)

Day two of hiking was the most physically profane because we essentially scaled a "fourteener" (14,000 foot mountain in Colorado). With each breathtaking step, we slowly climbed in elevation, and the landscape around us ascended to divine comparisons of mountains as cathedrals. We could not help but stop often. As the air became thinner, inhaling became a holy experience. Each gulp of breath felt both sacred and profane. After several hours of climbing that morning, we had hiked over 3,900 feet up from our campground to reach Dead Woman's Pass, which is nearly 14,000 feet above sea level. Several of the mountain peaks towering around us were near 20,000 feet high.

There is something spiritual about hiking in the mountains. Maybe it is simply the lack of oxygen combined with the happy brain endorphins from a physical workout. Whatever it is makes me smile and

Breathtaking view of Phuyupatamarca ("the place above the clouds")
within the Andes Mountains.
Photo credit 2016 Mick Beltz.

breath deeper just remembering those experiences. There is a deep, satisfying feeling of accomplishment in standing atop a mountain and looking back on how far you have come. Then taking in the vista of sky and rocky crags surrounding me, it is breathtaking. I feel my soul lift in sacred joy.

One Incan site that I found particularly captivating was a semi-circular lodge called Runkuraqay, which is composed of two divided rooms forming a half-moon shape. Our guide described how it was a rest stop for travelers and messengers. The ancient Incans would send verbal messages along the trail we were hiking, between Cusco and Machu Picchu and beyond. The messengers would run the trail, covering a roundtrip 60 mile distance with a fully memorized message and reply in a single day. The lodge was one of their stopping points to transfer a message to the next runner. Our support crew were descendants of those mountain runners, and we were amazed each day by their fleet-footed abilities. They seemed to fly down the stone steps, carrying all of our gear including tents, a camp kitchen, food, most of our clothing and other personal items, and even a portable toilet. We would leave camp about an hour before the crew each day and they easily caught up with us in a few hours, jogging by us carrying 50 pound packs while we huddled to the side of the trail so as not to slow them down.

As we descended to lower elevations, crossing from the mountain cloud forest into the tropical jungle, we marveled that we were exploring the far western edge of the Amazon River watershed. This change in ecosystem brought opportunities to find the sacred in small things. All along the trail my eyes were searching for orchids and other wildflower cousins. We found their bright colors occasionally punctuating scraggly grasses or bursting out of cracks in the walls of the ancient ruins. I frequently scolded myself to pay better attention to the path and the mundane movement of my feet because one distracted step could ruin the magic of the adventure with an ankle sprain or a tumble down a rocky slope and a helicopter ride back to civilization. But I could not stop seeking those delicate little prizes.

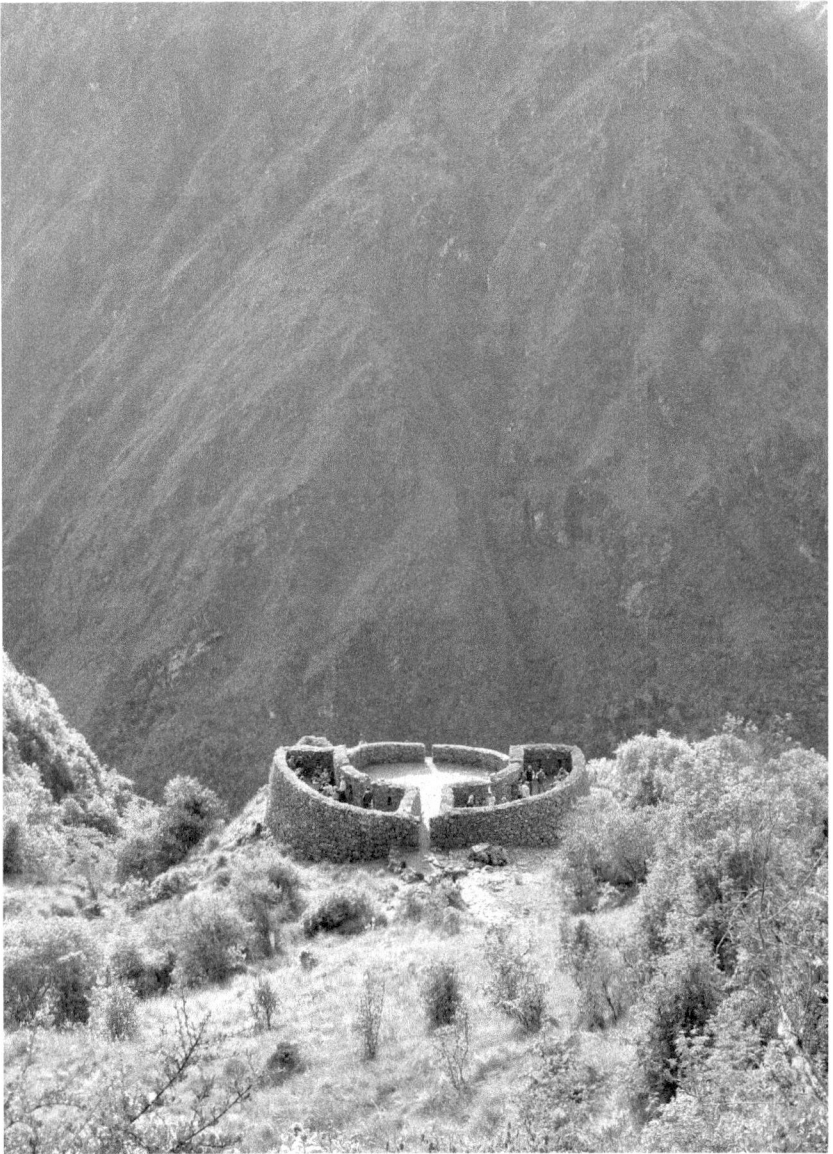

Ruins of Runkuraqay, a rest stop for ancient trail runners.
Photo credit 2016 Mick Beltz.

Sadly, there were frequent sightings of "tissue flowers" along the trail as well. Small, white wads of toilet paper blossoms, often in clusters, and the occasional solitaire. These telltale litter blooms are reminders of the profound challenges involved in managing great numbers of people concentrated in a place. Nobody wants to see tissue flowers, much less step in what was left behind with them. Human waste is not only disgusting to encounter, but it is also hazardous. It can draw animals toward trails, increasing the risk of injury to humans and wildlife. Waste can also contain parasites and disease-causing microbes that can live outside our bodies for weeks or months, increasing the risk of disease transmission to future visitors. People can take individual responsibility and carry a small hand trowel to dig a cathole and bury their own poop if needed. But realistically, not many people enjoying popular trails and parks are that conscientious. Regardless of whether it is a crowded city park or a protected wilderness, more people requires more planning.

Toilet facilities are one of the most mundane necessities wherever people gather, but they are so essential that people get understandably upset if the lines are too long or the porta potties run out of toilet paper. Parks and trails around the world have developed both mundane pit toilets and **creative composting toilets** to manage this essential, unmentionable need.[12] For example, one of the most innovative, beautiful views of mountains and wildflowers I have ever encountered was from the seat of an open-air pit toilet. Located somewhere in the Cascade Mountains of Washington state, it may be the best throne experience imaginable. No walls, no roof, no profane odors, and pristine nature set before you in sacred glory. The trail comes up through a small cluster of trees behind the pit toilet, which provides a quiet screen of privacy and allows anyone approaching to see when the seat is occupied, but the user will not be disturbed by seeing them. It made the necessity so enjoyable that it was difficult to admit when I was finished and should return to the campsite in the woods.

After four breathtaking days traversing the Andes Mountains, we were rewarded for our efforts as we arrived at the Sun Gate ruins with the early morning sun just peeking over the mountains. The Sun Gate was one of the Incans' defensive observation towers to guard the city, and it was very well positioned. To the east, we had an awe-inspiring view of sunrise, towering peaks, and the valley we had just climbed out of, while to the west was a commanding overlook of the city of Machu Picchu, hidden in clouds. Machu Picchu sits on a steep mountain ridge over 7,900 feet above sea level.

Machu Picchu was a sacred center and fortress for the Incan Empire. Mark Adams retraces the steps of historian and explorer Hiram Bingham III, who stumbled into the lost city in 1911 with the help of local people who had been visiting it and farming on its terraces for generations. Bingham had visited Cusco a few years earlier and learned of a "four-hundred-year-old unsolved mystery. When the Spanish conquistadors had invaded in the sixteenth century, a group of Incas withdrew to a hidden city high in Peru's impenetrable cloud forest, carrying with them the sacred treasures of their empire" (p 3). The city and its people were long forgotten, so well hidden by the tropical forest and lost from collective knowledge, that most historians had written off the mystery as a myth. Bingham thought the experts were wrong. After years of scouring obscure texts and maps for clues, and tramping around the mountains with local guides, he eventually found the spectacular ruins of Machu Picchu (but it was not the fabled lost city he was seeking).

As we nibbled on a bit of breakfast at the Sun Gate, we watched the ruins of Machu Picchu slowly emerge from the mist, like a myth being revealed in a story. The leafy green mountains and vibrant blue sky played hide and seek behind the clouds for some time, but eventually we saw the first tour groups snaking their way along the paths and grass-covered avenues like small, colorful strings of beads. We rallied our tired muscles and joined the postcard scene.

View of Machu Picchu from the Sun Gate with Huayna Picchu in the background.
Photo credit 2016 Mick Beltz.

Touring Machu Picchu was both sacred and profane. The site was picture perfect and underwhelming at the same time. Part of the mundane was our guide's lackluster tour, but partly the ancient city also felt surreal. We had explored smaller versions of it and other ruins along the trail, and now it seemed less special by comparison. But that may have been due to what I call the "tourist effect," my feeling that a place seems disappointing when there are lots of people milling around it with you.

Instead of giving in to disappointment, we decided to hike a few more miles up and down more stone steps, by climbing the neighboring peak, Huayna Picchu. Adams describes it well: "From afar, and in photographs, it's difficult to see that Huayna Picchu is covered in stonework, temples and terraces that cling to the slope like baby monkeys. . . . Sets of granite steps wound like a DNA helix several hundred feet to the summit" (p 192). From its top, we could overlook the entire city, seeing it from the ancient peoples' perspective. There we found the sacred of Machu Picchu. The panoramic view took my breath away. The Incans literally carved civilization out of the side of mountains. Given the abundance of temples and other stonework at the summit, the ancient Incans must have enjoyed this heavenly overlook also. We could see the full scale of Machu Picchu's layout with an incredible number of terraces lining the slopes of the mountain, giving the city a green and tan striped skirt. The tourists were too small to see and the activities of daily life seemed far away. As my eyes took in the full scope of the surrounding mountains, Machu Picchu seemed like a small gem hidden amidst the vivid forest and soaring peaks, and I understood how this sacred city stayed safely hidden from the profane mundaneness of the modern world for centuries.

As we hiked back to civilization, my mind drifted between the sacred and the profane. The soreness of muscles and feet increased each day as the miles added up. On the final stretch, the pains made me more aware of the routine features of life. The historian Eliade argued that humans have long regarded nearly all of our bodily activities (eating, sex and reproduction, sleep and dreaming) as having spiritual meaning, perhaps allowing us to experience the work of the gods, and communicate with them, in our daily lives. For non-spiritual humans who see the world as "desacralized," this might mean that daily life is filled with mundane, profane activities and perhaps they feel life is lacking something special. But maybe we have simply lost sight of the sacred. The jungle of daily responsibilities has overgrown our ability to sense the sacred in daily life and given us a false impression that the busy-ness we are overwhelmed by is actually important.

Each day along the Inca Trail, we explored incredible ruins representing the daily lives of ancient people. Wandering through those remnants of walls, I could imagine people going about their mundane day-to-day activities. Are we so different? Remove the technology of any era and we essentially have the same fundamentals in life. We wake, eat, poop, work, socialize, gather food, cook, eat again, and sleep. We create holidays to celebrate what we value as sacred, and to break up the mundaneness of life. On this basic level, I find it comforting to think we are similar to our ancestors. In other ways, the idea is depressing. No matter what era of human history we live in, we seem to get stuck in the mundane routines of daily life.

Caught up in our daily rituals, we seem to always lose sight of the sacred, both the big questions and the beauty in small details. Modern society is plagued by questions of how to manage the mundane needs of billions of people. How do we properly reduce and dispose of our waste? How do we make sure everyone has enough food? What about equal access to electricity and the internet? I keep wondering: why can't we learn more from our predecessors' mistakes and their wisdom? Surely there are lessons we can draw on from our ancestors on how to avoid wars, develop resilient communities, use natural resources more sustainably, and create and protect equality amongst people? Maybe we are not looking for the lessons our many ancestors could teach us. Maybe we need to expand our kincentric awareness and tap into the values handed down by those who follow Pachamama to recognize that Mother Earth is sacred and should be valued simply for herself, in addition to what she provides for humans. Sherri Mitchell highlights that Indigenous knowledge "recognizes the familial relationship and acknowledges that all life is both sovereign and interdependent, and that each element within creation (including humans) has the right and the responsibility to respectfully coexist as coequals within the larger system of life" (p 19).

The Incan people and the ruins of their ancient cities still have lessons to teach us about valuing nature as sacred and recognizing the importance of the profane/mundane necessities in our modern era. For example, the Smithsonian's National Museum of the American Indian has a teaching guide for 11-14 year-old students that helps share some of the Incan's wisdom about making sure that a society has enough food and water for everyone.[13] The incredible engineering involved in the Incans' terraced gardens prevented soil erosion, and ingenious water canals provided drinking water and irrigation for farming on steep mountain slopes. In fact, small family farms in many parts of the Andes Mountains still use these techniques today, and some of the ancient canals still flow with drinkable water.

Perhaps life is like hiking in the mountains, our progress as a species depends on one's perspective. When focused on the uphill climb, we only pay attention to the path in front of us and our immediate surroundings. But once we reach a good place to pause and rest, we can look back and appreciate how much we have accomplished, consider and correct mistakes we have made, and use the knowledge we gained along the way. Then, onward—there's more trail to cover. We need to keep moving forward, but don't neglect those opportunities to pause and reflect. That is how we can pass on lessons we have learned and make course corrections to protect the important sacred and profane components of our world.

Endnotes

1 https://en.wikipedia.org/wiki/Sacred%E2%80%93profane_dichotomy (https://perma.cc/VS9P-LWM6)
2 https://www.native-art-in-canada.com/turtleisland.html (https://perma.cc/74CS-387A)
3 https://en.wikipedia.org/wiki/Pachamama (https://perma.cc/EB5Z-YPEV)
4 https://www.pachamama.org/about/origin (https://perma.cc/X5BC-PBMX)
5 http://www.worldfuturefund.org/Projects/Indicators/motherearthbolivia.html (https://perma.cc/9QE5-7BAL)
6 http://whc.unesco.org/en/list/1459 (https://perma.cc/25AZ-T4E8); http://www.bbc.com/news/world-latin-america-27958466 (https://perma.cc/D5Q3-KV6R)
7 http://whc.unesco.org/en/list/274 (https://perma.cc/D4T6-7H5V)
8 http://whc.unesco.org/en/criteria/ (https://perma.cc/5FNW-PJAP)
9 https://en.wikipedia.org/wiki/Everyone_Poops (https://perma.cc/CN9U-WLLT)
10 https://en.wikipedia.org/wiki/Squat_toilet (https://perma.cc/JZC7-DCAW)
11 https://sdgs.un.org/topics/water-and-sanitation (https://perma.cc/XN4C-L2WU)
12 https://www.insidescience.org/news/inside-controversial-world-composting-toilets (https://perma.cc/UX6S-8HDZ)
13 https://americanindian.si.edu/nk360/inka-water/pdf/Full-Lesson-InkaRoad-WaterManagement-ENGLISH.pdf (https://perma.cc/EB6M-PK8L)

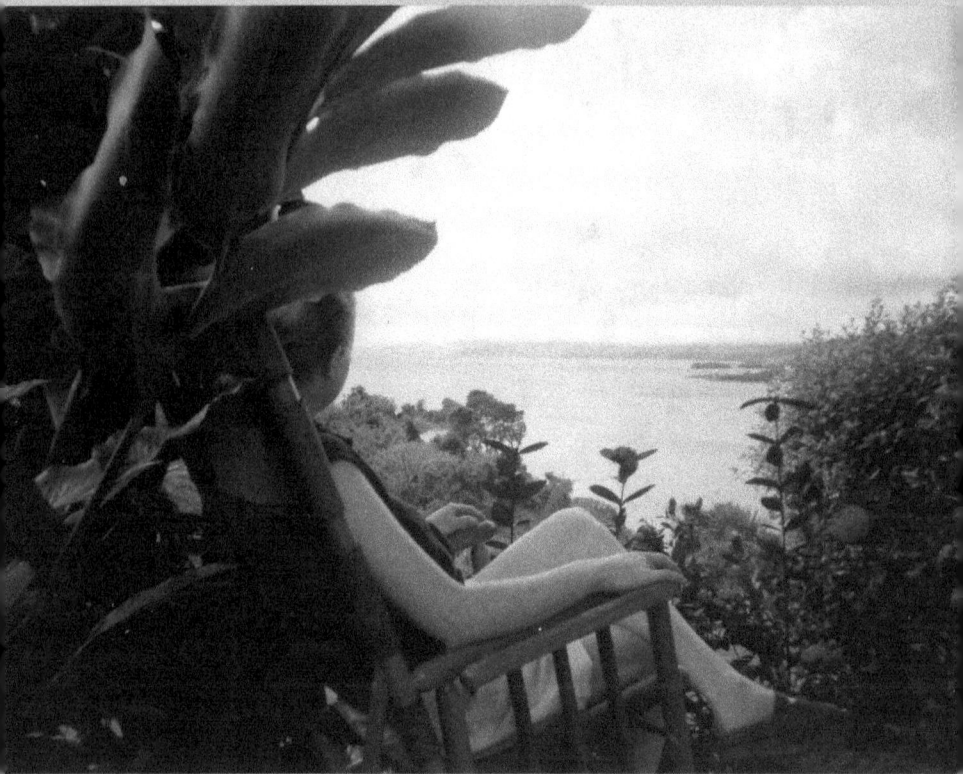

The author appreciating the view of Lake Arenal.
Photo credit 1998 Mick Beltz.

Choosing a Sustainable and Resilient Future

Lake Arenal watershed, Costa Rica, December 1998

December 1998. I am experiencing one of those time-space warps made possible by airplane travel. Yesterday we were in 10 degree Fahrenheit, snow covered Minnesota, having spent a week celebrating Christmas with my family. Now I listen to gentle sheets of rain pummel the wooden roof of our tiny bungalow. The floor tiles are pleasantly smooth and warm under my bare feet. Seating myself in a leather-backed rocking chair on the porch, I shift slightly for my best view overlooking the lush tropical landscape of Costa Rica. My eyes follow the hilly slopes down to the shoreline of Lake Arenal, a long reservoir lake covering 33 square miles. The rain shower is passing quickly. Low clouds of mist hover in my field of vision, obscuring portions of the lake and opposite shore.

Within a quarter hour, sunshine is poking holes in the clouds with patches of blue sky becoming more brilliant. My eyes are drawn upslope, as if following a sheer curtain that is rising, and the magnificent Arenal Volcano slowly emerges center stage. This is one of those places where I could be happy if the annoyingly steady march of time suddenly paused for a while.

I am very intrigued by Costa Rica, a small country with big sustainability ambitions. I believe its smallness encourages people to think big.

In 1949, Costa Rica abolished its military and invested that funding into education and health care. Apparently, the military was considered weak and ineffective, so using that money elsewhere was not controversial. Then in 1994, Costa Ricans made another innovative decision—they amended their national constitution to incorporate the **right to a healthy environment** for all residents.[1] These bold actions

White-nosed coati.
Photo credit 1998 Rebecca J Romsdahl.

have undoubtedly contributed to Costa Rica's designation as the happiest country in the world in 2009, 2012, and 2016.[2] This is significant because happiness is often confused with money in attempts to measure wellbeing. Gross domestic product (GDP), the total monetary value of finished goods and services produced within a country during a given time period, is often used to measure a society's progress, success, wellbeing, and overall worth. But is a country really only as good as the sum of money it gets for its labor and the stuff is produces? Absolutely not. GDP leaves out incredibly important aspects of life like human and environmental health, education, equity, and happiness.

A curious little gang of pizotes (white-nosed coatis) approached our car on soft padded feet, squeaking amiable to each other. They look like a raccoon crossed with a large house cat. These pizotes were looking for treats. As one, then two, then three stood on their back feet with their hand-like paws outstretched, it became obvious that many visitors entering the park have stopped here and given bits of food to these mischievously cute critters. We waved goodbye to the gang and entered Manuel Antonio National Park on the Pacific coast. The three of us—my partner, his father, and I—wanted to see more of Costa Rica's biodiversity, so we had gone to the park for a day trip rather than go souvenir shopping with the rest of the family.

Costa Rica added to its sustainability and resilience credentials in 1997 by becoming the first nation to establish Payments for Environmental Services. Through this program, the government pays private landowners for being good environmental stewards. Four services are recognized by the program.

- Carbon storage. Landowners can reduce greenhouse gas emissions, such as by reforesting their property and letting the trees grow into maturity. This increases carbon storage as the trees pack it away in their dense, woody trunks and branches.
- Hydrological services. These are important and can be recognized through activities like protecting streams from erosion and pollution.

- Biodiversity conservation. Landowners can plant new trees and manage a reforested area to promote a diverse variety of trees and plants that provide habitat for a greater variety of insects and animals.
- Scenic beauty. This might seem obvious, like when you think about the value of a house on lakefront property. But scenic beauty is also a cultural value, and I think this is often overlooked by government and business decision makers.

This payment program also provides incentives for landowners to manage natural resources in ways that protect and improve the environment overall.

Building on this impressive leadership, Costa Rica set a **world record** in 2017.[3] They declared success in reaching 300 consecutive days of generating the nation's electricity from renewable energy sources, a combination of wind, hydro, and solar. After proving their ability to run on green energy, a **National Decarbonization Plan** was announced by President Carlos Alvarado Quesada and Costa Rica's world famous Christiana Figueres, the former Executive Secretary of the United Nations Framework Convention on Climate Change (she orchestrated the successful Paris Climate Agreement in 2015).[4]

Through this decarbonization plan, Costa Rica was the first nation to declare a carbon neutral plan, with a target date of 2085. Other nations, like the United Kingdom, have since established their own plans with more ambitious mid-century targets, like 2050. A carbon neutral target means trying to reduce all greenhouse gas emissions as low as possible in all sectors of a nation's economy and society. At the same time, Costa Rica will also implement strategies to pull emissions out of the atmosphere and store them in carbon sinks, such as wetlands protection, soil renewal, planting more trees, and potentially using new technologies. Costa Rica's ambitious plan begins to outline changes needed in transportation, energy supply, agriculture, forests, and waste management. Given that these are big, complex systems in any country, it is not surprising that the plan does not provide details about how and when these changes will happen. But Costa Ricans are proud of their global environmental leadership, so businesses and individuals are already working on changing what they can do themselves. There will be many challenges, of course. Gaps between wealthy and poor residents will make some goals more difficult to achieve, such as transitioning to electric vehicles. Many of the proposed changes will not be easy, but worthy ones rarely are.

Costa Rica is unusual in many ways. Geography and geology place it on top of the Ring of Fire, which is a horseshoe-shaped path crowning the Pacific Ocean with volcanos, earthquake zones, and deep ocean trenches. These are the surface signals of the unrelenting, unseen shifting of massive tectonic plates that form the thin layer of solid earth we call home. The horseshoe stretches from the southwest coast of South America, up the coastline to Alaska, and across the Bering Sea to trace the island chains of Japan, the Philippines, and Indonesia, and then southward to New Zealand. This incredible geology creates the narrow landmass of Central America, and Costa Rica's boundaries encircle a biodiversity hotspot, meaning it has an amazing number of unique plants and animals. Costa Rica's unusual political history has helped it make distinct decisions to recognize the value of the natural environment.[5] It has the highest percentage of protected green space in the world (25% of its territory) in 29 national parks and other biological reserves.

Manuel Antonio National Park was one of the first national parks created by the Costa Rican government. It was established in 1972, and it is an example of a park in a working landscape, as it has agriculture lands on three sides. At a trailhead, we stopped to watch several white-faced capuchin monkeys hanging out in the trees. One cocked her head, watching me watching her. I am not sure who was more curious, though it was probably me, since she likely saw plenty of humans every day.

A few hundred feet into the forest, we were loudly greeted by a band of mantled howler monkeys moving through the trees above us. Their glossy black fur was striking against the vivid green leaves, and it allows them to hide in shadows when they are sitting still. A flash of bright red hindquarter caught my eye, and I burst into giggles. I quickly covered my mouth, feeling like a small child caught looking at a dirty picture. Their vocal abilities were superb and can be heard clearly for three miles even in dense forests! One raised his mouth skyward, formed a perfect "O" with his lips, and sang a series of low pitched, throaty, melodious yowls, reminding me of a Gregorian Monk chanting a sacred song. We continued hiking up into the jungle, admiring the lush emerald-green vegetation of the tropical lowland rain forest. After a long history of logging and agriculture, Manuel Antonio National Park is one of only two large areas that preserve this type of forest along the entire Pacific coast of Central America. The other is Corcovado National Park, which is on a peninsula of Costa Rica.

About half an hour later, we quietly walked through a dense section of trees and a movement above caught my eye. I stopped to pinpoint who or what I saw. I found it and silently clapped my hands in delight—a small red-backed squirrel monkey! She was slowly walking along a branch, hand over hand, foot over foot. I had been hoping to find one of these cute critters. Native to Central America, they are an endangered population because they can only live in and around this Park and Corcovado National Park, where their forest habitat is protected.

Whenever I am hiking, I probably spend more time looking at the trail just ahead of me than I do looking around at the landscape. That has saved me countless times from tripping over a stone or surfaced tree root. That day, this habit also worked in my favor for wildlife viewing. I spotted a small line of green leaf bits steadily marching along the top of a large fallen tree branch. Squatting down to take a closer look, I found a crew of **leafcutter ants** busy at work.[6] They were hiking their own trail, like a two-lane highway, with some ants bringing leaves back to the nest and others heading out for more leaves.

Leafcutter ants are native to South and Central America, Mexico, and parts of the southern United States. Many people might think they are just insects, but leafcutter ants are remarkable organisms. They are even similar to humans in two ways. One, they have evolved to organize themselves into **complex civilizations** where different individuals have different roles in society.[7] Starting from scratch, a new queen ant searches for a suitable underground spot to form her colony. If she is successful, within just a few years her offspring will help build a subterranean city that can rival any human metropolis. Some of these ant colonies have been measured as having a central city of 98 feet across and suburbs extending to a radius of 260 feet (covering 320 to over 6,000 square feet). What humans can see of their city is the aboveground dome of excavated soil. Some of these domes can rise to heights of six feet.

The second way that leafcutter ants are similar to humans is through farming. These ants were **farming for millions of years** before humans learned how to garden.[8] Leafcutter ants grow food for their entire colony, which could include eight million individuals. There is a lot of hard work involved and every ant has an important role to play. You might see one set of ants hauling bits of leaf, flower, and grass back to their colony. Interestingly, the ants cannot digest plants. Instead, these are the tools they use to grow their food. Once inside the nest, a different set of ants chew the plant bits into a substance like paper-mache that acts as the soil. And what are they growing? Fungus, essentially mushrooms, but not the cute little stem and hat versions. Their fungal gardens mostly contain threadlike hyphae, what we might consider the roots of mushrooms. It is tempting to say that these ants invented organic agriculture. They developed a way to use natural materials to grow a nutritious, unlimited food supply. This is an important part of their success because a large colony consumes roughly the same amount of plant materials as a full-grown cow! Before leaving her family nest, a young queen ant will take a bit of fungus and tuck it into a pocket in her mouth. Then she uses that to start the garden for her new colony. It reminds me of how people will share a bit of sourdough bread starter with a friend or relative. It also reminds me that we are part of the same natural world and have more in common with our animal relatives than we think.

After an hour or so of hiking through the jungle, we began to emerge. Openings between the trees offered us postcard views of a sandy beach and waves of bright blue ocean washing ashore. As the trail led us down through mangrove trees and onto the sand, I was enthralled. Costa Rica had given me remarkable wildlife, gorgeous tropical jungle, and soft sand to wiggle my toes in as the Pacific Ocean circled my ankles. Was this reality, or had I landed somewhere over the rainbow? Had I escaped to a nameless paradise island? The thought was very pleasing, and I closed my eyes to savor it for a few minutes while listening to the waves.

I often think about the idea that change is constant, but many people do not like changes in their lives. If we could embrace the idea of change, maybe the US and other nations could be more like Costa Rica, developing big goals and big plans to protect the environment. What do we want our future to look like? This brings to mind the *Choose Your Own Adventure* books from my childhood. I would always flip to the back of the book to find out which ending I might enjoy the most, and then I would read that storyline. If more nations would look ahead toward their future and choose the more resilient, sustainability-focused storyline that Costa Rica is planning, I believe we could have more happiness in this world.

Endnotes

1 https://www.nytimes.com/2018/09/21/climate/costa-rica-zero-car-bon-neutral.html (https://perma.cc/B8FX-GAHU)
2 http://happyplanetindex.org/countries/costa-rica (https://perma.cc/7QV8-59XZ)
3 https://www.independent.co.uk/news/world/americas/costa-ri-ca-electricity-renewable-energy-300-days-2017-record-wind-hy-dro-solar-water-a8069111.html (https://perma.cc/J2BQ-FMLT)
4 https://climateactiontracker.org/countries/costa-rica/ (https://perma.cc/K53F-G3SN)
5 https://www.mdpi.com/2071-1050/10/2/296 (https://perma.cc/RF7D-7QVF)
6 https://en.wikipedia.org/wiki/Leafcutter_ant (https://perma.cc/8M-SA-ZT2S)
7 https://www.google.com/books/edition/The_Leafcutter_Ants_Civ-ilization_by_Inst/NqE4MmJiUiAC?hl=en&gbpv=1&printsec=frontcover (https://perma.cc/8WBE-WYL9)
8 https://www.pbs.org/wgbh/evolution/library/01/3/l_013_01.html (https://perma.cc/L9BC-EKC2)

Snow wave cresting over the porch.
Photo credit 2019 Rebecca J Romsdahl.

Reflections on Snow

Red River of the North watershed, United States, February 2019

Last night, the moon was nearly full, save for a thin sliver. The sky was clear, with stars like tiny, brilliant diamonds winking against black velvet cloth. This is the type of winter night where the air is so frigidly cold that it feels like the vacuum of space has descended upon us. I treasure these moonlit winter nights because they create striking, stark shadows of bare tree branches, like a museum display of Shodo art (Japanese calligraphy) painted across the smooth, white canvas of snow on my backyard.

If we must endure the frigid temperatures, I want a thick blanket of snow everywhere. I like it clean and white, so frequent snowstorms are welcome. Wrapping myself in layers of fleece and putting on a hat, scarf, wool mittens, downyfilled windproof coat, and insulated boots, I sometimes wonder if this is how it feels to put on a spacesuit. Stepping outside my nest, I embrace my Minnesota-Scandinavian heritage as the negative temperatures freeze my nose hairs causing them to stick together, while the snow creaks and squeaks under my footsteps.

I pause, lifting a mittened hand to block the sun, and marvel at the twin sundogs in a dazzling blue sky. Heaps of fluffy snow weigh down pine branches and dark, eye-shaped scars peer out of the white trunks of birch trees in my backyard. My boots are not tall enough, but I release my inner ten-year-old self, laughing as I sink knee-deep in the snow, tromping toward the bird feeders. Cold, wet patches suddenly bloom on my wool socks. I hustle through the steps of emptying old seed remnants out of the two feeders and refilling them with fresh

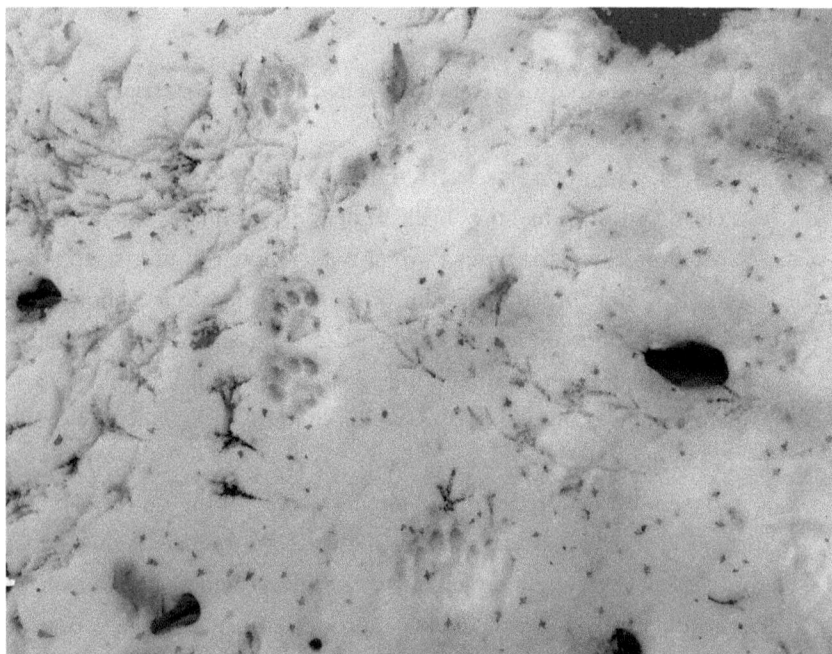

Tracks in snow.
Photo credit 2019 Rebecca J Romsdahl.

seeds. As my nose and cheeks begin to sting, I recall a news article about the genetics of being a redhead and how extremely sensitive we are to changes in temperature. But on a day that will only reach -15 degrees Fahrenheit by midafternoon, I sympathize with the critters who live in my yard. Five minutes of deep freeze and I am back in the **hygge** (cozy) warmth of my house.[1]

Heavy clouds hang low in the sky tonight, muffling the city noises. The calm air holds the **"smell of snow,"** that mysterious scent of expectant snowfall.[2] Cloudy winter nights combine with city lights to affect a strange, diffuse snow-glow that is bright as day. I often wonder if this is how well my cats see at night. Some of these nights produce a warm golden glow, while others seem pinkish.

I wake to a fresh layer of snow, several inches thick. It looks like this will be the day we set a new local record for February snow accumulation. I believe the old record was around 22 inches. Surveying the outside world from my windows reveals a treat. Tracks in the snow!

There are mice living under our front porch. They have tunneled through the snow wave that covers the three-panel window of our half basement and is cresting over the porch. The mice tracks emerge from beneath a pile of branches that is now mostly hidden by snow wave. Our neighborhood has plentiful cottontail bunnies who leave trails of scat around the house and tracks across the yard to their favorite gaps between fences. Hungry birds have left trails of abstract art across the patio table and under the feeders. I consider songbirds my fellow travelers as they fly hundreds or thousands of miles migrating between their summer and winter homes.

There are not as many regular visitors at my feeders this winter. In recognizing this, I fear we have lost the lessons learned from Rachel Carson's work in her famous book, *Silent Spring*. After World War II, she became concerned with the toxic impacts of widespread use of pesticides, especially DDT (Dichlorodiphenyltrichloroethane). She put a spotlight on the harmful effects that pesticides were causing, from cancers in humans to the death of wildlife, specifically birds. She wrote, "On the morning that had once throbbed with the dawn chorus of robins, catbirds, doves, jays, wrens, and scores of other bird voices, there was now no sound" (p 2). Talking with friends who are also amateur birders, I find they have noticed a similar lack of birds throughout the seasons over the last few years.

We have a theory to explain this increasing absence. But we also have a growing concern. Our city has seen rapid housing development south of my neighborhood and increasing traffic on the nearest multilane street. These changes may be causing our bird friends to move to new locations. Scientists have also recorded alarming declines in bird population across North America.[3] Since 1970, we have lost nearly three billion individual birds in their breeding populations! Grassland birds in my home ecosystem have dropped by 53%. Common birds that we would see in our backyards, such as finches, sparrows, and warblers, have been hit the hardest. The birds are disappearing due to a variety of negative climate and habitat changes, as well as the overuse of pesticides. These threats are killing some birds directly, while others die of starvation, and many are prevented from breeding and raising healthy chicks. Are we seeing these impacts reduce the number of birds in our own neighborhoods as well? I fear we are.

The science also shows a clear map for reversing these negative trends. Researchers found that some types of birds are doing well. The population numbers of ducks, geese, eagles, hawks, and wild turkeys have all grown in the last 30 years. In other words, the birds that we have been specifically protecting through organizations, dedicated conservation funding, and laws are doing well. This is good news. We can build on the success of these past efforts as blueprints for protecting the rest of our feathered friends.

Today is an unusual delight. The cold snap this week has brought feathered friends back to my feeders. My two cats sit on a shelf in the sunroom looking out the window, tails twitching. We love watching the birds in our yard. There are splashes of color from a pair of cardinals, and riotous chatter from a charm of nearly 30 redpolls. They are competing with our shrinking little crew of dark-eyed juncos, whose feathers are fluffed against fierce 40-mile-an-hour gusts of wind. The delicate nature of black-capped chickadees is amusing as they grab a single sunflower seed, fly to a branch, and apply patient determination to peck it open and devour the prize. A solitary red-breasted nuthatch sneaks in when the crowd has momentarily scattered because somebody got spooked. A downy woodpecker flits from tree to tree, keeping an eye on the busy traffic.

The winter season can be marked as truly deep when a trio of ravens descends on our bird feeding station in the empty hours of midday. They are enormous creatures, holding onto the stem of the shepherd's hook while trying to scoop seeds out of the small feeder with their long, black beaks and digging through the spills in the snow beneath. These ravens must by very hungry for I have never witnessed them at our feeders before this.

When I next tromp out to refill the feeders, I find that somebody has left beautifully mysterious markings of wingtips in the snow. Were the ravens seeking more seeds or has our neighborhood sharp-shinned hawk returned too early from her wintering grounds? I continue to ponder this while I eat lunch from a seat facing the windows, overlooking the feeders. The glare off the snow is blinding and makes me smile behind my sunglasses. This is how I cope with cabin fever.[4]

Endnotes

1 https://norskbloggen.no/how-to-hygge-seg-norwegian-style/ (https://perma.cc/7CQJ-G96Z)
2 http://physicsbuzz.physicscentral.com/2016/01/podcast-physics-and-smell-of-snow.html (https://perma.cc/XV93-FVMZ)
3 https://www.allaboutbirds.org/news/vanishing-1-in-4-birds-gone/?__hstc=161696355.f29dc4ae1c9296de93e4450c291b-42de.1610482641896.1618001845915.1620068999121.3&__hssc=161696355.1.1620068999121&__hsfp=3889324403&_gl=1*18us-fvk*_ga*MTM3MjE3MzYzNS4xNjEwNDgyNjQy*_ga_QR4N-VXZ8BM*MTYyMDA2ODk5Ny4xLjAuMTYyMDA-2ODk5Ny42MA..#_ga=2.11737399.209790609.1620068998-1372173635.1610482642 (https://perma.cc/5Q2U-C6PX)
4 https://www.theguardian.com/science/2020/sep/26/dreading-a-dark-winter-lockdown-think-like-a-norwegian (https://perma.cc/SPL3-LHX6)

Wandering through the Scottish Highlands on a path to Ardvreck Castle ruins.
Photo credit 2013 Mick Beltz.

Wanderlust and Meandering Thoughts

River Lune watershed, United Kingdom, September 2013

Humans have always traveled. Wanderlust is a fundamental trait of our species, and some say we have **restless genes.**[1] Over thousands of generations, our early human ancestors walked out of the African savannas into Europe and Asia; perhaps they eventually walked across the Bering land bridge all the way from northern top to southern tip of the Americas. We were nomadic hunters and gathers much longer than we have been settled farmers and city dwellers. Throughout the centuries we have travelled on religious pilgrimages and journeys of self-discovery. We have even leapt off our planet to wander across the surface of the moon, and we have sent reconnaissance robots to tell us about the landscape of Mars. Will the first humans walk on the Red Planet during my lifetime? Travel is a sort of kinship amongst people. It has helped me understand how similar we all are underneath our outward differences.

As my partner and I toured around the United Kingdom in 2013, exchanging travel stories with the British people we met, many expressed surprise and jealously, saying they had not traveled much in their own country. Several people told us that when going on holiday (vacation), they tended to pack up the family and jump on a plane heading to the Mediterranean, the United States, or elsewhere. After a handful of these conversations, I was struck by how different this was from American culture. I have rarely met another American who has not traveled outside their home state to explore other parts of the country.

One of the important factors in this different approach to travel can be illustrated by the price of petrol (gas). In October, we rented a little purple Peugeot 107 for a weekend trip to the Scottish Borderlands. This car is not much bigger than a double bed, gets very good gas mileage, and only holds about eight gallons of fuel. Petrol prices were around £1.35 per liter, which translates to roughly $10.00 per gallon, so it cost us approximately $65.00 to fill the tank of that tiny car. By comparison, most Americans get upset when gas reaches $3.00 per gallon. This is a significant difference in price and shows the dominance of America's car culture, which is also reflected in the way many Americans take vacation. They pack the family in the car and take a week-long road trip across the country. In the UK, the much higher gas prices accomplish the intended goal of discouraging extra driving, but the unintended outcome is that it seems to promote vacations by air travel, particularly as discount airline companies offer ticket prices cheap enough to compare with filling a car's gas tank.

This is troublesome for the UK because the government has committed to cutting its greenhouse gas emissions by 57% (from 1990 levels) by 2032 and becoming net-zero by 2050. This is one of the most ambitious national goals currently being attempted by any nation. But there is also support in the government for expanding air travel by 60% during the same timeframe. This **conundrum** produces a good deal of media discussion and widespread criticism.[2] Some experts have called for measures to actively curb the rising demand for air travel and to increase domestic tourism in the UK. My first reaction to reading that was disagreement. From my American perspective, it seems wrong for government to actively discourage people from participating in the global community or creating policies that limit global opportunities to those who are wealthy enough to afford more expensive air travel.

This gut reaction surprised me because it contradicts my environmental common sense. Society should be cutting back on air travel overall in order to reduce greenhouse gas emissions. Yet, I know firsthand how valuable international travel is for people to be able to experience different cultures and meet others with different

Dunstanburgh Castle ruins with cows and sheep grazing in the foreground.
Photo credit 2013 Mick Beltz.

worldviews. I am torn by these seemingly opposite values, and I have not yet found a good way to reconcile them. Given my discussions with British people, I would encourage more domestic tourism for the UK. It is a beautiful country with such variety in a small space, from seascape to landscapes, distinct English, Scottish, Welsh, and Irish cultures, foods, and rich history to explore. But I completely understand the desire to explore new places. Travel is about stepping outside your comfort zone and seeing the world from new perspectives. It's in our genes. Fulfilling that desire is part of why I travel.

During our trip to the Scottish Borderlands, we walked along the northeast coast of England to visit the ruins of **Dunstanburgh Castle.**[3]Lovely photos portray the sparse remains of a few walls and the skeletal silhouette of the castle gatehouse, but the visuals cannot capture the whole experience. There were so many sensory connections that create a visceral memory for me, and it is much richer than just a picture in my mind. The fierce north wind chilled my face, making me feel like I would transform into a marble statue if I stood still too long. The roar of two-meter waves crashing on rocks was the only thing I could hear above the wind. Despite the nature of that wind, the air held a tangy smell and tasted of sea salt. I could have stood for hours watching the undulation of frothy, thick, caffé latte-colored seafoam along the shore being blown in fluffy masses, tumbling inland across the landscape. Balancing all this was the bewildering experience of walking amidst the cows and sheep, peacefully grazing right down to the rocky shoreline of this wild seascape, with the romantic castle ruins behind them.

How will global travel change as nations continue to develop plans for reducing greenhouse gas emissions? Train travel is being promoted in many nations, especially where electric trains are supported and popular, like Japan and China. Carbon offsets are becoming more common opportunities with air travel. Basically, this means you donate a certain amount of money to a project that is doing mitigation work, such as planting trees, to compensate for the amount of carbon emissions you will create by flying on your next trip. But there are a variety of problems with carbon offsets, including how to measure the mitigation efforts, corruption, and questions about whether they just allow business to continue as usual instead of actually reducing the use of fossil fuels.

If nations are going to get serious about reducing greenhouse gas emissions from all activities, including travel, then we all may need to reassess how often we travel, how far, and on what transportation. But if society collectively begins to discourage long-distance international travel, which is mostly done via air, would we risk becoming more insulated within our own national borders, increasingly relying on the internet and social media to show us the world and introduce us to new people and cultures? I hope not. I do enjoy the virtual travel provided online by photos and stories of remote, beautiful places. But they cannot bring the same sense of wonder that I have experienced through travel.

If we are honest with ourselves, we don't always need to travel far to refresh our perspectives on our familiar daily world. One of my hopes is that more people will take time to tour their own beautiful countries. But I also hope we find a way to maintain global travel opportunities as nations cut their greenhouse gas emissions.

May 2020. Lockdown. The days blur together. To wander is to be human, but now only my thoughts wander. The Covid-19 pandemic has silenced travel and kept many people in their homes for weeks or even months. Whether strolling through neighborhood parks or hiking rainforest mountains in a distant land, when will we wander again?

Maybe we need to embrace the wonders of technology. When I lived in the United Kingdom for half a year, I cherished the miracle of Skype; it allowed me to "visit" my family, seeing and hearing them in real time. In lockdown, we have transformed the way we work, go to school, shop—anything that can be done online is now a reality. I recently had the unique experience of attending a wedding conducted entirely online; it was distracting to have glimpses into the homes of people who were attending from different countries around the world. Even gatherings with friends and family have become screentime events, even if they are within walking distance.

Some days, I am thankful that technology allows me to have a much-needed teatime or happy hour drink with friends. Many other days, I dread the next Zoom meeting, when I feel tethered to my chair until my back aches and my eyes are strained. In the virtual world, there is nothing to separate the workday and the weekend, so we keep working. But it is not productive work, it is distracted. The global news is a 24-hour horror show. I try to avoid it, but I'm entranced by it, like trying to look away from a sputtering plane. Will it crash and explode or miraculously survive a hard landing?

My partner and I canceled our annual spring break trip to Las Vegas as we watched the dominoes fall and everything across the United States shut down. My conference trip to Los Angeles was canceled, and the conference event was later converted into an online experience. Eventually, the university semester ended. Now there is so much extra time. My dad summed it up well once when I asked how his weekend was: "Stale." This has made winter's hangover and the slow greening of spring in the Red River Valley feel even more drawn out than usual.

We are very lucky though; we are privileged. My partner and I have academic jobs that allow us the flexibility to work from home, and we live in a smallish city in a rural area, so we are not locked away indoors. We have found quiet distractions in the backyard. We watch puffy clouds drift across the sky, listening as migrating birds pass through and give way to breeding residents competing melodiously for territory. Strolls along the river walk show the passage of time as spring flood waters rise and retreat. Sitting on the early spring grass, I make plans for the summer garden.

But my thoughts wander, meandering like a prairie stream.

There is so much uncertainty. How long will we need to teach remotely? I don't mind working from home, but I don't feel as productive. Will we catch the virus and get sick? How widespread will the economic cuts be? Will we lose our jobs? What day is today? Maybe I should get groceries tomorrow, since mid-week is quiet in the store. Will science ever find what animal this new coronavirus came out of? I find nature so beautiful that I want to protect it, and yet it is completely indifferent to us humans. How dangerous is Covid-19? Will we lose family members or friends to this pandemic?

Life is short. I try to keep my focus on the present and revel in the experiences of every day, good and bad. I embrace the people and passions I love.

Travel is one of my passions, but for now it is part of history. Instead, just going to the grocery store has become a carefully planned outing. To avoid anxiety, we don't go out for groceries on weekends, we wear masks, and we bring hand sanitizer.

I have a bit of germaphobia. I think of it as a healthy amount, but I also avoid scary zombie films because they give me disease filled nightmares. Given this, I have struggled with the idea of making the six-hour drive to visit my family, exposing myself and my elderly parents to potential Covid-19 infection. I cannot fathom getting on a plane or train filled with people. The thought of sharing crowded spaces with potentially infected people ties my stomach in knots. Thoughts of future travel are put out of mind entirely.

Meandering, restless thoughts.

The wanderlust that propels my partner and I to explore is not easily bottled up. It might become unsettling to a degree that requires a traditional American road trip just to scratch the itch. Westward to the Rocky Mountains, or eastward to the siren call of Lake Superior? But nagging questions linger: Is the risk of Covid-19 infection too great? What precautions would be best for a road trip? Camping seems low risk, right?

How long is this horrible pandemic journey, and then where do we go from there?

People keep saying, "These are strange times." I agree, but what do we mean by that? There is often an undertone of lightness, as if to imply, "This won't last long. Don't worry, we'll be back to normal soon." But this pandemic is uncharted territory. We are lost and nobody seems to have a useful map. As a society, we need to recognize that going "back to normal" is too dangerous. The pandemic and the resulting economic crisis are bigger than we want to admit.

Lockdown, staying at home, and physical distancing this year have given us time and space to be present in the moment. They have given us time to observe the slow melt of snow, to watch the reawakening of small green blades of grass, and to reflect on our relationship with the world. The entire world also became **quieter and cleaner** as human transportation and other activities slowed or stopped.[4] As most people have been forced to pause their normal life, I find myself seeking hopeful ideas and thinking a great deal about how this crisis can be an opportunity.

When societies experience sudden, dramatic disruptions like the Covid-19 pandemic, they often implement big policy ideas that in normal times would seem radically outrageous, such as giving each American adult $1,200 to help offset the economic crisis. If that were established as a monthly payment, it would be what sustainability studies calls a Universal Basic Income. It would provide a way to level the economic playing field so that people have a little more security and resilience in their home budget in case of a sudden emergency or don't feel forced to work a second job just to pay the bills. As I watch big ideas unfold in different cities around the world, I feel this is a time of **opportunity**, a time to reimagine the world we want to live in after the crisis.[5] There will be significant changes that come out of this quest to survive.

Which changes made during lockdown will become permanent? Some days my thoughts billow out larger and broader, like summer clouds over big sky country. Will face masks become another safety feature of travel, like seatbelts? The thought of wearing a face mask for a 12-hour flight makes my nose itch. Will the custom of greeting people with a handshake be replaced with something like a head nod

Crowd watching the Prague Astronomical Clock.
Photo credit 2019 Mick Beltz.

or an elbow bump? Will international travel become unpopular, too expensive, and too risky? We are living through a unique moment in history, and it has the potential to encourage transformational changes.

Even before the pandemic, global tourism may have reached a tipping point. Critics call it **overtourism**.[6] Some tourism hotspots, such as Barcelona, Spain, have seen local residents demonstrating against tourism and demanding policy changes from local governments. Residents and local leaders **agonize** over the benefits of tourist money flooding into their communities versus the burden put on small businesses and city services that struggle to accommodate increasing visitor demands and crowds.[7] Swelling numbers of tourists also disrupt the unique sense of place they have traveled to experience. But tourism is big business, eight trillion dollars per year, **employing nearly one in ten people worldwide!**[8] That level of money holds immense power and helps explain why tourism has become a nightmare for many local people.

When we stayed in Prague, Czech Republic, in June 2019, our small hotel was located in the heart of the old city. We saw and heard some colorful examples of what many residents in popular tourist cities complain about. There were dozens of hen and stag (bachelorette and bachelor) parties mixed in with the other tourists on the Friday night and Saturday night of our stay. Most of them were drunk. Some were loud and rowdy into the wee hours of the night. We had left the windows open for cool night air while we slept. But I woke after 2:00 am and had to close them to shut out drunken singing and loud talking from the street below. It is hard to imagine having to deal with that type of disruption to your home life on a regular basis for months each year.

Residents of some popular tourist cities feel like they are being occupied by foreign invaders during high season. It is easy to understand why when you consider the numbers. For example, in 2017 there were 30 million overnight visitors in Barcelona, which has a resident population of only 1.6 million. Another overtourism hotspot is **Venice**, Italy.[9] When my partner and I stayed in Venice in March of 2006 (off-season), it was quiet and lovely, with drizzly spring weather. The canals were

View of San Giorgio Maggiore Island from Venice's iconic square, Piazza San Marco.
Photo credit 2008 Mick Beltz.

nearly empty while we enjoyed a romantic gondola ride. At an outdoor café, we sat alone with our thoughts, sipping hot, strong cappuccinos and admiring the stunning architecture of Saint Mark's Cathedral. We were the only guests staying at our B&B hotel in the heart of the city.

But there were already signs of strain. Venice's resident population has fallen by nearly 100,000 people from 50 years ago. As of 2020, there are only 55,000 residents in the historic city (this does not count the 200,000 people who live in the mainland extensions of the metro area). Our hotel owners and the employees did not live in the city because it was too expensive. Then in 2017, a decade after our visit, Venice had 36 million international tourists. Many of these people arrived in Venice by cruise ship. This subset of the tourism industry has been especially awful. Companies have built enormous ships that tower over many of the places they visit, spoiling and often completely blocking beautiful views. These ships also displace so much water that they cause structural damage to the Venetian canals and historic buildings, as well as small ports in other locations.

An estimated 32,000 cruise ships disgorge tourists daily into Venice between April and October. I imagine the crowds flowing like a zombie horde, slowly spewing into Saint Mark's Square and rapidly clogging the narrow side streets, 400 bridges, and walkways until everyone feels trapped.[10] These visitors are most often traveling on package tours, meaning they have paid the cruise line companies for onboard transportation, meals, and entertainment. This means they generally do not spend much time or money in the places they visit. They create crowds, take a few photos, use the toilet facilities, and leave a lot of trash in their wake. During the peak month of August, cruise ship tourists add a great deal more stress to an already stressed Venice, on top of over 460 thousand day-trippers and two million overnight guests coming in from the mainland. As my parents would say, "Uff-da! That's too many people!"

One Venetian commented how an online search result for Venice in Airbnb, which shows the available vacation rentals as little red dots on a map, made it look like her city was bleeding to death. Scientists have cautioned that our expanding human **impacts** on the planet are coming to resemble an **infestation**.[11] For example, the more tourists visiting a place, the more trash is left behind, which can overwhelm local capacity to dispose of it properly. In Venice, local leaders are working on proposals to help challenge the idea that this World Heritage City is now just an open-air museum. They want to create jobs outside tourism and start limiting tourist numbers during peak months. They have also limited the size and number of cruise ships in some of the busiest canals.

Cruise line companies have **behaved badly** for decades. They have evaded laws on workplace safety, environmental protections, and avoided paying their fair share of taxes in their home countries. The ships release tons of pollution from untreated wastewater, diesel fuel, and greenhouse gas emissions. Companies have also been negligent about ensuring sanitary, safe living conditions for guests and staff, which have led to horrible norovirus, and now coronavirus, outbreaks on ships.

As world leaders were slowly recognizing the new coronavirus as a global pandemic, travelers were still setting sail on their scheduled vacations. Some cruise companies even started using the Covid-19 news coverage as part of their advertising by playing on people's concerns: "Don't worry, catching the coronavirus is not a risk in warm, sunny weather. Join our cruise to South America or the Caribbean Islands! Here is our discount price." Too many people wanted to believe this idea and then got caught in a nightmare. Thousands of tourists on more than 40 ships were **detained** for weeks as countries hastily closed borders, trying in vain to keep the pandemic out.[12] Nearly 80 passengers died from Covid-19, some before they could be evacuated from the ships.

The bad conduct of cruise line companies may now bring their demise.[13] Over 100,000 cruise line employees were trapped aboard ships for months because of Covid-19, confusion about how to repatriate them to their home countries, and who should pay the costs of that travel. Employees committed suicide on stranded ships, lawsuits are piling up, and governments have refused to include the industry in financial assistance policies related to the pandemic. Covid-19 has changed everything. Perhaps it provides an opportunity to say good-bye to the cruise line industry, or at least reduce its oversized negative impacts.[14]

My partner and I have tried over the years to minimize our travel impacts, both environmentally and socioeconomically. We have scheduled most of our trips to fall during the off-peak season of the places we visited. Admittedly, this is also because we do not like crowds. We believe strongly in slowing our pace and that less is more. We try to focus our visits in one or two places when we travel to a country or region. We also slow down and spend multiple days in the same location so we can absorb more about that place.

Day trips off a cruise ship or taking a cheap flight for a weekend getaway were not sustainable before the pandemic. And now they are a high risk to public health. Plus, these types of trips are just snapshots. You could get the same experience and cause fewer negative impacts through an online virtual tour. During the first wave of the pandemic lockdown, my partner and I experimented with this idea. The miracles of technology! We purchased an Oculus virtual reality headset and started revisiting some of our favorite places using an app, rightly named *Wander*. From our living room, we have skipped around London, England; Córdoba, Spain; and Kyoto, Japan. We also play a game of "Guess Where You Are." One of us picks three locations where we have traveled. The other person then gets two chances to guess where they are viewing. This type of virtual travel is amazing, even though it is limited to a visual perspective.

Placing the headset over my eyes feels like clicking a switch in my brain. I allow myself to be mentally transported. With the press of a button on the handheld controller, I am suddenly standing on a familiar cobblestone street looking uphill and downhill at shops. My cheeks turn up in a wide smile as I recognize High Street, part of the Royal Mile in Edinburgh, Scotland. Another press of the button and I "walk" toward The World's End pub. My partner places a dram of Jura whisky in my hand. I cannot sit in the pub to enjoy my drink, but I sip and let the strong flavors enhance my memories as I continue "strolling" uphill toward the castle, marveling at the 360-degree virtual view.

What might global travel look like after we emerge from the Covid-19 pandemic? Now is the time to rethink how, where, and why we wander for pleasure across this beautiful planet.[15] Could sustainability principles help us reimagine our wanderlust? Perhaps. I hope we will seriously consider them. But as long as the global tourism industry focuses primarily on making money, it will remain a supergrowth industry and thereby also remain a part of the problem that makes our privileged lifestyles unsustainable. Ecotourism has been promoted as a strategy for making travel more sustainable. But in my experience, I do not believe it is the magic answer. I say this because the ecotourism industry is driving urban development in the Galapagos Islands and tourists have been loving National Parks to death for over 50 years in the US.[16]

Whenever we feel it is safe to travel again, there will still be a high risk for a rebound effect. After spending a year or longer in various phases of lockdown, reevaluating our lives and our values, many of us will want to get away from home. Lots of people will want to tackle their global bucket list of adventures before they get too old. Tourism is likely to explode, similar to how outdoor recreation did in the summer of 2020. There are concerns that we may see overtourism spread to other locations and extend throughout the year. This may be driven by people's basic enjoyment of exploring new places and recreation in the natural world, but it will also be pushed by the tourism industry as a plan to get the economy "back to normal."

But the Covid-19 pandemic has changed everything. There is no going "back to normal." Now is the time to imagine a more sustainable and resilient future for travel and tourism. There are no easy answers, so the tourism industry needs to be involved in this reimagining and all travelers need to be willing to take a step back. We should consider how we can be better global citizens. And what's a good place to start? Make a positive difference: reduce the number of trips, take a train instead of a plane, stay in small, family-owned hotels, stay longer, buy from local businesses, get to know a community, and support the local economy.[17]

We can also embrace the miracles of technology a bit more. The global lockdowns have made **virtual experiences more common** and increased the variety of activities.[18] For example, Discover Puerto Rico has offered online Samba dance lessons. If you want a taste of fame, you can have a virtual reality experience of being onstage and singing your favorite songs as a member of the **Beatles**.[19] Or, if you feel more like relaxing under a canopy of stars, you can download a virtual planetarium experience and gaze longingly into the far reaches of the Milky Way while sitting comfortably on your sofa. For a greater sense of adventure, NASA is developing ways that we can **visit Mars** from the safety of home.[20] And if you just need a reason to smile, you can join the adventures of the **tiny goats** who visit other animals around their home zoo in Oregon.[21] These adorable goats have brought me tiny bits of joy, even on difficult days.

Before the Covid-19 pandemic, we were planning to visit Russia in the summer of 2020. Maybe I can enjoy an Oculus tour of Red Square in Moscow while listening to Tchaikovsky's classical music. But you do not need a virtual reality headset to enjoy exploring the world. There are online virtual tours of **world-class museums** including the Vatican Museums,[22] the British Museum, and the **Smithsonian Natural History Museum**.[23] You can even take a virtual stroll through the **Louvre** art museum in Paris to view the famous Mona Lisa painting.[24] For people who might be nervous about the idea of hiking down into underground caverns, but are still curious, they can explore the caves of Carlsbad Caverns in New Mexico via online **virtual tours of National Parks**.[25] The **Open Heritage project** offers opportunities to visit World Heritage Sites virtually.[26] The project has created 3D models of 26 heritage locations in 18 countries that **can be toured online**.[27] One of these is the 1,000-year-old Temple of Kukulcán in the Mayan city of Chichén

Itzá, Mexico. I have not traveled to Mexico yet, so this seems like a good virtual tour to explore when I need a warm place to escape from winter.

Even international exchange programs—my favorite way to explore and learn about a new place—may become more virtual. I recommend exchange trips for every high school and college student, but not everyone has the financial resources to afford an in-person, physical travel exchange. As we rethink global travel, one proposal for sharing cultural exchanges taps into our technology capacity. International education programs at universities are proposing **online study abroad** classes, wherein students can enroll with an instructor and classmates from around the world.[28] This would allow them to experience not only the content of classes from different countries, but also the different teaching and learning styles based in different cultures. This type of program could expand the number of students who have access to life-changing experiences through international study. With a few revisions to policies, it could also allow students to use their US-based financial aid and apply the credits directly toward their graduation requirements.

Despite all the advances we have made in our digital world, we should also be mindful of the impacts our technology has on the living world. Think of the chemicals and minerals needed to make our computers, the electricity to run them, the toxic plastics and waste left behind when we are done using them. Rebecca Solnit reminds us that "the physical landscape of Silicon Valley is now everywhere, not only in the attempts to clone its success but in the spread of its products and its waste throughout the globe, the outside world being ravaged by [our] retreat to the interior" (p 63). We have been grounded for now, locked away in our Zoom meetings and escaping reality through videos, online gaming, and virtual visits. But this is temporary. We will eventually emerge from the Covid-19 pandemic and reengage with the real world. When that time comes, we will set our feet in motion again.

Travel is as essential as hugs and books, says Eric Weiner.[29] It is food for the soul. He argues that it is not natural for humans to be as sedentary as we have become. The whole point is to get out there and embrace the variety that makes the world so colorful. My restless bones agree. I will always prefer in-person, physical travel, especially spending several weeks, months, or even a year living in a new country. I enjoy being immersed in and trying to learn a new language. I enjoy tasting new foods, dancing to new music, learning about different cultures and arts, walking new paths, and expanding my understanding of the rich diversity of this world.

That said, staying home during a pandemic is good for public health. It is also a good time to learn to be mindful about the impacts of tourism on the places we will visit later. To be better global citizens, we may need to curb our wanderlust a bit. Staying home more often could help restore the ecology of our planetary health, which is also good for human health. At the same time, I want to remain optimistic that crisis inspires creative ideas. Staying closer to home can be a good balance with exploring our world through more virtual options. When we tire of virtual travel, we can wander more locally and explore our home watersheds. To do my part, I will embrace my Norwegian heritage more and practice friluftsliv, or "free-air life," communing with the great outdoors in my neighborhood and region.[30]

As our thoughts meander and we dream about life after Covid-19, we will need to make choices that move us toward more sustainable relationships with the natural world and how we travel through it. Going back to what was normal before lockdown is not a realistic option. Although my low-tech Magic 8-Ball is not very reliable at predicting the future, it does say "Outlook Good." The Covid-19 pandemic has opened a window of opportunity for reimagining our wanderlust in new ways. Now we need to take advantage of it and make changes happen.

Endnotes

1 https://www.nationalgeographic.com/magazine/2013/01/rest-less-genes/ (https://perma.cc/FE3K-8VLS)
2 http://www.theguardian.com/environment/2013/oct/08/can-we-fly-more-and-meet-carbon-targets (https://perma.cc/94X9-8WS6)
3 https://www.english-heritage.org.uk/visit/places/dunstanburgh-castle/history/ (https://perma.cc/HCU4-GEHK)
4 https://www.theatlantic.com/science/archive/2020/04/coronavirus-pandemic-earth-pollution-noise/609316/ (https://perma.cc/Q3HJ-WLGF)
5 https://www.zurich.com/knowledge/topics/global-risks/is-the-coronavirus-showing-us-how-we-can-transition-to-a-low-carbon-world (https://perma.cc/5KD9-4UHD)
6 https://theconversation.com/overtourism-a-growing-global-problem-100029 (https://perma.cc/FF4U-B8R9)
7 https://www.theguardian.com/commentisfree/2017/aug/05/only-governments-can-stem-tide-of-tourism-sweeping-the-globe (https://perma.cc/JJE3-V2J4)
8 https://www.un.org/en/coronavirus/it-imperative-we-rebuild-tourism-sector (https://perma.cc/NVR4-YNAK)
9 https://www.cnn.com/travel/article/venice-tourism-overcrowding-intl/index.html (https://perma.cc/5NTQ-6NKE)
10 https://www.businessinsider.com/disappointing-photos-show-venice-italy-expectation-vs-reality-2018-12#many-of-venices-tourists-come-to-the-city-by-way-of-massive-cruise-ships-28 (https://perma.cc/QS8R-XS6N)
11 https://en.wikipedia.org/wiki/Impacts_of_tourism (https://perma.cc/R48Q-KSN4); https://www.theguardian.com/commentisfree/2017/aug/11/tourism-tipping-point-travel-less-damage-destruction (https://perma.cc/BK6L-BLTJ)
12 https://www.miamiherald.com/news/business/tourism-cruises/article242565281.html
13 https://theconversation.com/this-could-be-the-end-of-the-line-for-cruise-ships-135937 (https://perma.cc/ZMZ4-VRS7)
14 https://www.dw.com/en/can-cruises-kick-start-the-decarbonization-of-shipping/av-57016833 (https://perma.cc/7CAD-ZPX7)
15 https://theconversation.com/the-end-of-global-travel-as-we-know-it-an-opportunity-for-sustainable-tourism-133783 (https://perma.cc/7DFF-4P5J)
16 https://www.outsideonline.com/2292951/have-50-years-overcrowded-parks-taught-us-nothing (https://perma.cc/P5W8-NJRC)

17 https://www.cnn.com/travel/article/pandemic-travel-environment-impact/index.html (https://perma.cc/FH4T-TV9U)

18 https://www.insider.com/museums-theme-parks-offer-virtual-tours-ideal-for-social-distancing-2020-3#take-a-guided-virtual-walking-tour-through-one-of-many-us-national-parks-from-the-badlands-to-yellowstone-3 (https://perma.cc/D2R4-QHDX)

19 http://m7virtual.co.uk/become-the-beatles-vr/ (https://perma.cc/MJY2-KV7T)

20 https://informal.jpl.nasa.gov/museum/360-video (https://perma.cc/P697-JYVU)

21 https://www.oregonzoo.org/news/2018/05/zoo-launches-new-web-series-about-tiny-goat-visits (https://perma.cc/R7T3-QDW6)

22 https://www.mentalfloss.com/article/75809/12-world-class-museums-you-can-visit-online (https://perma.cc/R99Q-QMAX)

23 https://naturalhistory.si.edu/visit/virtual-tour (https://perma.cc/DQ3U-7WDS)

24 https://www.louvre.fr/en/visites-en-ligne (https://perma.cc/A58H-HZKL)

25 https://www.travelandleisure.com/trip-ideas/national-parks/virtual-national-parks-tours (https://perma.cc/TE9K-M7GN)

26 https://www.nbcnews.com/mach/science/now-you-can-visit-world-heritage-sites-virtual-reality-ncna867881 (https://perma.cc/EDA3-5PLG)

27 https://www.cyark.org/projects/ (https://perma.cc/8F2V-ZQY8)

28 https://theconversation.com/heres-a-new-way-to-do-study-abroad-during-the-covid-19-pandemic-and-beyond-138931 (https://perma.cc/267X-KAWK)

29 https://www.nationalgeographic.com/travel/article/why-travel-should-be-considered-an-essential-human-activity? (https://perma.cc/66VZ-KY3Y)

30 https://www.theguardian.com/fashion/2020/sep/23/fjord-focus-is-norways-friluftsliv-the-answer-to-surviving-a-second-lockdown?CMP=Share_iOSApp_Other (https://perma.cc/K7J6-X382)

Afterword One
Acknowledgements

This collection would not be possible without my best friend, navigator, and partner in life, Mick Beltz. I love traveling the world with you and look forward to many more adventures. Your support throughout the process of developing, writing, organizing, and revising this collection has helped me finally turn this book into a reality.

My appreciation is extended to the two anonymous reviewers whose feedback was tremendously helpful and greatly valued. I also want to thank Andrea Herbst-Horner for her tremendous work in copy-editing the final draft. Her suggestions and revisions help give the manuscript a polished finish. Many thanks as well to Bill Caraher for encouraging me to publish these essays in a collection and all his tireless work throughout the publishing process.

My thanks also to friends and family who listen to our travel stories, enjoy our photos, and share our wanderlust.

References and Suggestions
for Learning More

Adams, Mark. *Turn Right at Machu Picchu: Rediscovering the Lost City One Step at a Time*. Plume, 2012.

Ambrose, Stephen E. *Undaunted Courage: Meriwether Lewis. Thomas Jefferson, and the Opening of the American West*. New York, Simon & Schuster, 1996.

Benson, Melinda Harm, and Robin Kundis Craig. *The End of Sustainability: Resilience and the Future of Environmental Governance in the Anthropocene*. University Press of Kansas, 2017.

Brown, Gabe. *Dirt to soil: One family's journey into regenerative agriculture*. Chelsea Green Publishing, 2018.

Carson, Rachel. *Silent Spring*. Houghton Mifflin, 1962.

Darwin, Charles. *Narrative of the Surveying Voyages of His Majesty's Ships Adventure and Beagle Between the Years 1826 and 1836, Describing Their Examination of the Southern Shores of South America, and the Beagle's Circumnavigation of the Globe. Journal and remarks. 1832–1836*. Vol. 3, London, Henry Colburn, 1839. Available online: http://darwin-online.org.uk/content/frameset?itemID=F10.3&viewtype=text&pageseq=1

Eliade, Mircea. *The Sacred and the Profane: The Nature of Religion*. Houghton Mifflin Harcourt, 1959.

Ellis, Erle C. "Sharing the land between nature and people." *Science*, vol. 364, no. 6447, 2019, pp. 1226-1228. doi:10.1126/science.aax2608.

Fitter, Julian, et al. *Wildlife of the Galapagos*. Princeton University Press, 2002.

Gómez-Limón, José A., et al. "Eco-efficiency assessment of olive farms in Andalusia." *Land Use Policy*, vol. 29, no. 2, 2012, pp. 395-406. doi. org/10.1016/j.landusepol.2011.08.004.

Irving, Washington. *Tales of the Alhambra*. Editor Miguel Sánchez, 1982.

Leopold, Aldo. *A Sand County Almanac and Sketches Here and There*. Special Commemorative Edition, New York, Oxford University Press, 1989.

Little, Amanda. *The Fate of Food: What We'll Eat in a Bigger, Hotter, Smarter World*. Harmony Books, 2019.

Mahoney, Rosemary. *Down the Nile: Alone in a Fisherman's Skiff*. Little, Brown and Company, 2007.

Marris, Emma. *Rambunctious Garden: Saving Nature in a Post-Wild World*. Bloomsbury USA, 2013.

McGraw, Seamus. *Betting the Farm on a Drought: Stories from the Front Lines of Climate Change*. University of Texas Press, 2015.

Minter, Adam. *Secondhand: Travels in the New Global Garage Sale*. Bloomsbury Publishing, 2019.

Mitchell, Sherri. "Indigenous prophecy and Mother Earth." *All We Can Save: Truth, Courage, and Solutions for the Climate Crisis*, edited by Ayana Elizabeth Johnson & Katharine K. Wilkinson, One World, 2020. pp. 16-28.

Morse, Kathryn. *The Nature of Gold: An Environmental History of the Klondike Gold Rush.* University of Washington Press, 2009.

Pearce, Fred. "Weather makers." *Science*, vol. 368, no. 6497, 2020, pp. 1302-1305. doi.org/10.1126/science.368.6497.1302.

Primack, Richard B., et al. "The impact of climate change on cherry trees and other species in Japan." *Biological Conservation*, vol. 142, no. 9, 2009, pp. 1943-1949. doi.org/10.1016/j.biocon.2009.03.016.

Raworth, Kate. *Doughnut Economics: Seven Ways to Think Like a 21st-Century Economist.* Chelsea Green Publishing, 2017.

Runte, Alfred. *National Parks: The American Experience*, 3rd ed., University of Nebraska Press, 1997.

Sakurai, Ryo, et al. "Culture and climate change: Japanese cherry blossom festivals and stakeholders' knowledge and attitudes about global climate change." *Biological Conservation*, vol. 144, no. 1, 2011, pp. 654-658. doi.org/10.1016/j.biocon.2010.09.028.

Sanderson, Eric W., et al. "From Bottleneck to Breakthrough: Urbanization and the Future of Biodiversity Conservation." *BioScience*, vol. 68, no. 6, 2018, pp. 412-426. doi:10.1093/biosci/biy039.

Shenker, Jack. *The Egyptians: A Radical Story.* Allen Lane, 2016.

Solnit, Rebecca. *Storming the Gates of Paradise: Landscapes for Politics.* University of California Press, 2007.

Tinch, David M. N., *Shoal and Sheaf: Orkney's Pictorial Heritage.* Blackstaff Press, 1988.

Vossen, Paul. "Olive Oil: History, Production, and Characteristics of the World's Classic Oils." *HortScience*, vol. 42, no. 5, 2007, pp. 1093-1100. doi.org/10.21273/HORTSCI.42.5.1093.

Wapner, Paul. *Is Wildness Over?* John Wiley & Sons, 2020.

Weiner, Jonathan. *The Beak of the Finch: A Story of Evolution in Our Time*. Vintage, 2014.

Zelikova, Jane. "Solutions underfoot." *All We Can Save: Truth, Courage, and Solutions for the Climate Crisis*, edited by Ayana Elizabeth Johnson & Katharine K. Wilkinson, One World, 2020. pp. 287-92.

Podcasts

These podcasts and specific episodes inspired my thinking about and writing of *Mindful Wandering*.

Costing the Earth
- Podcast homepage: https://www.bbc.co.uk/programmes/b006r4wn
- "Covid-19: The environmental impact": https://www.bbc.co.uk/programmes/m000h7yb
- "Plastic Burnout": https://www.bbc.co.uk/programmes/m000gsmd
- "Plastic Gardens": https://www.bbc.co.uk/programmes/m0009jl4
- "Zero Carbon Orkney": https://www.bbc.co.uk/programmes/p07pzk6f/p07pzlmc

Living Planet
- "Drowning in plastic": https://www.dw.com/en/living-planet-drowning-in-plastic/av-55662415
- "Rethinking farming": https://www.dw.com/en/living-planet-rethinking-farming/av-56839563
- "Sustainability and the city": https://www.dw.com/en/living-planet-sustainability-the-city/av-56698341
- "To fly or not to fly? The truth behind carbon offsetting": https://www.dw.com/en/living-planet-to-fly-or-not-to-fly-the-truth-behind-carbon-offsetting/av-56454824

On the Green Fence
Season 4 (2021) explores the future of travel and how various sectors are trying to reduce their environmental impacts.
- Podcast homepage: https://www.dw.com/en/on-the-green-fence/a-55160456

Science Friday

Degrees of Change: this series examines climate change and a variety of responses to it.

- "Eating Smarter in a Warmer World": https://www.sciencefriday.com/segments/eating-smarter-in-a-warming-world/
- "How the Fashion Industry Is Responding to Climate Change": https://www.sciencefriday.com/segments/doc-climate-and-fashion/
- "How Native American Communities Are Addressing Climate Change": https://www.sciencefriday.com/segments/native-american-communities-climate-change/
- "How Soil Could Save the Planet": https://www.sciencefriday.com/segments/soil-capture-carbon-dioxide/
- "'Resilience' Looks at How Things Bounce Back": https://www.sciencefriday.com/segments/resilience-looks-at-how-things-bounce-back/

The Experiment

- "The Problem with America's National Parks": https://www.wnycstudios.org/podcasts/experiment/episodes/national-parks-native-americans

Throughline

- "A Symphony of Resistance": https://www.npr.org/2021/05/17/997660501/a-symphony-of-resistance

39 Ways to Save the Planet

- Podcast homepage: https://www.bbc.co.uk/programmes/m000qwt3
- This podcast series explores a variety of innovative ideas that people are working on to manage the climate crisis, help protect the natural environment, and improve human relationships with Planet Earth.

About the Author

Rebecca J. Romsdahl, PhD, is a translational ecologist, educator, writer, and professor in the Department of Earth System Science & Policy at the University of North Dakota. Her research and teaching examine links between social, ecological, and policy factors when scientists, stakeholders, and decision makers work together to solve environmental problems.

www.ingramcontent.com/pod-product-compliance
Lightning Source LLC
Chambersburg PA
CBHW062047270326